D0284450

How Robert E. Lee
Lost The Civil War

ST. JOHNS COUNTY PUBLIC LIBRARY SYSTEM
1960 PONCE DE LEON BLVD.
ST. AUGUSTINE, FLORIDA 32084

How Robert E. Lee

Lost The Civil War

Edward H. Bonekemper, III

Sergeant Kirkland's Press
Fredericksburg, Virginia

Copyright 1997 by Edward H. Bonekemper, III

ALL RIGHTS RESERVED -- No part of this book may be repro-
duced or transmitted in any form or by any means, electronic or
mechanical, including photocopying, recording, or by any information storage and retrieval system, without permission in
writing from the publisher.

Published & Distributed by
**Sergeant Kirkland's Museum
and Historical Society, Inc.**
912 Lafayette Blvd.
Fredericksburg, Virginia 22401-5617
Tel. (540) 899-5565; Fax: (540) 899-7643
E-mail: Civil-War@msn.com

Manufactured in the USA

The paper in this book meets the guidelines for permanence and
durability of the Committee on Production Guidelines for Book
Longevity of the Council on Library Resources, Inc.

Library of Congress Cataloging-in-Publication Data
Bonekemper, Edward H.
How Robert E. Lost the Civil War / by Edward H. Bonekemper, III
p.   cm.
Includes bibliographical references and index.
ISBN 1-887901-15-9 (alk. paper)
1. Lee, Robert E (Robert Edward), 1807-1870—Military leadership. 2. Generals—Confederate States of America—Biography. 3. Command of troops. 4. Strategy—History—19th cen-
tury. 5. United States—History—Civil War, 1861-1865—
Campaigns. I. Title.

E467.1.L4B655   1998
973.7'3'092—dc21
[B]   97-18213
                                                       CIP
            1 2 3 4 5 6 7 8 9 10

Cover design and page layout
by Ronald R. Seagrave.
Edited by Pia Seija Seagrave, Ph.D.
Frontispiece
Robert E. Lee, 1865 (Library of Congress)

Dedication

This book is dedicated to my loving and patient wife, Susan,
and as a memorial to my fellow Civil War buff,
Alfred W. Weidemoyer.

Table of Contents

Acknowledgements

During my seven years of work on this book, I have been encouraged, stimulated, challenged and assisted by a great many people. My wife, father-in-law, parents, co-workers and friends have patiently listened to me excitedly describe each new idea and discovery as I read and thought about Lee and the Civil War. Without their support, this book would not have been possible.

My wife tolerated my using my days off to write this book instead of working around the house. Al Weidemoyer, my late father-in-law, and I shared over one hundred Civil War books and jointly concluded that Lee has been greatly overrated. I owe a special debt to my mother, Marie Bonekemper, who taught me to love reading even before I went to school, and my father, Ed Bonekemper, who taught me the typesetting, printing, and newspaper businesses when I was in my early teens.

The Library of Congress staff was as helpful to me as they have been to millions of other researchers and authors. Even more beneficial have been the critical reviews of my manuscript by a splendid and varied group of professionals and friends. Especially helpful were the keen and thoughtful criticisms provided by Dr. Edwin Baldrige, former chairman of the history department at Muhlenberg College, and Dr. Harold Wilson, chairman of the history department at Old Dominion University. Ed Baldrige recently completed 40 years of inspired and humor-filled teaching, and Harold Wilson has always been a tough, but fair, critic of his students' writing.

Other indispensable reviewers were Jim MacDonald, Mary Crouter and Steve Farbman. Jim's four Buckeye great-grandfathers all fought for the Union, and Jim brought to bear his professionalism and Civil War expertise to improve my manuscript. Mary and Steve, my attorney colleagues, know what good writing is all about and helped clarify my thinking and expression.

I also must acknowledge several other readers who provided valuable feedback: Dr. Virginia Litres, Jeffrey Baldino, Bill Holt, Ken Holt, Dore Hunter, and Al Roberts. My boss, Judy Kaleta, graciously allowed me to adjust my work schedule to facilitate my writing this book. Historian and author Mac Wyckoff and Dr. William C. McDonald provided vital, thorough and critical reviews of my manuscript that significantly improved its quality.

Absolutely essential were the confidence, perseverance and skills of my publisher, Ronald R. Seagrave, and my editor, Dr. Pia Seagrave.

Lastly, vital to this book are permissions to publish excerpts from the following publications:

From *Fighting for the Confederacy: The Personal Recollections of General Edward Porter Alexander*. Edited by Gary Gallagher. Copyright(c) 1989 by the University of North Carolina Press. Used by permission of the publisher.

From Fleming, Martin K., "The Northwestern Virginia Campaign of 1861: McClellan's Rising Star -- Lee's Dismal Debut," *Blue & Gray Magazine*, X, Issue 6 (Aug. 1993), 10, 62. Copyright(c) 1993 by Blue & Gray Magazine. Used by permission of the publisher.

Although this book could not have been completed without the generous assistance of all these people and institutions, I am solely responsible for any errors that remain.

Preface

Lee's Fatal Flaws

Robert E. Lee is often described as one of the greatest generals who ever lived. He usually is given credit for keeping vastly superior Union forces at bay and preserving the Confederacy during the four years of the American Civil War (1861-65).

This book presents a contrary view, a side of the coin infrequently seen. It relies upon previously-published sources but extracts from them a more critical analysis of Lee's Civil War performance. It goes beyond any of the earlier critics of Lee by describing all of Lee's strategic and tactical errors, analyzing their cumulative effect, emphasizing the negative impact he had on Confederate prospects in both the East and the West, and squarely placing on him responsibility for defeat of the Confederates in a war they should have won. More attention is given to developments in the West than in most books about Lee because events there spelled the ultimate military doom of Lee's army and because Lee himself played an often-overlooked role in those events.

The cult of Lee worshippers began with former Civil War generals who had fought ineffectively under him. They sought to polish their own tarnished reputations and restore southern pride by deliberately distorting the historical record and creating the myth of the flawless Robert E. Lee.[1]

In his capacity as the Confederacy's leading general and President Jefferson Davis' primary military advisor for virtually the entire war, however, Lee bears considerable responsibility for the war's outcome. Even more significantly, Lee's own specific strategic and tactical failures cost the Confederates their opportunity to outlast the Union, to cause President Abraham Lincoln's electoral defeat in 1864, and, thereby, to win the war.

The war was winnable through a conservative use of Confederate resources, but Lee squandered the Confederacy's precious manpower

---

[1]. See Appendix I herein, Historians' Treatment of Lee. On the "transcendental" myth of Lee, see Fuller, J.F.C., *Grant and Lee: A Study in Personality and Generalship* (Bloomington: Indiana University Press, 1957) [hereafter Fuller, *Grant and Lee*], pp. 103-8.

and its opportunity for victory.[2] The South's primary opportunity for success was to outlast Lincoln, and deep schisms among Northerners throughout the War made Confederate victory a distinct possibility. Northerners violently disagreed on slavery, the draft and the war itself. To exploit these divisions and in order to prevail, the Confederates needed to preserve their manpower, sap the strength of the North, make continuation of the war intolerable, and compel recognition of the Confederacy's independence.

The South was outnumbered by a ratio of 4 to 1 in terms of white men of fighting age and could not afford to squander its resources by engaging in a war of attrition.[3] Robert E. Lee's deliberate disregard of this reality may have been his greatest failure.

The possibility of a Confederate victory through a defeat of Lincoln at the ballot box in 1864 is demonstrated by the fact that, during August 1864, Lincoln himself despaired of winning reelection that coming November.[4] Had Lee not squandered Rebel manpower during the three preceding years, that 1864 opportunity for victory could have been realized.

Lee's strategy and tactics dissipated irreplaceable manpower -- even in his "victories." His losses at Malvern Hill, Antietam, and Gettysburg, as well as his costly "wins" at Second Bull Run and Chancellorsville -- all in 1862 and 1863 -- made possible Ulysses S. Grant's and William Tecumseh Sherman's successful 1864 campaigns against Richmond and Atlanta and created the aura of Confederate defeat that Lincoln exploited to win reelection. If Lee had performed differently, the North would have been fatally split, Democratic nominee (and "out-to-pasture" Union Major General) George B. McClellan might have defeated Lincoln, and the South could have negotiated an acceptable settlement with the compromising McClellan. Although some have contended that McClellan would not have allowed the South to remain outside the Union,[5] he often had demonstrated his reticence to engage in the offensive warfare necessary for the Union to prevail; he

---

[2]. "The weaker side can win; the South almost did." Hattaway, Herman and Jones, Archer, *How the North Won: A Military History of the Civil War* (Urbana and Chicago: University of Illinois Press, 1983, 1991) [hereafter Hattaway and Jones, *How the North Won*], p. ix.

[3]. *Ibid.*, p. 114; Nevins, Alan, *Ordeal of the Union*, 8 vols. (New York and London: Charles Scribner's Sons, 1947-50) [hereafter Nevins, *Ordeal*], IV, p. 488, citing Appleton's *Annual Cyclopaedia* (1861).

[4]. Nevins, *Ordeal*, VIII, pp. 92-6.

[5]. Davis, William C., *The Cause Lost: Myths and Realities of the Confederacy* (Lawrence: University Press of Kansas, 1996), pp. 142-7.

also had demonstrated great concern about southerners' property rights in slaves.

Lee's strategy was defective in two respects.[6] First, it was too aggressive.[7] With one quarter the manpower resources of his adversary, Lee exposed his forces to unnecessary risks and, ultimately, lost the gamble.[8] Second, Lee's strategy concentrated all the resources he could obtain and retain almost exclusively in the eastern theater of operations, while fatal events were occurring in the "West" (primarily in Tennessee, Mississippi and Georgia).[9] Historian Archer Jones provides an analysis tying together Lee's two strategic weaknesses:

> More convincing is the contention that if the Virginia armies were strong enough for an offensive they were too strong for the good of the Confederacy. They would have done better to

---

[6]. For details of Lee's defective strategy, see Chapter 12, "Overview."

[7]. "Like Napoleon himself, which his passion for the strategy of annihilation and the climactic, decisive battle as its expression, [Lee] destroyed in the end not the enemy armies, but his own." Weigley, Russell F., *The American Way of War: A History of United States Military Strategy and Policy* (New York: MacMillan Publishing Co., Inc., 1973) [hereafter Weigley, *American Way of War*], p. 127.

[8]. "Even some generals who enjoy high reputations or fame have actually been predominantly direct soldiers who brought disaster to their side. One such general was Robert E. Lee, the beau ideal of the Southern Confederacy, who possessed integrity, honor, and loyalty in the highest degree and who also possessed skills as a commander far in excess of those of the Union generals arrayed against him. But Lee was not, himself, a great general. Lee generally and in decisively critical situations always chose the direct over the indirect approach." Alexander, Bevin, *How Great Generals Win* (New York and London: W.W. Norton & Company, 1993) [hereafter Alexander, *Great Generals*], pp. 25-6. "Of all the army commanders on both sides, Lee had the highest casualty rate." McPherson, James M., *Battle Cry of Freedom: The Civil War Era* (New York: Ballantine Books, 1988) [hereafter McPherson, *Battle Cry of Freedom*], p. 472.

[9]. Lee operated in an area of 22,000 square miles, while the western theater consisted of 225,000 square miles in seven states. Connelly, Thomas Lawrence, "Robert E. Lee and the Western Confederacy: A Criticism of Lee's Strategic Ability," *Civil War History*, 15 (June 1969), pp. 116-32 [hereafter, Connelly, "Lee and the Western Confederacy"], p. 118. ". . . a very real criticism of Lee is that while he managed to defend Richmond for almost three years, he allowed the rest of the Confederacy to be slowly eaten away." Katcher, Philip, *The Army of Robert E. Lee* (London: Arms and Armour Press, 1994), [hereafter Katcher, *Army of Lee*], p. 27. ". . . [Lee's] thoughts were always concentrated on Virginia, consequently he never fully realized the importance of Tennessee, or the strategic power which resided in the size of the Confederacy." Fuller, *Grant and Lee*, p. 255. Although defenders of Lee contend that he was merely an eastern army commander for most of the war, he frequently advised President Davis on national issues, including military strategy. Connelly, Thomas Lawrence, *The Marble Man: Robert E. Lee and His Image in American Society* (New York: Alfred A. Knopf, 1977) [hereafter Connelly, *Marble Man*], pp. 202-3.

spare some of their strength to bolster the sagging West where the war was being lost.[10]

Just as significant as his flawed strategy were Lee's tactics, which proved fatally defective.[11] His tactical defects were that he was too aggressive on the field,[12] he frequently failed to take charge of the battlefield,[13] his battle plans were too complex or simply ineffective,[14] and his orders were too vague or discretionary.[15]

The results of Lee's faulty strategies and tactics were catastrophic. His army had 121,000 men killed or wounded during the war -- 27,000 more than any Union or Confederate Civil War general including that alleged "butcher," Union Lieutenant General Ulysses Simpson Grant,

---

[10]. Jones, Archer, *Confederate Strategy from Shiloh to Vicksburg* (Baton Rouge and London: Louisiana State University Press, 1991), p. 29.

[11]. For details concerning Lee's tactical weaknesses, see Chapter 12, "Overview."

[12]. General James Longstreet said, "In the field, [Lee's] characteristic fault was headlong combativeness... He was too pugnacious." Wert, Jeffrey D., *General James Longstreet: The Confederacy's Most Controversial Soldier--A Biography* (New York: Simon & Schuster, 1993) [hereafter Wert, *Longstreet*], p. 296.

[13]. Lee explained his approach to a Prussian military observer at Gettysburg: "I think and work with all my powers to bring my troops to the right place at the right time; then I have done my duty. As soon as I order them into battle, I leave my army in the hands of God." To interfere later, he said, "does more harm than good." Connelly, *Marble Man*, p. 199; Piston, William Garrett, "Cross Purposes: Longstreet, Lee, and Confederate Attack Plans for July 3 at Gettysburg" [hereafter, Piston, "Cross Purposes"] in Gallagher, Gary W., *The Third Day at Gettysburg & Beyond* (Chapel Hill and London: The University of North Carolina Press, 1994) [hereafter, Gallagher, *Third Day*], pp. 31, 43. "What Lee achieved in boldness of plan and combat aggressiveness he diminished through ineffective command and control." Glatthaar, Joseph T., *Partners in Command: The Relationships Between Leaders in the Civil War* (New York: Macmillan, Inc., 1994) [hereafter, Glatthaar, *Partners in Command*], p. 35. "Lee's battlefield control was minimal." Piston, William Garrett, *Lee's Tarnished Lieutenant: James Longstreet and His Place in Southern History* (Athens and London: The University of Georgia Press, 1987) [hereafter, Piston, *Lee's Tarnished Lieutenant*], p. 36.

[14]. Glatthaar, *Partners in Command*, p. 35.

[15]. "Lee's failure adequately to order his generals to perform specific actions or discipline them if they failed was probably his greatest character defect... One of his staunchest defenders [Fitzhugh Lee] agreed:'He had a reluctance to oppose the wishes of others, or to order them to do anything that would be disagreeable and to which they would not consent.[']" Katcher, *Army of Lee*, p. 26. "Every order and act of Lee has been defended by his staff officers and eulogists with a fervency that excites suspicion that, even in their own minds, there was need of defence to make good the position they claim for him among the world's great commanders." Bruce, George A., "Lee and the Strategy of the Civil War," pp. 111-38 [hereafter, Bruce, "Lee and Strategy"] in Gallagher, Gary W. (ed.), *Lee the Soldier* (Lincoln and London: University of Nebraska Press, 1996) [hereafter Gallagher, *Lee the Soldier*], p. 117.

and about 90,000 more than any other Confederate general.[16] Although Lee's army inflicted a war-high 135,000 casualties on its opponents, 60,000 of those occurred in 1864 and 1865[17] when Lee was on the defensive and Grant was engaged in a deliberate war of adhesion (achieving attrition and exhaustion) against the army Lee had fatally depleted in 1862 and 1863.[18] Astoundingly (in light of his reputation), Lee's percentages of casualties suffered were worse than those of his fellow Confederate commanders.[19]

During the first 14 months that Lee commanded the Army of Northern Virginia, he took the strategic and tactical offensive so often with his undermanned army that he lost 80,000 men while inflicting only 73,000 casualties on his Union opponents.[20] Although daring and sometimes seemingly successful, Lee's actions were inconsistent with the North's 4:1 manpower advantage and were fatal to the Confederate cause. By 1864, therefore, Grant had a 120,000-man army and additional reserves to bring against Lee's 65,000 and, by the sheer weight of his numbers, imposed a fatal 46 percent casualty rate on Lee's army while losing a militarily tolerable 41 percent of his own replaceable men, as Grant drove from the Rappahannock to the James River and created a terminal threat to Richmond.[21]

By June, 1864, Lee's diminished forces were tied down by Grant at Richmond and Petersburg. In the following month, Sherman reached Atlanta. Atlanta fell on September 1, and the Shenandoah Valley was lost in October. Lincoln was reelected in November. The South was doomed, Sherman was marching through Georgia, and Confederate soldiers were dying, near starvation and deserting in droves.

---

[16]. McWhiney, Grady and Jamieson, Perry D., *Attack and Die: Civil War Military Tactics and the Southern Heritage* (Tuscaloosa and London: The University of Alabama Press, 1982) [hereafter McWhiney and Jamieson, *Attack and Die*], pp. 19-23.

[17]. *Ibid.*, p. 19.

[18]. "Though Lee was at his best on defense, he adopted defensive tactics only after attrition had deprived him of the power to attack. His brilliant defensive campaign against Grant in 1864 made the Union pay in manpower as it had never paid before, but the Confederates resorted to defensive warfare too late; Lee started the campaign with too few men, and he could not replace his losses as could Grant." *Ibid.*, pp. 164-5.

[19]. Major Confederate generals' percentages killed and injured were: Lee, 20.2%; Joseph E. Johnston, 10.5%; Braxton Bragg, 19.5%; P.G.T. Beauregard, 16.1%; Earl Van Dorn 8.5%; Jubal Early, 11.2%; and John Bell Hood, 19.2%. *Ibid.*, pp. 19-21. See Chapter 12, "Overview," for more comparative statistics. Also, see Appendix II herein, "Casualties in the Civil War."

[20]. *Ibid.*, p. 19; Livermore, Thomas L., *Numbers & Losses in the Civil War in America, 1861-65* (Millwood, N.Y.: Kraus Reprint Co., 1990, reprint of Bloomington: Indiana University Press, 1957) [hereafter Livermore, *Numbers & Losses*], pp. 82-103.

[21]. McWhiney and Jamieson, *Attack and Die*, p. 19; Livermore, *Numbers & Losses*, pp. 110-6.

The time had come to end the war, but Lee did nothing. Revered and loved by his troops and the entire South, Lee certainly had the power to bring down the curtain on the great American tragedy. His resignation would have brought about an even more massive return of southern soldiers to their homes and would have destroyed the Army of Northern Virginia's, and, ultimately, the Confederacy's, will to fight. But he did nothing. For five more months after Lincoln's reelection, up until the last hours at Appomattox, Lee continued the futile struggle. The result of Lee's failure to resign was continued death and destruction throughout the South. This senseless continuation of the slaughter was Lee's final failure.[22]

---

[22]. Although the morale of some in the Confederacy remained high until the end, many realized that defeat was becoming increasingly likely in late 1864 and early 1865. Massive desertions from Lee's army reflected, among other things, the likelihood of defeat. See Chapters 10 and 11.

Chapter 1

The Making of the Man and Soldier

"The Lees of Virginia." That simple phrase conveys the historical burden that fell on Robert Edward Lee. Most of his ancestors had been rich, famous and, most importantly, respected.

But, despite a romantic record as a Revolutionary War officer, Lee's father had disgraced the family name. His war record actually was tainted. Henry Lee, III, proudly known as "Light- Horse Harry" Lee, had been court-martialed twice. He had ordered a deserter hanged and then, cruelly, had the man's severed head delivered to General George Washington.[1] Finally, he had resigned from the army in 1782 while engaged in a love affair.

But it was Henry Lee's profligate spending of his two wives' money that brought dishonor and disgrace to him and the family. In 1782, he married his cousin, Matilda Lee, and spent their (her) money so foolishly that she hired an attorney to put the remaining assets in trust for their two sons. After her sudden death, Henry married Ann Hill Carter of the famous and wealthy Virginia Carters -- over the strong and wise opposition of Ann's father. That 1793 marriage re- sulted in the birth of five children, including Robert E. Lee (the fourth child and third son) on January 19, 1807, but ended in another financial disaster. The grand Stratford Hall plantation, Robert Lee's birthplace, was reduced from 6,600 acres to 236 acres under the profligate management of Light-Horse Harry.[2]

Harry had, thus, squandered a second family fortune, passed bad checks (including one to George Washington), fraudulently sold to his brother land that he no longer owned, and served two jail terms totaling a year for failure to pay his debts. Four relatives cut him out of their wills. In 1813, Lee's father, desperate to escape his debtors, fled the

---

[1]. Nagel, Paul C., *The Lees of Virginia: Seven Generations of an American Family* (New York and Oxford: Oxford University Press, 1990) [hereafter Nagel, *Lees of Virginia*], pp. 161-4; Connelly, *Marble Man*, pp. 176-7.
[2]. *Ibid.*, pp. 164-82; Thomas, Emory M., *Robert E. Lee: A Biography* (New York and London: W.W. Norton & Company, 1995) [hereafter Thomas, *Lee*], pp. 23-9.

country. Five years later, the mortally-ill Light-Horse Harry tried to return to Virginia to die but, instead, perished on Cumberland Island off the Georgia coast while on his return journey.[3]

As if that disgrace were not sufficient, Light-Horse Harry's son, Henry IV (Robert E. Lee's half-brother), earned the sobriquet "Black-Horse Harry" by impregnating his wife's sister, Betsy McCarty, who also was his ward. That 1820 indiscretion became public the next year when she obtained a court order ending the guardianship. The court said that "Henry Lee hath been guilty of a flagrant abuse of his trust in the guardianship of his ward Betsy McCarty." The scandal reached national proportions a decade later when President Andrew Jackson attempted to name Black-Horse Harry consul to Algiers. Because of his previous misconduct, the Senate, in executive session, unanimously defeated the nomination. By then Black Horse Harry, like his father, had fled the country. He never returned.[4]

The notoriety and prodigality of Robert's father and half-brother brought shame and humble circumstances to the small family of Robert, his mother and siblings. After his 1807 birth at stately Stratford Hall in Westmoreland County on Virginia's Northern Neck (east of Fredericksburg), Robert and the rest of the family moved to Alexandria in 1810. This forced move followed the 1809 imprisonment of Light-Horse Harry because of his bad debts. Thereafter, Robert and his mother lived in borrowed homes courtesy of wealthy relatives.

From a very early age, Lee cared for his frail mother, Ann Carter Lee, and his two sisters until he left their Alexandria home to go to West Point in 1825. When he departed Alexandria, his mother reportedly said, "How can I live without Robert? He is both son and daughter to me."[5] Having struggled to live until Robert's return, she died in 1829, about a month after he had returned to Alexandria as a graduate of West Point and an officer in the United States Army.

Restoration of his family's honor became a driving force in the life of Robert E. Lee. At West Point, where he and five of his peers spent four years without receiving a single demerit, Lee's classmates tagged him "the Marble Model." Lee finished second in the Class of 1829.[6]

Upon his mother's death, Lee inherited ten slaves. Two years later, in July 1831, Lee married Mary Anne Randolph Custis, the only child of George Washington's adopted son, and, thereby, went a long way toward reestablishing his aristocratic credentials. His marriage also

---

[3]. Nagel, *Lees of Virginia*, pp. 164-84; Thomas, *Lee*, pp. 24-36; Connelly, *Marble Man*, p. 177.

[4]. Thomas, *Lee*, p. 40; Nagel, *Lees of Virginia*, pp. 207-26; Connelly, *Marble Man*, p. 177.

[5]. Thomas, *Lee*, p. 44.

[6]. *Ibid.*, pp. 36-55.

gained him access to the grand, 1,100-acre Arlington House plantation, which he made his permanent home until the Civil War. Between 1832 and 1846, the Lees had seven children, two of whom became Civil War major generals; another became a captain in Lee's army.

Lee served in a variety of engineering posts in Virginia (Fort Monroe), New York (Fort Totten), Maryland, Georgia and Missouri. While Lee was on duty around the country, Mary and the children often remained at the Custis family estate in Arlington, across the Potomac from Washington and just north of Alexandria. Mary had been a pampered child and could not tear herself away physically or emotionally from her doting parents and the luxurious estate. She and Robert were separated for most of their married lives. They shared a depressing and strained marriage, and suffered through increasingly debilitating illnesses (she for 30 years and he for his final eight).

The highlight of Lee's pre-Civil War career was his heroic experiences in the Mexican War (1846-48). There he garnered experience and exposure as a member of General-in-Chief Winfield Scott's staff. Scott, rivaled only by General Zachary Taylor as America's hero during the Mexican War, led the victorious campaign from Vera Cruz to Mexico City. Demonstrating initiative, intelligence, and bravery, Lee was a hero in several battles, particularly Cerro Gordo, Contreras, Churubusco, and Chapultepec; he received three brevet (temporary) promotions in recognition of his sterling performance. Lee emerged from the war with the brevet (temporary) rank of colonel. General Scott even talked of insuring Lee for five million dollars if the nation ever went to war.[7]

On the down side, however, his Mexican War experiences may have given Lee an erroneous impression of what could be accomplished by daring, perhaps rash, frontal assaults. He actively participated in a series of successful attacks upon positions defended by poorly-trained infantry armed with unrifled, inaccurate, short-range, muzzle-loading muskets. At Cerro Gordo, for example, the Americans attacked successfully, even against some field works, and emerged victorious with losses of only five percent. Similarly, they incurred insignificant casualties in their successful, war-winning assault on the Mexican fortress of Chapultepec, just outside Mexico City. There was to be little resemblance between those heroic and victorious charges of the Mexican War and the deadly, disastrous frontal assaults of the Civil War.[8]

---

[7]. Thomas, *Lee*, pp. 113-42.

[8]. *Ibid.*, pp. 140-1.

Lee's heroic Mexican War adventure may have been the only time he enjoyed his pre-Civil War military career. It, perhaps, made him believe that he had partially restored his family's honor. The Mexican War experience, however, probably created in Lee's mind an unrealistic confidence in the success that could be achieved through offensive warfare. The capture of Mexico City, for example, by an army of 9,000 opposed by 30,000 defenders and a hostile populace may have been misleadingly easy. Any confidence gained by this experience was misplaced because of the basic incompetence of Santa Anna's Mexican Army and the soon-to-be-outmoded weaponry used by the Mexican defenders against the American assaults.

The relatively small number of troops on both sides also distinguished that struggle from the later Civil War. The Americans invading Mexico could be managed by a commanding general with a small staff. Lee, later, would make the mistake of attempting to manage a force many times as large as Scott's with the same, small, personal staff. In addition, Scott's strategic position in Mexico was similar to the North's position, not the South's, in the Civil War. Unlike the Confederacy fifteen years later, Scott had to conquer the Mexicans and win the war and, therefore, was compelled to take the offensive. Also, as Scott moved farther from Vera Cruz, retreat became a less viable option and attack became increasingly necessary. Scott, at Mexico City, unlike Lee at Malvern Hill, Antietam, Chancellorsville, and Gettysburg, had to engage the enemy directly. These strategic and tactical distinctions seem to have escaped Lee in the 1860s.

During the early 1850s, Lee served as Superintendent of West Point. In 1855, he became the lieutenant colonel of the just-formed 2nd Cavalry Regiment and embarked on a western tour of duty, once again far removed from his wife and children. His colonel was Albert Sidney Johnston, and they joined John Bell Hood and Edmund Kirby Smith of the same famed regiment as four of the Confederacy's eight four-star generals. In fact, the 2nd Regiment furnished eleven generals to the Confederacy and eight to the Union.

Throughout the 1850s, Lee was depressed and thought of himself as a failure; promotions were slow, accomplishments were few, and his marriage was characterized by duty more than love.[9] Despite, or perhaps because of, his long separations from his wife, Colonel Lee, in early 1859, advised fellow officer Winfield Scott Hancock's wife, Almira Russell Hancock, to accompany her husband to his California post

---

[9]. Thomas, *Lee*, pp. 175-90 (Chapter 14, "How Hard It Is to Get Contentment"); Nagel, *Lees of Virginia*, pp. 241-62.

because separated young couples "...cease to be essential to each other."[10]

Meanwhile, the increasing sectional dissension concerned Lee. In 1857 he deplored the growing national discord and expressed his concern about certain northerners who seemed dedicated to "...interfere with & change the domestic institutions of the South."[11]

While on leave in Arlington, in October, 1859, Lee had the opportunity to put down John Brown's ill-fated and poorly-planned slave insurrection and raid on Harper's Ferry, Virginia. Lee's men captured Brown and freed his hostages. The efficiency of Lee's actions at Harper's Ferry enhanced his military reputation in Washington and Virginia. Brown's subsequent hanging, for treason against the Commonwealth of Virginia, made him a martyr in the eyes of northern abolitionists.

In 1860, Lee returned to duty in Texas, where he watched, with interest and apprehension, the accelerating rift between the North and South. His correspondence made it clear that he would go wherever the Commonwealth of Virginia went. In December, 1860, he tellingly wrote, "As an American citizen, I prize the Union very highly & know of no personal sacrifice that I would not make to preserve it, save that of honour."[12] By January, he made it clear, in other letters, that his honor compelled him to side with Virginia: "If the Union is dissolved, I shall return to Virginia & share the fortune of my people," and "If the Union is dissolved, I shall return to Virginia and share the misery of my native state..."[13]

On the eve of the Civil War, Robert E. Lee was one of the finest officers of the United States Army, a military hero of the nation's previous war, an officer convinced of the advantages of offensive warfare, and a man obsessed with a need to prove himself and to uphold the honor of his family name.

---

[10]. Jordan, David M., *Winfield Scott Hancock: A Soldier's Life* (Bloomington and Indianapolis: Indiana University Press, 1988, 1996) [hereafter Jordan, *Hancock*], p. 27.

[11]. Thomas, *Lee*, p. 173, citing Lee to Edward Childe, January 9, 1857.

[12]. *Ibid.*, p. 186, citing Lee to Rooney Lee, December 3, 1860.

[13]. *Ibid.*, citing Lee to Annette Carter, January 16, 1861, and Lee to Markie Williams, January 22, 1861.

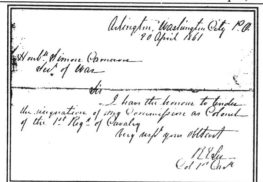

On April 20, 1861, Robert E. Lee sent this letter to Secretary of War Simon Cameron, resigning as colonel of the First U.S. Cavalry. (National Archives and Records Administration)

That same day, Lee also wrote to his old chief Bvt. Lt. Gen. Winfield Scott explaining his difficult decision to resign from the army and sending his heartfelt wishes for their past association. (Eleanor S. Brockenbrough Library, The Museum of the Confederacy, Richmond, Virginia)

Chapter 2

1861: Failure In Western Virginia

With the November, 1860, election of Abraham Lincoln, southern state leaders became aware that slavery in U.S. territories, and, thus, slavery itself, was in serious political trouble. There was no northern interest in President James Buchanan's December, 1860, proposal of pro-slavery constitutional amendments which were intended to avoid secession and war.[1] Led by South Carolina, seven states (South Carolina, Mississippi, Alabama, Georgia, Louisiana, Florida and Texas) seceded from the United States before Lincoln's March 4, 1861 inauguration. On February 9, Jefferson Davis was elected provisional president of the Confederate States of America; he was inaugurated nine days later.

During those critical months, Lieutenant Colonel Robert E. Lee, U.S. Army, was on duty in San Antonio, Texas. On February 13, the same day Virginia's Constitutional Convention initially voted against secession by one vote, Lee was ordered to report to Washington. He made the long trek from Texas to Virginia and arrived at his Arlington home March 1, 1861. It is clear, from Lee's Texas correspondence and letters he wrote while journeying to Virginia, that he intended to cast his lot with the Commonwealth of Virginia. Critical to Lee's determination of his future, therefore, was Virginia's decision on whether or not to secede. That decision awaited military developments.

Meanwhile, U.S. military installations were falling into state and Confederate hands throughout the South. The prominent exception was Fort Sumter in Charleston, South Carolina, the cradle of the Confederacy. Lincoln refused to surrender the fort, ordered it re-supplied, and maneuvered the southern forces into firing on the fort -- thereby placing the stigma for actual initiation of hostilities on the Confeder-

---

[1]. Nevins, Allan, *Ordeal of the Union*, IV, pp. 352-4; Savage, Douglas, *The Court Martial of Robert E. Lee: A Historical Novel* (Conshohocken, Pennsylvania: Combined Books, Inc., 1993) [hereafter Savage, *Court Martial*], p. 60.

ates.[2] On April 12, the very day that Confederates fired on Fort Sumter, a delegation from Virginia arrived at the White House to talk to Lincoln about avoiding war. Lincoln told them, "You are too late."

After the fall of Fort Sumter, Lincoln issued an April 15 public proclamation seeking 75,000 volunteers to suppress the rebellion in South Carolina. Two days later, the members of Virginia's Convention reversed their earlier vote and decided to secede -- subject to later confirmation by popular vote. On April 18, Lincoln and his General-in-Chief, Winfield Scott, through Francis Blair, offered Colonel Lee command of the Union Army, but he declined. Lee immediately went to pay his respects to Scott, his 75-year-old mentor, who told Lee he was making the biggest mistake of his life.[3]

That night, Lee drafted and signed his resignation from the United States Army; the document was hand-delivered to General Scott the next day. Immediately after signing his resignation, Lee penned a letter to his brother in which he tellingly said, "Save in defense of my native State, I have no desire ever again to draw my sword."[4]

On April 22, Lee traveled to Richmond, where Governor John Letcher formally offered him a commission as a major general in the Virginia Militia and command of the "...military and naval forces of Virginia."[5] Lee promptly accepted the Virginia command. On the 23rd, Virginia's Constitutional Convention gave Lee a hero's welcome. Unfortunately for the Confederacy, Lee would forever be committed to promoting the military interests of the Old Dominion -- with little regard to the impact on other theaters of battle.

Lee was commissioned a brigadier general in the Provisional Army of the Confederate States on May 10. For one month, until Davis took charge, Lee was Commander-in-Chief of the Confederate forces. He spent several months recruiting, training, and provisioning the Virginia Militia; building a unified force of 40,000 from numerous disparate units of 18,000 men; integrating them into the Provisional Army of

---

[2]. For details of the Fort Sumter situation and conflict, see Hendrickson, Robert, *Sumter: The First Day of the Civil War* (Chelsea, Michigan: Scarborough House, 1990).

[3]. Nagel, *Lees of Virginia*, p. 267; Thomas, *Lee*, pp. 187-8. The offer to Lee is a reflection of General Scott's admiration for Lee, who had performed heroically under Scott during the Mexican War.

[4]. Lee to Sydney Smith Lee, April 20, 1861, Dowdey, Clifford and Manarin, Louis H., *The Wartime Papers of R.E. Lee* (New York: Bramhall House, 1961) [hereafter Dowdey and Manarin, *Papers*], p. 10.

[5]. Union General Winfield Scott, also a native Virginian, had received the first offer of this position but declined. Allan, William, "Memoranda of Conversations with General Robert E. Lee," pp. 7-24, [hereafter Allan, "Conversations"] in Gallagher, *Lee the Soldier*, p. 10.

the Confederate States, and serving as the primary military advisor to President Davis. He remained in Richmond until late July.[6]

While assembling his Virginia army, Lee moved to occupy a crucial position by sending troops under Colonel Thomas Jonathan Jackson to Harper's Ferry, Virginia, on May 1. Later that same month, on May 23, Virginians formally voted to secede, 97,000 to 32,000, but it became clear that western Virginians did not share the majority sentiment. Lincoln reacted swiftly to developments in Virginia. On the same day as the secession vote, 13,000 Union troops, under Brigadier General Irvin McDowell, crossed the Potomac and occupied the Lees' Arlington plantation. Mrs. Lee, who had fled with her daughters, wrote letters of protest to General Scott and others.

On May 24, Union troops moved south from Arlington and occupied Alexandria. There was one death on each side: a Union colonel was shot by a tavern-keeper when the officer tried to replace a Confederate flag on the roof of Alexandria's Marshall House with a United States flag; the tavern-keeper was immediately shot by Union troops. The bloodshed had begun.

On June 1, Brigadier General Pierre Gustave Toutant Beauregard (a Louisiana native with the most romantic name of any Civil War general) was appointed commander of the Confederate Army of the Potomac in northern Virginia (then known as the "Alexandria Line"). The next day, there was skirmishing at Arlington Mills and Fairfax Court House.

Far to the northwest, on May 30, Union troops moved south from Wheeling, Virginia, and occupied Grafton, Virginia, to protect the Baltimore and Ohio Railroad. On June 2-3, two Union columns moved south from Grafton and surprised the Confederates at Philippi in that same western Virginia area. In what became known as "the Philippi races," the Confederates rapidly fled. It was becoming clear that western Virginia was vulnerable to Union incursions and perhaps a Union takeover. Lee sent his own adjutant, Brigadier General Robert S. Garnett, to take command. With ominous prescience, Garnett complained, "They have not given me an adequate force. I can do nothing. They have sent me to my death."[7] Between July 10 and 13, Union troops swept over the remaining Confederates in the area with victories at Rich Mountain, Laurel Hill, and Carrickford (or Carrick's Ford). Gar-

---

6. Thomas, *Lee*, pp. 189-98; Nagel, *Lees of Virginia*, pp. 268-71.

7. Fleming, Martin K., "The Northwestern Virginia Campaign of 1861: McClellan's Rising Star -- Lee's Dismal Debut," *Blue & Gray Magazine*, X, Issue 6 (Aug. 1993), pp. 10-17, 48-54, 59-65 [hereafter Fleming, "Northwestern Virginia Campaign"], p. 16.

nett, the first general officer to die in Civil War combat, was killed during the retreat from Laurel Hill.

Although Major General George McClellan was in command of the Union troops who won all these battles, he was present at and directly responsible for none of them, behaved timidly, and overestimated enemy strength throughout the brief campaign.[8] The one thing he did successfully was promote his own alleged achievements via the telegraph wire that he, without precedent, had dragged along behind his troops.

Demonstrating the Union pressure being brought to bear all over Virginia, some northern troops moved up the lower Virginia Peninsula from Fort Monroe on Hampton Roads. They did not get far, however. On June 10, Confederates forced a Union retreat at Bethel Church (Big Bethel), south of Yorktown.

On the northern Virginia front, the Confederates abandoned Harper's Ferry on June 14 as Union Generals McClellan and Robert Patterson advanced toward them from the west and north. Lee, as the de facto chief of staff, ordered a concentration of Confederate forces near Manassas Junction, an obvious Union target if the Northerners were to move toward Richmond.

Pressure built toward a major battle. To maintain public support in the North and to utilize the original 90-day enlistees, Lincoln and his cabinet met on June 29 with Generals Scott and McDowell to discuss plans for military action. The drumbeat for action continued as Congress convened on July 4 at the President's request. Lincoln sent Congress a message blaming the war on the South, urging a declaration of war, and requesting an additional 400,000 troops.

Although worried about the readiness of his men, McDowell moved toward Fairfax Court House with 40,000 troops on July 14. Northwest of Manassas, Beauregard requested augmentation of his 22,000 soldiers. Jefferson Davis ordered Brigadier General Joseph E. Johnston to move to Beauregard's aid from near Harper's Ferry. Hapless Union General Patterson was supposed to hold Johnston in place or immediately pursue him if he moved; Patterson failed to do either and was unaware that his adversary was moving by foot and rail to join Beauregard at Manassas.

After some minor skirmishing at Blackburn's Ford on July 18, the First Battle of Bull Run, or Manassas, was fought on July 21. Union

---

8. Waugh, John C., *The Class of 1846: From West Point to Appomattox: Stonewall Jackson, George McClellan and Their Brothers* (New York: Warner Books, Inc., 1994) [hereafter Waugh, *Class of 1846*], p. 265.

forces took the offensive, attacked the Rebel left flank, and met with initial success. But the tide of battle turned, and the Union attackers were repulsed and routed -- primarily due to the undetected movement of Johnston's (including Brigadier General Thomas Jackson's) forces from the Shenandoah Valley to the Manassas battlefield. Jackson's stalwart performance on the Confederate left earned him the name "Stonewall" and promotion to major general that October. While Davis rushed to the scene of the battle (and, thus, became involved in a dispute about who was responsible for the victorious Rebels not immediately taking Washington), a frustrated Lee remained in Richmond.

A major impact of the Confederate victory at Manassas was the feeling of superiority and over-confidence throughout the South. A September 27, 1861, *Richmond Examiner* editorial expressed these feelings:

> The battle of Manassas demonstrated, at once and forever, the superiority of the Southern soldiers, and there is not a man in the army, from the humblest private to the highest officer, who does not feel it... The enemy...know now that when they go forth to the field they will encounter a master race. The consciousness of this fact will cause their knees to tremble beneath them on the day of battle.[9]

Shortly after First Manassas, Lee's first opportunity to command Southern forces resulted in disaster. Already he had failed to prevent Yankee occupation of the western counties of Virginia, which then seceded from the Confederacy and ultimately became the State of West Virginia. Initially, Lee remained in Richmond while his outnumbered northwestern Virginia forces interspersed defeats at Philippi, Rich Mountain, and elsewhere with consistent retreats. By July 2, a legislature for western Virginia convened at Wheeling and had received U.S. recognition. On July 24, Union forces, under Brigadier General Jacob D. Cox, advanced and forced the retreat of Confederates from Charleston to Gauley Bridge in the southern part of the area that was to become West Virginia.[10]

After those defeats and the death of Garnett, Lee, in July, named Brigadier General William Wing "Old Blizzards" Loring to command the Army of the Northwest. Not realizing that the Federals already

---

[9]. Wiley, Bell Irvin, T   Road to Appomattox (Baton Rouge and London: Louisiana State University Press, 1994; originally Memphis: Memphis State College Press, 1956) [hereafter Wiley, *Road to Appomattox*], p. 47.

[10]. An excellent synopsis of the fighting in western Virginia is found in Fleming, "Northwestern Virginia Campaign," *supra*.

held the key position of Cheat Mountain, northwest of Staunton and Monterey, Lee ordered Loring to hold that position. Although Loring had only arrived in the area on July 22, Lee left Richmond for northwest Virginia on July 28. Lee was under orders from Jefferson Davis to inspect and consult on the campaign plan.[11]

Lee's unannounced arrival at Loring's headquarters probably disconcerted Loring, who only recently had assumed command and had discretionary orders on how to handle the situation. Nonetheless, Lee's arrival was less troubling than the inadequate supplies, widespread illness, and terrible weather -- all of which hampered Loring's ability to push the Yankees back over the Alleghenies. Because Lee failed to compel or cajole Loring into attacking the enemy before it increased its strength and fortified its position, critics, including pro-Lee historian Douglas Southall Freeman, have criticized him for being too much the gentleman and too little the general.[12]

The cold mountain weather caused Lee to grow his famous beard, and, on August 31, he was promoted to full general retroactive to June 14 -- the third senior general in the Confederacy (junior only to Adjutant General Samuel Cooper and Albert S. Johnston). With this additional encouragement, Lee replaced Loring as commander-in-fact. Lee became personally involved in scouting for attack routes on the Union stronghold, the Cheat Mountain Summit Fort, and allowed Colonel Albert Rust of the 3rd Arkansas Infantry to convince him of the utility of a rugged route to a vantage point that commanded the Union position.

In his perceptive analysis of this northwest Virginia campaign, Martin Fleming comments on that decision and its reflection of a weakness on the part of Lee:

> Rust was very confident that he could lead his men to this vantage point without losing the important element of surprise and argued his point. Lee acquiesced, revealing his weakness of sometimes being more of a gentleman than a forceful leader.
>
> Lee was not a stern commander. He tended to avoid personal controversy and worked best with commanders with whom he was familiar, giving them broad discretion in

---

[11]. On Lee's western Virginia experiences, see Freeman, Douglas Southall, *R.E. Lee*, 4 vols. (New York and London: Charles Scribner's Sons, 1934-5) [hereafter Freeman, *R.E. Lee*], I, pp. 531-604; Newell, Clayton R., *Lee vs. McClellan: The First Campaign* (Washington, D.C.: Regnery Publishing, Inc., 1996) [hereafter Newell, *Lee vs. McClellan*].

[12]. Freeman, *R.E. Lee*, I, pp. 552-3; Newell, *Lee vs. McClellan*, pp. 216, 232.

carrying out their orders. These qualities, and other manly traits for which history remembers him, earned Lee great respect and loyalty in the rank and file of the Army of Northern Virginia. However, such traits sometimes caused problems, and during the campaign in northwestern Virginia problems arose with Loring, and later with Generals [Henry Alexander] Wise and [John Buchanan] Floyd in the Kanawha Valley. But none were as costly as Lee's decision to allow Albert Rust to embark on his risky mission.[13]

Forecasting the mistake-prone approach he would take in the Seven Days' Battle the following year, Lee devised a complicated battle plan calling for a coordinated, six-column assault on Cheat Mountain and nearby Camp Elkwater. After marches of up to 2½ days, three columns were to converge on each of the two Union positions; the attack on Cheat Mountain was to serve as the signal for the companion assault. To succeed, everything had to go well; however, it did not. Early on September 12, Colonel Rust's wet, tired, and hungry men foolishly exposed their presence by attacking Federal supply wagons a half-mile from the Cheat Mountain fort. Even worse, Union prisoners convinced Rust that he was outnumbered, and his 1,500-man force ultimately was routed by 200 Yankee skirmishers. The small amount of noise made by this farce of a battle failed to alert the other Rebel columns -- including the three commanded by Lee at Camp Elkwater -- that the time for fighting had arrived.

Long after Lee's attacks were to have started in earnest, Union scouts discovered the Rebel threat and prepared their defenses. No serious attack ever took place. Lee, with 10,000 troops, had failed to dislodge 3,000 Yankees. The next day, Lee sent his aide-de-camp, Lieutenant Colonel John A. Washington, and his son, William Henry Fitzhugh "Rooney" Lee, to scout Union positions for an opportunity to salvage something from all those efforts. The result was that Washington was killed by Union pickets.

After two days of skirmishes, Lee withdrew his forces from the Cheat Mountain area and switched his attention to the Kanawha Valley in southern West Virginia. A few weeks later, on October 3, Union troops moved from Cheat Mountain and defeated a Rebel force at

---

[13]. Fleming, "Northwestern Virginia Campaign," p. 62. Freeman and Newell share Fleming's judgment that Lee seriously erred in relying upon Colonel Rust for this critical assignment. Freeman, *R.E. Lee*, I, p. 575 (referring to Rust as "an unskilled volunteer"); Newell, *Lee vs. McClellan*, pp. 232-3.

Greenbriar, Virginia, thereby completing the rout of Lee's Confederates in the midst of Virginia's Allegheny Mountains.

During August and September, Lee failed to exercise his authority and resolve a blood feud between two subordinate generals, Brigadiers John Buchanan Floyd and Henry Alexander Wise. They spent more time bickering with each other than fighting Yankees in the Kanawha Valley. Lee allowed this intolerable situation to continue by declining their specific requests that he issue orders to straighten out the mess and, instead, by referring the matter to Richmond.[14] Lee preferred not to get involved -- to the detriment of the Confederate cause in southwest Virginia.

When he moved southwest to the Kanawha Valley, Lee faced Brigadier General William S. "Old Rosey" Rosecrans. But Lee arrived there too late to accomplish anything. Union forces under General Cox had moved (in a southeasterly direction) up the Kanawha River from below Charleston in July. After losing a skirmish at Cross Lanes on August 26, Cox's outnumbered forces had been reinforced by Rosecrans, who had replaced McClellan when he was transferred to Washington. On September 10, Rosecrans' troops had defeated 2,000 Confederates at Carnifax Ferry, and the losers had retreated to Meadow Bluff, where Lee found them when he arrived. After an October 3, four-hour battle at Camp Bartow, the opposing armies fought again in early November and, eventually, went into winter quarters. On October 30, Lee left western Virginia for the last time -- his efforts there having been less than noteworthy.[15]

In western Virginia, Lee had demonstrated two of his common tactical mistakes: he had failed to take charge of the battlefield and he had issued overly complex and ineffective orders. The press and the public justifiably criticized Lee's performance as weak and vacillating. Nevertheless, after the war, Jefferson Davis found Lee blameless for the western Virginia failures:

> ...If his plans and orders had been carried out, the result would have been victory rather than retreat... Yet, through all this, with a magnanimity rarely equalled, he stood in silence, without defending himself or allowing others to de-

---

[14]. Freeman, *R.E. Lee*, I, p. 594; Newell, *Lee vs. McClellan*, p. 238; Fuller, *Grant and Lee*, pp. 137-8.

[15]. "[Lee's] habit of issuing broad orders and leaving details to his subordinates had led to a series of lost opportunities as the Confederate military leaders in western Virginia delayed and bickered." Newell, *Lee vs. McClellan*, p. 263.

fend him, for he was unwilling to offend anyone who was striking blows for the Confederacy.

"If only his plans and orders had been carried out!" No more sympathetic assessment could any general ask.

While Lee was struggling in the Virginia mountains, ominous developments were occurring in the West and Deep South. Confederate Major General Leonidas Polk committed a grave political error by foolishly violating Kentucky's neutrality on September 6. Three days later, Ulysses Grant moved troops into Paducah, Kentucky, at the vital juncture of the Tennessee and Ohio Rivers. On September 16, Confederate forces abandoned Ship Island off the Mississippi coast, thereby providing the Northerners with a useful operational base in the Gulf of Mexico.

Contemporaneous developments augured ill for Confederates in the West. In late 1861, Richmond authorities were demanding that most meat and grain raised in Tennessee be sent to the troops in Virginia and instructing General Albert S. Johnston, commander of the Confederacy's Army of Tennessee, to reserve Rebel supplies in Nashville solely for those same Virginia soldiers. Because of distance and, perhaps, a lack of concern, Richmond remained ignorant of the weakness in arms, manpower, and supplies of the Army of Tennessee.[16]

Lee, meanwhile, needed an opportunity to redeem himself. Perhaps the "Granny Lee," "Great Entrencher," and "King of Spades" sobriquets Lee acquired after his western Virginia experience created a resolve on his part to demonstrate his aggressiveness when he had another opportunity to command.[17] A new assignment came on November 6, two days after Jefferson Davis was elected to a six-year term as President of the Confederate States of America. Davis dispatched Lee to the Southeast, but Lee's new position gave him no opportunity for offensive action. In his new assignment, Lee was to be responsible for improving the coastal defenses of South Carolina, Georgia, and Florida. The fact that Davis found it necessary to write letters on Lee's behalf to the governors of South Carolina and Georgia indicates the low esteem in which Lee was held at that time. Davis explained Lee's situation: "Lest the newspaper attack should have created unjust and unfavorable impressions in regard to him, I thought it desirable to write to

---

[16]. Connelly, Thomas Lawrence, *Army of the Heartland: The Army of Tennessee, 1861-1862* (Baton Rouge and London: Louisiana State University Press, 1967), pp. 11, 93-4.
[17]. Newell, *Lee vs. McClellan*, p. 262.

Governor Pickens [of South Carolina] and tell him what manner of man he was who had been sent to South Carolina."[18]

The situation in the Southeast was deteriorating badly because of developments on the Union side. Lincoln had replaced McDowell with George McClellan as commander of the Division of the Potomac on July 27, 1861. The Union Army, under the leadership of McClellan, was rebuilding after the Bull Run disaster and going on the offensive along the Atlantic Coast. A Union expeditionary force captured Forts Clark and Hatteras on the North Carolina coast and gained control of strategically located Hatteras Inlet at the southern end of that state's Outer Banks. In lower South Carolina, an expeditionary force compelled the evacuation of Forts Beauregard and Walker and then occupied Port Royal, an ideal shelter for Union blockade vessels between Charleston and Savannah.

Farther south, shortly after receiving his new orders, Lee arrived at Fort Pulaski on the Savannah River, fifteen miles east of the vital port city of Savannah. As a second lieutenant, he had been one of the engineers involved in the start of the fort's construction in 1829. Lee pronounced the 25-million-brick, 7½-foot-thick walled fort impervious to artillery fire. However, a 30-hour Union bombardment on April 10-11, 1862, proved him wrong. Rifled artillery destroyed the walls, exposed the powder magazine, and brought about the surrender of 385 men and the fort. The early 1862 fall of Fort Pulaski ended virtually all Confederate blockade-running through Savannah.[19] During his four months in South Carolina, Georgia, and Florida, Lee realized that, with the exception of a few strongholds, it was impossible to defend the coast against combined Union naval and army forces. Therefore, he concentrated his efforts on building defenses inland at points unreachable by the Union navy.[20]

While Lee worked on defenses in the Southeast, developments were occurring in Washington that would affect Lee's future. On November 1, 1861, General Winfield Scott resigned as General-in-Chief of the Union Army, and, four days later, Lincoln replaced him with George McClellan. "Little Mac" had succeeded in driving Scott out of

---

[18]. Davis, Jefferson, *The Rise and Fall of the Confederate Government*, 2 vols. (New York: Da Capo Press, Inc., 1990; reprint of 1881 edition), p. 376; Thomas, *Lee*, p. 212, citing Jefferson Davis to Joseph E. Brown, November 6, 1861. Freeman also concluded that Davis wrote to the two governors because of strong opposition to Lee. Freeman, *R.E. Lee*, I, p. 607.

[19]. Thomas, *Lee*, pp. 215-6; Weigley, *American Way of War*, p. 101.

[20]. On Lee's service in the Southeast, see Freeman, *R.E. Lee*, I, pp. 605-31; Thomas, *Lee*, pp. 212-7 (Chapter 17, "Low-Country Gentlemen Curse Lee").

Washington and was to be both Lincoln's hope and nemesis for the following two years. During Lee's four months in the Southeast, McClellan devised a grand scheme for capturing Richmond that would create the opportunity, in 1862, for Lee to emerge from the shadows and move to center stage.

Chapter 3

Early Summer 1862:
Slaughter on the Peninsula

Throughout the winter of 1861-2, Lincoln grew increasingly impatient about the inaction on the part of McClellan in the East and Major General Henry Wager Halleck and Brigadier General Don Carlos Buell in the West. This led him to issue his January 27, 1862 General War Order Number One directing a general movement of Union forces against the "insurgent forces" on February 22.[1] In the same vein, Lincoln issued a January 31 Special War Order Number One directing seizure of a railroad position southwest of Manassas Junction.

In early February, Lincoln and McClellan debated whether to march the Union army south toward Richmond or to ferry troops to the southeast of Richmond to launch an assault from there. Meanwhile, between February 7 and 10, General Ambrose Everett Burnside consolidated Union control of the Outer Banks and North Carolina's sounds by capturing Roanoke Island. That same month, in contrast to the inactive McClellan, Union forces made significant progress in the West. On February 3, Grant launched his campaign against Fort Henry on the Tennessee River and nearby Fort Donelson on the Cumberland.[2] By the afternoon of February 6, Fort Henry had fallen to Union Flag Officer Andrew Hull Foote's gunboats before the arrival of Grant's 15,000 troops. On February 11 and 12, Brigadier Generals Grant and John Alexander McClernand marched on and encircled Fort Donelson and Dover, Tennessee, with 40,000 Union troops. The land attack commenced on the 13th, and a gunboat assault followed the next day. After repelling the gunboats, the Confederates attempted a breakout on the 15th, initially drove back the Blue troops, fatally hesitated, and then were driven back in by Grant's counter-attack. Grant insisted on "un-

---

[1]. Hattaway and Archer, *How the North Won*, p. 93.
[2]. For details of Grant's campaign, see Cooling, Benjamin Franklin, *Forts Henry and Donelson: The Key to the Confederate Heartland* (Knoxville: The University of Tennessee Press, 1987).

conditional and immediate surrender," which he obtained on February 16, 1862. Grant's campaign resulted in the first major victory for the North, capture of 12,500 of 15,000 Confederates, Union control of the Tennessee and Cumberland Rivers, the South's loss of the bulk of both Kentucky and Tennessee, and a veritable knife driven into the left side of the Confederacy.

On March 4, Lee was replaced by Major General John Clifford Pemberton as commander of the Confederate Department of South Carolina, Georgia and East Florida. Although he thus far had failed to achieve any operational success, Lee became military advisor to President Jefferson Davis. On March 13, Davis designated Lee to be in charge of "the conduct of military operations in the armies of the Confederacy." By making Lee his advisory chief of staff, Davis thwarted his congressional opponents who had tried to force Davis to appoint Lee Secretary of War. In Lee's new advisory position, his only responsibility until June 1, he did little to bring about the national unity of command so necessary to Confederate defense and success. Instead, Lee focused on the East.

Yielding to the supposed military expertise of McClellan, Lincoln on March 8 approved his plan for a campaign against Richmond via the Virginia Peninsula between the James and York rivers. However, in his second General War Order, Lincoln required that sufficient troops to defend the Union capital be kept near Washington. That same day the southern ironclad CSS Virginia (formerly the USS Merrimack) wreaked havoc on the Union fleet in Hampton Roads. That evening, however, the just-completed Union ironclad, USS Monitor, arrived on the scene after its hasty maiden voyage from the famous Brooklyn Navy Yard. The next day, March 9, the two vessels fought to a draw in the first battle between ironclad ships, and the perceived threat of the Virginia to Washington and the entire northeast coast came to an end.

Also on March 9, McClellan's troops moved out of Alexandria only to make the embarrassing discovery that the Confederates had abandoned their Manassas camps and left behind a collection of log "Quaker cannons," which had played a role in causing McClellan to overestimate enemy strength. It was only two days later that Lincoln removed McClellan from his General-in-Chief position and put Secretary of War Edwin Stanton in charge of overall coordination of military activities. As Commander of the Army of the Potomac, McClellan continued planning his Peninsula Campaign. On March 13 Stanton advised him to get on with it but to ensure that Washington and Manassas Junction were protected.

At long last, Little Mac moved out, by water, for the Peninsula on March 17. He suffered a severe setback four days later and many miles away. At Kernstown, Virginia, in the northern Shenandoah Valley, Stonewall Jackson's 4,000 troops unwittingly attacked a vastly superior force of over 9,000 Union infantry. Although Jackson suffered a tactical defeat and retreated, he won a major strategic victory. Lincoln and Stanton perceived Jackson as a threat to Washington or Harper's Ferry and took preventive action. They held back Major General Nathaniel P. Banks' army at Harper's Ferry and had Major General McDowell's troops remain at Fredericksburg. Thus, they deprived McClellan of tens of thousands of additional troops for his campaign against Richmond.

By April 1, McClellan had moved 12 divisions of the Army of the Potomac to the Peninsula. These joined Major General John E. Wool's 12,000 troops at Fort Monroe and began the long, deliberate trek up the Peninsula. On April 3, Lincoln discovered that "Little Mac" had planned on leaving fewer than 20,000 troops to guard Washington. Having been disconcerted by Jackson, Lincoln ordered retention of an additional corps at the capital. Nevertheless, McClellan had about 110,000 Union troops to begin his siege of Yorktown the next day. General Joseph Johnston had only 17,000 Confederates to defend Yorktown and an eight-mile line across the Peninsula from the York River on the northeast to the James River on the southwest. Although Johnston wanted to retreat immediately to the Richmond area, Lee convinced Davis that Johnston must be ordered to contest McClellan's advance up the Peninsula.

Meanwhile, another Confederate General Johnston--Albert Sidney--launched a massive, but poorly planned and executed, surprise attack on April 6 against General Grant's troops at Shiloh (Pittsburg Landing), Tennessee, on the Tennessee River. In a March 26 letter, Lee had encouraged Albert Sidney Johnston to take the offensive: "I need not urge you, when your army is united, to deal a blow at the enemy in your front, if possible, before his rear gets up from Nashville." In a day-long battle, the Rebels pushed the Yanks back toward the river, encountered stiffening resistance, and lost General Johnston to a bullet in the leg, lack of prompt medical attention, and a lethal loss of blood.

Late that day and throughout the next day, Grant was greatly reinforced by Major General Don Carlos Buell. Grant went on the offensive, recovered the ground lost the prior day and compelled the Rebels to retreat to Corinth, Mississippi. Although both sides claimed victory at Shiloh, the Rebel offensive actually was a costly bloodbath for each. The Union lost 13,000 men, and the Confederates almost 11,000. The massive casualty lists from Shiloh were harbingers of similar tragedies to occur in the East.

The Confederacy suffered another significant setback in the West on April 24 and 25, 1862. Union Flag Officer David Farragut fought his fleet past two forts on the Mississippi and captured New Orleans, the major city and port of the Deep South.

In Richmond, meanwhile, the need for additional manpower in the military became so apparent that President Davis, on April 16, signed the Confederate Conscription Act drafting all white men between 18 and 35 years old and extending all enlistments for the duration of the war.[3] Concerned about the manpower disparity between North and South, Generals Lee and Joseph Johnston had successfully urged Davis to obtain passage of this legislation. However, a contemporaneous Exemption Act opened the door for those in many occupations to avoid the draft. There was a disparity between the law and reality; many southerners required to serve in the military failed to sign up. The law, however, did allow a draftee to hire a substitute, and the escalating cost of substitutes led to the perception and complaint that the struggle was "a rich man's war and a poor man's fight."

During mid-April Lee demonstrated his manpower priorities. On April 10 Lee advised his southeastern successor, John C. Pemberton, of the critical need for troops in the West: "Send, if possible...If Mississippi Valley is lost Atlantic states will be ruined."[4] For once Lee recognized the importance of the West -- so long as the troops going there were not from Virginia. More typically, ten days later he requested Pemberton to send troops to Virginia.[5]

Realizing the serious threat that McClellan on the Peninsula and McDowell at Fredericksburg posed to Richmond and Johnston's army, Lee wrote to Stonewall Jackson on April 21.[6] In that letter and another on April 25, Lee turned Jackson loose (with reinforcements under Major General Richard S. "Old Baldy" Ewell) on a brilliant diversionary campaign that prevented the Union forces in Virginia from uniting against Johnston.[7] Reflecting the essence of their relationship, Lee only had to advise Jackson of the goals and options and then could leave the execution to Jackson: "I cannot pretend at this distance to direct operations depending on circumstances unknown to me and requiring the exercise of discretion and judgment as to time and execution, but sub-

---

[3]. Hattaway and Jones, *How the North Won*, p. 113; Wiley, *Road to Appomattox*, p. 56.

[4]. Lee to John C. Pemberton, April 10, 1862.

[5]. Lee to John C. Pemberton, April 20, 1862, Dowdey and Manarin, *Papers*, p. 150.

[6]. Lee to Thomas J. Jackson, April 21, 1862, Dowdey and Manarin, *Papers*, p. 152.

[7]. Lee to Thomas J. Jackson, April 25, 1862, Dowdey and Manarin, *Papers*, pp. 156-7.

mit these suggestions for your consideration."[8] Lee's strategy would bear fruit through Jackson's execution of it during the following several weeks. Lee and Jackson were an excellent match because Jackson -- unlike many of Lee's other subordinates -- generally thrived under Lee's hands-off approach.[9]

Back on the Virginia Peninsula, Johnston, outnumbered 6 to 1 and having held out as long as possible by bluffing McClellan into grossly overestimating the Confederate "strength," finally evacuated Yorktown on May 3. The next day Union troops moved in and once again found a collection of "Quaker cannons." On May 5, however, the Yankees finally had a successful day on the Peninsula. In a battle at Williamsburg, they took advantage of Brigadier General Jubal A. Early's excessive aggressiveness, decimated Confederate troops and inflicted 1,700 casualties, while suffering fewer than 500 themselves.[10]

Fearing that they were about to be outflanked, Confederate forces abandoned Norfolk and its valuable shipyard and naval facilities on May 9. Lincoln, who had been on the Peninsula since May 7, prodded McClellan to get moving toward Richmond and personally oversaw the May 10 occupation of Norfolk. Over the course of the next week, McClellan at last made some real progress advancing on Richmond. President Davis' wife and many others fled the city, and Johnston retreated across the nearby Chickahominy River.

Although accompanying Union naval forces, including the Monitor, were repelled on May 15 at Drewry's Bluff seven miles below Richmond on the James River, a coordinated land assault on the Confederate capital appeared to be shaping up nicely. On May 17, McDowell at Fredericksburg was ordered to head south with his 20,000 men to connect with McClellan's right flank. Three days later, McClellan, still awaiting McDowell, had troops as close as eight miles from Richmond and appeared to be poised for attack. McDowell, however, was not speeding to McClellan's side and was still in Fredericksburg on the 23rd, when he met there with Lincoln. As Lee had accurately presumed and because of Lincoln's omnipresent fears for the security of Washington, the President precluded McDowell's merger with McClellan.

Lincoln's fears reflected developments on the other side of the Blue Ridge Mountains. With a force of 10,000 moved secretly into the Virginia mountains west of Staunton, Stonewall Jackson had begun his

---

8. *Ibid.*, p. 157; Glatthaar, *Partners in Command*, p. 23.

9. The Seven Days' Battle was the major exception.

10. Detailed accounts of the Peninsular Campaign, including the Seven Days' Battle, are in Sears, *To the Gates of Richmond: The Peninsular Campaign* (New York: Ticknor & Fields, 1992); Freeman, *R.E. Lee*, II, pp. 8-250; and Nevins, *Ordeal*, VI, 34-64, 119-38.

classic Shenandoah Valley Campaign with a May 8 victory over 6,000 Union troops at McDowell. After climbing 20 miles over the rugged Shenandoah Mountains in less than a day, pushing those Union forces back to Franklin, and blocking the road between Franklin and Staunton, Jackson's men quickly slipped back into the Valley for their brilliant general's next move. This came on the 20th when Jackson joined forces with Ewell and moved to the Luray area in the center of the Valley to threaten Nathaniel Banks' army.

On the 23rd of May Jackson sprung the surprise attack that convulsed the North and canceled all attempts to reinforce Little Mac on the Peninsula. Jackson's men, keeping Massanutten Mountain between them and Banks' main army, struck 1,400 Yankees at Front Royal. They killed, injured or captured three-quarters of them and drove the remainder northward across both branches of the Shenandoah. This put Jackson's and Ewell's 16,000 troops in a position to cut off Banks' entire army. The next day Lincoln reacted predictably, ordering Major General John C. Fremont to close in on Jackson's rear by moving east from Franklin and, even more significantly, ordering McDowell to send his 20,000 troops west from Fredericksburg into the Shenandoah Valley instead of south to the Peninsula.

On the 25th Jackson pressed his forces northward toward Winchester in a bloody but unsuccessful attempt to cut off Banks completely. The effort, which forced Banks to retreat all the way to Williamsport, Maryland, on the Potomac River, cost Banks 1,000 men and Jackson 400. It was now clear to Lincoln that he was not going to be able to send any additional troops to McClellan, who had an insatiable appetite for reinforcements. Realizing that and concerned about Jackson's forceful foray, Lincoln, also on the 25th, ordered McClellan to get on with his attack on Richmond or to return and defend Washington. Possibly in response, McClellan initiated minor offensive actions north of Richmond at Hanover Station on the 27th and Ashland on the 29th. Richmonders breathed a sigh of relief when they learned on the 28th that McDowell was heading to the Shenandoah Valley instead of Richmond. Lee's strategy had worked.

Meanwhile Jackson's 16,000 men were keeping an amazing 60,000 Union troops occupied in the Shenandoah. After chasing Banks across the Potomac, Jackson threatened Harper's Ferry before finally retreating. With Union armies closing in from the north (Banks), east (McDowell and Brigadier General James Shields) and west (Fremont), Jackson's foot-soldiers conducted one of their patented marches southward "up" the Valley on the last two days of May and eluded their pursuers with minimal conflict and casualties. Jackson had done his job.

A few days earlier on the Peninsula it was Joseph Johnston, not McClellan, who launched a major attack. On May 31, in the Battle of Fair Oaks (Seven Pines), Joe Johnston assaulted 30,000 entrenched Union troops isolated on one side of the Chickahominy River. The seemingly simple plan of attack proved too complicated. Uncoordinated marches and attacks resulted in high Confederate casualties and Union retreats but in no Confederate breakthrough or capture of large numbers of Union soldiers. Committing errors that Lee would often repeat, Johnston had given his generals verbal orders, failed to ensure that Major General James "Old Pete" Longstreet understood his orders, and failed to oversee execution of his orders.

Late in the day, however, an event occurred that changed the character of the war. Johnston was seriously wounded by flying shell fragments and succeeded by Major General Gustavus W. Smith. Within hours, Smith suffered a stroke, and that night Davis replaced him with Robert E. Lee. One early post-war northern historian concluded that when Lee assumed command of that army, "he found in command of its various divisions and brigades the best military talent the South possessed or that was to be developed during the war."[11]

To avoid naming another general-in-chief who might interfere with his playing that role, Davis kept Lee in that position and simply added an army command to Lee's duties. The next day Lee issued Special Orders No. 22 referring for the first time to the Army of Northern Virginia. From June 1, 1862, until April 9, 1865, Lee would command that army.

The Battle of Fair Oaks continued the next day with a disastrous Confederate assault and retreat. Although ordered from Richmond to the battlefield at 8 a.m., Lee mysteriously delayed until 2 p.m. his arrival on the battlefield, which was only six miles from Richmond. The two days of Rebel frontal assaults at Fair Oaks resulted in 4,400 Union casualties but a total of 5,700 for the undermanned and attacking Confederates.[12] Would a lesson be learned from this experience? Later in June the Seven Days' Battle, under the command of Lee, would tell.

When McClellan learned that Lee had replaced Joe Johnston as commander of the Confederate forces defending Richmond, he must have been pleased. Less than two months before, he had written to Lincoln: "I prefer Lee to Johnston -- the former is too cautious and weak

---

[11]. Bruce, "Lee and Strategy," in Gallagher, *Lee the Soldier*, pp. 111-2.
[12]. Livermore, *Numbers & Losses*, p. 81.

under grave responsibility -- personally brave and energetic to a fault, yet he is wanting in moral firmness when pressed by heavy responsibility and is likely to be timid and irresolute in action."[13] Not only had Little Mac failed to detect Lee's propensity for aggressiveness, but in fact he attributed to Lee the very traits that made McClellan a failure as a Civil War general.[14]

McClellan was not alone in his judgment of Lee at the time Lee replaced Johnston. Because of Lee's lack of prior battlefield success, many southerners were not pleased by his appointment. The *Richmond Examiner* commented: "Evacuating Lee, who has never yet risked a single battle with the invader, is commanding general."[15] What impact might comments like that have on Lee? Did he have something to prove?

Some insight into how badly McClellan had misjudged Lee comes from a conversation that June between Longstreet's chief of artillery, Brigadier General E. Porter Alexander, and Captain Joseph C. Ives of Jefferson Davis' staff. To Alexander's question whether Lee would be sufficiently audacious, Ives responded:

> Alexander, if there is one man in either army, Federal or Confederate, who is, head and shoulders, far above every other one in either army in audacity, that man is General Lee, and you will very soon have lived to see it. Lee is audacity personified. His name is audacity, and you need not be afraid of not seeing all of it that you will want to see.[16]

After the war, Alexander wrote that Lee had been as audacious as Napoleon -- and perhaps had surpassed him in audacity.[17]

While Lee took about four weeks to strengthen his Richmond area forces, significant events occurred elsewhere. On the Mississippi River on June 6, Union naval forces won a major one-hour battle, sank seven of eight Confederate vessels, and accepted the surrender of Memphis.

---

13. Reardon, Carol, "From `King of Spades' to `First Captain of the Confederacy': R.E. Lee's First Six Weeks with the Army of Northern Virginia," pp. 309-30 in Gallagher, *Lee the Soldier*, p. 312.

14. McClellan, with resources to spare and the necessity to win, should have been aggressive but was not; Lee, with scarce resources and only needing a deadlock, should have been defensive but was not.

15. Connelly, *Marble Man*, p. 17.

16. Gallagher, Gary W. (ed.), *Fighting for the Confederacy: The Personal Recollections of General Edward Porter Alexander* (Chapel Hill: University of North Carolina Press, 1989) [hereafter Alexander, *Fighting for the Confederacy*], p. 91.

17. *Ibid.*, pp. 91-2.

The Union now controlled all of the vital Mississippi except the southern stretch from Vicksburg to Port Hudson.

Closer to Lee, Jackson continued to flee frustrated and angry Union forces until he turned on his pursuers and repelled them in bloody battles. He and Ewell managed to keep the troops of Union generals Fremont and Shields separated by the South Fork of the Shenandoah River and to defeat each of them, respectively, in engagements at Cross Keys on June 8 and Port Republic on June 9. Total casualties were 900 for Jackson and 1,600 for the Yankees. Those battles brought an end to Jackson's famous and effective diversionary Valley Campaign. At the cost of 2,500 casualties and 600 prisoners, he had inflicted 3,500 casualties and captured 3,500 prisoners, 10,000 small arms and nine cannon. Most significantly, Jackson had carried out Lee's strategy and performed his primary mission of preventing a massive coalition of Union armies against Richmond and its defenders. Now Lee, at the suggestion of Davis, had other plans for Jackson and his exhausted men.

Lee realized that he needed to maximize his forces in the Richmond area without letting Lincoln and his generals comprehend what was happening. Therefore, on June 15, he sent 10,000 troops west from Richmond in what appeared to be an effort to reinforce Jackson. Lee made sure that this activity appeared surreptitious but was in fact known to the enemy. At the same time, Lee executed his "real" plan and on the 16th ordered Jackson to proceed east expeditiously to join the Army of Northern Virginia. Barely a week after the end of his Valley Campaign, Jackson moved on June 17 toward the Chickahominy River northeast of Richmond.

Lincoln went for the bait. On June 18 he wrote to McClellan and urged him to attack the opposing Confederate lines, which had been weakened by the movement of 10,000 troops. McClellan, of course, saw this deployment as proof of his position that the gray forces greatly outnumbered his. Meanwhile, between June 12 and 15, Brigadier General Jeb Stuart embarrassed Little Mac by leading a cavalry ride completely around the Union army, capturing 165 prisoners and 300 horses, and exposing the inadequacy of Union communications. Lincoln's frustrations concerning recent developments led him, on June 17, to create the Army of Virginia and bring Major General John Pope in from the West to head it.

On June 25 McClellan at long last launched a feeble assault. With his Army still divided by the Chickahominy, he ordered an advance by the picket lines on his left (southern) flank near the James River. A furious but minor fight ensued with the Rebel defenders prevailing. They suffered only half of the Union's 500-plus casualties. This small struggle nevertheless was significant enough to rattle McClellan. That evening he sent a bizarre, panic-driven cable to Washington stating that Jackson was at Hanover Station (he was), that Beauregard's army (actually in Alabama) was in Richmond, that the Confederates had more than 200,000 men (more than double their true strength), that he expected to be attacked the next day (he was), that he could at least die with his army if it was destroyed by the overwhelming numbers, that any disaster would not be his fault, and that he could not get reinforcements even if he wanted them.

Even though Lee's and McClellan's armies were of about even strength, Lee planned to go on the offensive to save Richmond. Therefore, he devised a series of complicated, frontal-assault battle plans which resulted in severe casualties on both sides, especially the Confederate side, and the retreat of the Union forces in the Seven Days' Battle. For his offensive, Lee organized his army into divisions, including those under Major Generals Jackson, Longstreet, Ambrose Powell ("A.P.") Hill, and Daniel Harvey ("D.H." or "Harvey") Hill. By eliminating the two-wing concept of army organization, which Johnston had created to avoid Davis' prohibition on the use of corps in the army's organization, Lee undercut his ability to effectively manage his army that was about to grow to almost 100,000 troops.

Lee's problems began in the weeks and days preceding the offensive. Although Lee planned to cut off McClellan's army from its supply base to the north at White House Landing on the Pamunkey River (a tributary of the York River), Union capture of Norfolk had enabled McClellan to begin shifting his base to Harrison's Landing on the James River to his south. When Lee sent Jeb Stuart on his grandiose ride around McClellan's army, Little Mac realized the vulnerability of White House Landing and the necessity to move his base of supplies as quickly as possible.

Lee also underestimated the easily discernible exhaustion of both Jackson and his "foot cavalry." Between March 22 and June 9, at Lee's suggestion and with his full knowledge, Jackson's men had marched 676 miles; in their May 30-June 5 retreat from the Potomac alone, they had rapidly marched 104 miles. It therefore should not have surprised Lee when Jackson's tired troops took longer than originally contemplated to move, by marching and limited rail facilities, from the Valley to the Peninsula.

At Lee's critical pre-battle conference on June 23, an exhausted and overly optimistic Jackson said he would be on Lee's army's left, or north flank, early on June 25. Even though the offensive was delayed until June 26, Jackson would fail to arrive in time for the early morning assault. After the conference, Jackson rode in the rain all night to return to his exhausted men northwest of Richmond. In often rainy weather, it took Jackson's men three days to march the final 40 miles to their assigned position on the Confederate left. Lee, however, had sufficient information about the whereabouts of Jackson's troops to know that the timing of the offensive for early on the 26th was -- at the least -- a real gamble. But Lee was anxious to get on with it.

Thus, in his General Orders Number 75 on June 24, Lee set his complex, coordinated Mechanicsville attack for early on the 26th against Union Brigadier General Fitz John Porter's isolated corps north of the Chickahominy. Lee hoped to drive it back, break the Union supply-line from White House on the York River south to the Union army, and capture that supply base, as well as the Union supply trains at Cold Harbor. Those goals might have been achieved more efficiently and simply by going around the north flank of McClellan's army instead of launching a complicated frontal assault. In any event, Lee ordered Major General John B. "Prince John" Magruder to create a diversion south of the Chickahominy and Jackson, A.P. Hill, Longstreet and D.H. Hill, in that order from north to south, to attack Porter with their respective divisions.

Lee's complicated order was reminiscent of Cheat Mountain. Specifically, Jackson was to march from Ashland to the Slash Church on the 25th, camp west of the Virginia Central Railroad, march at 3 a.m. on the 26th, and capture Beaver Dam on the Yankee right flank and rear. When A.P. Hill heard Jackson's cannon, he was to cross the Chickahominy at Meadow Bridge and take Mechanicsville. As soon as Hill had moved sufficiently east to control the Mechanicsville Bridge, Longstreet and D.H. Hill were to cross that bridge and go to the support of Jackson and A.P. Hill respectively. The major problem with this battle plan was that, with a single error, the entire enterprise would collapse. Failure or disaster was likely, and both occurred.

Not surprisingly, Jackson failed to appear. Fatigued by their just-completed Valley Campaign, Jackson's men arrived at Ashland late on the 25th -- one day later than planned. Then, exhausted by their 20-mile, mud-encased march on the 25th, they failed to march at the ordered time of 3 a.m. on the 26th and did not begin leaving Ashland until 8 a.m. Not arriving at Hundley's Corner near Mechanicsville on the Confederate left flank until 5 p.m. that afternoon, Jackson, of course, was unable to carry out the planned morning assault that was to have initiated the entire Confederate offensive. Jackson himself had gotten only ten hours of sleep in four days and was physically ill for the next several days. Inexplicably, Lee apparently had taken no steps to stay informed of Jackson's location and simply waited for the battle plan to unfold. Instead it unraveled.

A.P. Hill grew impatient waiting for the sound of Jackson's non-existent attack, and decided to go ahead on his own. His men crossed the Chickahominy and entered Mechanicsville at 3 p.m. on the 26th, had some initial success and then were decimated by massed Union artillery and rifles. About 1,500 Rebels attacked 20,000 entrenched northerners at Beaver Dam and were slaughtered. Instead of halting the ill-advised offensive, Lee allowed D.H. Hill to enter the fray on A.P. Hill's right and come under the same deadly fire.

When Jackson finally arrived at Hundley's Corner near the Rebel left flank at 5 p.m., he decided his 20,000 men were not fit for fighting. He went into camp before sundown while the fighting raged three miles away and he was in a position to flank, or cut off the possible retreat of, the entrenched Union forces of Fitz John Porter. That evening Lee withdrew A.P. Hill's troops and prepared to attack again the next day.

Although it was a strategic success, the complex, intricately timed offensive planned by Lee had proven to be a tactical disaster. Lee had managed to get only 30 percent of his army involved in the assault. Of about 20,000 Union troops, only about 250 were killed or wounded. On the other hand, about 16,000 Confederates suffered 1,500 to 2,000 casualties.[18] In Brigadier General William Dorsey Pender's Brigade of A.P. Hill's Division, the 44th Georgia Regiment lost 264 of its 514 men (a 65% casualty rate).[19]

Mechanicsville provides a first opportunity to analyze the lethal effect of Lee upon the Army of Northern Virginia. Key statistics are provided by Thomas L. Livermore's *Numbers and Losses in the Civil War*. Livermore provides not only killed, wounded and missing statistics for both sides in many Civil War battles, but he also gives the numbers hit (killed and wounded) among each 1,000 soldiers and the number hit by each 1,000 soldiers engaged on each side. At Mechanicsville, the Union troops suffered light casualties and inflicted heavy casualties: only 16 of each thousand northerners were hit, while 95 of each 1,000 northerners killed or wounded a Confederate. Thus, the Union had a very favorable hit ratio of 16:95. On the other hand, the Confederates had a

[18]. Livermore, *Numbers & Losses*, p. 82

[19]. Fox, William F., *Regimental Losses in the American Civil War 1861-1865: A Treatise on the Extent and Nature of the Mortuary Losses in the Union Regiments, with Full and Exhaustive Statistics Compiled from the Official Records on File in the State Military Bureaus and at Washington* (Dayton, Ohio: Morningside House, Inc., 1985; reprint of Albany: Brandow Printing Company, 1898) [hereafter Fox, *Regimental Losses*] p. 556.

very negative hit ratio of 91:16; that is, 91 of every 1,000 Confederates were hit, but only 16 of every 1,000 Confederates killed or wounded a Union soldier.[20]

The Confederates' ratio compares very unfavorably with their fairly balanced hit ratios of 49:59 and 137:105 in the preceding (pre-Lee) battles at Williamsburg and Fair Oaks, respectively.[21] In those prior battles, the Army of Northern Virginia was hitting and being hit at about the same rate as the enemy. In Lee's first battle, on the other hand, they were being hit eight times as often as they were hitting the enemy. Livermore hit ratios also will be used to analyze many of Lee's later battles.

Jackson's failure to enter the fray on this first of the Seven Days presaged his disastrous non-involvement throughout the entire series of battles. Again and again in these consecutive days of bitter fighting, Jackson's men were late participants or non-participants -- due primarily to their commanding officer being in a stupor. Jackson slept for most of one afternoon of battle and fell asleep that night with food still in his mouth. Jackson's collapse probably resulted from extreme exhaustion brought on by his brilliant but fatiguing Valley Campaign and his lack of sleep while he oversaw his army's movement to the Peninsula. Between June 22 and 30, Jackson had very little sleep.[22]

Jackson's condition was so evident and debilitating that Lee should have been aware of it and taken corrective action. Lee may have been victimized by his practices of having a small staff and exercising lax battlefield oversight over his commanders. In any event, Lee either was or should have been aware of Jackson's incredible battlefield lapses from the very first day and should have placed him on sick leave, temporarily relieved him of command, or personally supervised Jackson's operations after the first day.

Although a tactical failure, the Battle of Mechanicsville was a major strategic success for Lee because it caused McClellan to panic and order the withdrawal of Porter -- over his objections -- across the Chickahominy, final abandonment of the White House Landing supply base, and then withdrawal of the Union army from the siege lines. Although he did not know it that night, Lee already had achieved his primary strategic objective -- relieving the siege of Richmond. While

---

20. Livermore, *Numbers & Losses*, p. 82.

21. *Ibid.*, pp. 80-1.

22. For details of Jackson's exhausted condition and lack of sleep, as well as an ambiguous conclusion about the cause of his failure on June 30 (one of many Jackson failures at Seven Days'), see Freeman, *R.E. Lee*, II, Appendix II-3, "The Reason for Jackson's Failure at White Oak Swamp, June 30, 1862," pp. 572-82.

ordering frontal attacks during the next several days, Lee ignored cavalry-obtained information indicating that McClellan's forces were retreating and were vulnerable to a flank attack on their James River base. Instead of going around McClellan's right flank and striking for the Evelington Heights overlooking Harrison's Landing, Lee attacked again and again.

Therefore, the next day (the 27th) A.P. Hill went on the offensive again, carried out a direct assault at Gaines' Mill for much of the day, and fought his division until it was no longer an effective fighting unit. Hill's problems were that Porter's forces had retreated during the night from Beaver Dam to another strong position east of Powhite Creek and that Jackson this time had barely entered the fray. That morning Lee had met with Hill and an exhausted Jackson to discuss a coordinated attack on the Union troops, which were being withdrawn from Mechanicsville for an ultimate retreat across the Chickahominy. It should have been apparent to Lee that Jackson was not in a competent state of mind.

Because of Jackson's failure to bring his men a few miles to the Confederate left flank, Hill once again fought alone for many long, bloody hours. The battle began at 11 in the morning and continued till dark. When Hill was suffering from withering artillery and small arms fire at Boatswain's Swamp, Lee finally sent his adjutant, Major Walter H. Taylor, at about 1 p.m. to prod the missing Jackson into action. It was another five hours until Jackson finally appeared and deployed. As the famed Louisiana Tigers were being driven from the battlefield, Ewell's Division (under Jackson) at last arrived to prevent a rout. During the middle of the afternoon, Lee ordered Longstreet's Division and Brigadier General John Bell Hood's and Colonel Evander McIvor Law's brigades to join the attack. Hood's 4th Texas Regiment lost 380 out of 500 men in the courageous charge, which succeeded in breaking the Union line.

Jackson, whose absence Ewell was unable to explain to Lee, finally entered the battle on the Confederate left at 6 o'clock. Lee's at-long-last-combined forces compelled Porter to retreat across the river at dusk. If Jackson had arrived and attacked Porter's right flank during the afternoon, Porter's retreat route across the Chickahominy would have been cut off and his forces isolated. Having escaped disaster, McClellan's forces now were in full retreat, and Lee's eagerness to assault continued unabated.

Lee's second offensive had again proven devastating to his own army. At Gaines' Mill (Boatswain's Swamp), the 39,000 Union troops had a total of 4,000 casualties and 2,800 missing, while the 33,000 Confederates had 8,800 killed or wounded. The Union had a favorable Livermore hit ratio of 117:256, and Lee's army suffered a negative 153:70 ratio.[23] In summary, five of every 40 Union soldiers in combat were hit, and ten of each 40 of them hit Confederates; on the other side, six of every 40 Confederates were hit while only three of every 40 Confederates hit the enemy. Thus, while the Union defenders were hitting their opponents at twice the rate of their own casualties, Lee's troops conversely were suffering twice the rate of casualties they were imposing.

On June 28 the Federals destroyed most of their huge stockpile of supplies at White House Landing, there were skirmishes at Garnett's and Golding's farms, and the Federal retreat toward the James River continued. Lee learned that all the Bluecoats had retreated south of the Chickahominy. He chose to continue attacking them directly instead of sweeping well around the east of them and cutting them off from embarking on vessels on the James River.[24]

On the 29th, Lee resumed his offensive against the retreating enemy. Once again Lee had a complicated plan of attack requiring coordination among many of his generals. This plan was not only complicated; it also was unwritten. Jackson was to cross the Grapevine Bridge over the Chickahominy and get behind (north and east of) the Union forces at Savage's Station. Major Generals Magruder and Benjamin Huger were to attack those forces from the west. Holmes was to seize Malvern Hill in front of the retreating Yankees. Due to a lackadaisical effort to rebuild or bypass the destroyed bridge, Jackson took all day to cross the river and never engaged the enemy.

Meanwhile, Magruder delayed his attack on particularly vulnerable troops of Brigadier General Edwin V. Sumner's 2nd Corps because Magruder mistakenly believed that Lee's orders required him to wait for Huger's arrival on his right flank. Magruder finally got Lee to order Huger to Magruder's flank. After his arrival on that flank, Huger departed without advising Magruder. Magruder went ahead with his unsupported attack at Savage's Station, and two brigades of his division were decimated by Sumner's corps before the latter retreated toward White Oak Swamp. The Union army left behind 2,500 wounded and sick. Due to lack of close on-scene coordination by Lee, lack of communication between Lee and his generals, and poor performance by all those generals,[25] Savage's Station became a major lost opportu-

---

[23]. *Ibid.*, pp. 82-3.
[24]. Alexander, Bevin, *Lost Victories: The Military Genius of Stonewall Jackson* (New York: Henry Holt and Company, 1992) [hereafter Bevin Alexander, *Lost Victories*], p. 114-6.
[25]. *Ibid.*, p. 131.

nity to strike the Bluecoats on the move. Freeman himself said, "The day's operations had been a failure, not to say a fiasco."[26]

More of the same occurred the next day. The Battle of Frayser's (Frazier's) Farm on June 30 was a classic example of the difficulty of coordinating a multi-divisional attack and the disastrous results of failure to do so. Jackson (with the divisions of Ewell, Brigadier General William Henry Chase Whiting and D.H. Hill) was to attack the Union army from the north as it retreated southward, while the other Rebel divisions were to attack that army's right flank from the west. Those other divisions were (from north to south) those of Major Generals Huger, Longstreet, A.P. Hill, and (Theophilus) Hunter Holmes.

After an early morning meeting with Lee, the totally fatigued Jackson failed until late in the day to get across White Oak Creek and Swamp, where the bridges (like Grapevine before them) not surprisingly had been destroyed. During an early afternoon artillery battle, Jackson slept under a tree and seemed unable to comprehend the news that his scouts had found a way through the swamp. Off on the far right, Huger delayed opening the attack and then inexplicably stopped firing. Once again Lee sent no couriers to the flanks to see what was amiss. He waited for his generals to carry out his grand plan. Two of them did. Longstreet and A.P. Hill slugged it out with the Federals they had attacked at Frayser's Farm. Unsupported on either flank, these 20,000 Butternuts took significant losses at the hands of 40,000 Yankees; they suffered 3,500 casualties.

Confederate General E. Porter Alexander thought that June 30, 1862, may have been the Confederates' best opportunity to win the war because the Confederacy was at its prime, especially in manpower, and had the chance to shock the North by capturing McClellan's army. He blamed Jackson for the lost opportunity but did not discount Lee's role:

> Yet it is hardly correct either to say that the failure to reap the greatest result was in no way Gen. Lee's fault. No commander of any army does his whole duty who simply gives orders, however well considered. He should supervise their execution, in person or by staff officers, constantly, day & night, so that if the machine balks at any point, he may be most promptly informed & may most promptly start it to work. For instance on Jun. 30 I think he should have been in person with Huger, & have had reliable members of his staff with Jackson on his left & Longstreet & others on his right,

---

[26]. Freeman, *R.E. Lee*, II, p. 176.

receiving reports every half hour or oftener, & giving fresh orders as needed.[27]

When confronted with the opinion that McClellan was about to escape, the frustrated Lee exclaimed, "Yes, he will get away because I cannot have my orders carried out."[28] It is interesting to compare Lee's hands-off approach to Grant's battlefield activism at both Fort Donelson and Shiloh during that same year.

The Rebels' delay on the 30th allowed McClellan to consolidate his forces in a dominating position on Malvern Hill near the James River. Malvern Hill became the scene of the most disastrous and unnecessary of Lee's frontal attacks during the Seven Days' Battle. After observing that Malvern Hill was a magnificent defensive position on which the Union infantry and artillery, including its siege and reserve train of 100 guns, could be assembled, and that it had protected positions for 300 guns which could sweep the narrow and obstructed approaches below, General Alexander offered a personal insight on the situation there:

> I don't think any military engineer can read this description of this ground without asking in surprise, & almost in indignation, how on God's earth it happened that our army was put to assault such a position. The whole country was but a gently rolling one with no great natural obstacles anywhere, fairly well cultivated & with farm roads going in every direction. Why was not half our army simply turned to the left & marched by the nearest roads out of the enemy's view & fire to strike his road of retreat, & his long, slow & cumbersome trains, a few miles below, while the rest in front could threaten & hold his battle array without attacking it.

> I have myself, on the ground afterward, discussed the feasibility of this in company with Gen. Wade Hampton, & [Major] Gen. J[eremy] F[rancis] Gilmer, chf. engineer, & we examined & found short, easy, & covered roads in every way favorable.

> But Gen. Lee, though himself distinguished as an engineer, & for engineer work, in Mexico, had but few engineer officers close to him, & seemed to have such supreme confidence that his infantry could go anywhere, that he took comparatively little pains to study out the easier roads.

> *In the Mexican War we fought with smooth bore, short range muskets, in fact, the character of the ground cut comparatively little*

---

27. Alexander, *Fighting for the Confederacy*, pp. 110-1.
28. Freeman, *R.E. Lee*, II, p. 202.

figure. But with the rifled muskets & cannon of this war the affair was very different as was proven both at Malvern Hill, & at Gettysburg...[29]

Not satisfied with the Union retreat virtually to the James River, Lee, ignoring the nearly unanimous advice of his corps commanders, launched a day-long series of suicidal attacks on July 1 by valuable veteran forces on strong Union positions. D.H. Hill had personally advised Lee of the height, vulnerable approaches, size and strength of Malvern Hill and added, "If General McClellan is there in force, we had better let him alone."[30]

Lee's usual lack of battlefield control and coordination resulted in Longstreet, A.P. Hill and Jackson being barely involved in the assault. A four-hour artillery duel resulted in the serial elimination of southern batteries when never more than sixteen Rebel guns were placed in action at one time and 90 of their guns were kept in reserve all day. Brigadier General William Nelson Pendleton, a vigorous post-war supporter of Lee, was Lee's Chief of Artillery directly responsible for this artillery fiasco.

After that artillery debacle, Union cannons and rifles decimated Rebel infantry attackers from Major Generals D.H. Hill's, Lafayette McLaws' and Huger's divisions. Their piecemeal attacks were brought about by a vague and flawed order Lee issued to his generals: "Batteries have been established to rake the enemy's lines. If it is broken as is probable, [Brigadier General Lewis Addison] Armistead, who can witness the effect of the fire, has been ordered to charge with a yell. Do the same."[31] The attacks continued even after the first ones had demonstrated the correctness of the advice of Lee's subordinates and the folly of continued infantry assaults on Union artillery and infantry firing down on the Confederates.

After the first failed attacks by five of D.H. Hill's brigades with a loss of 2,000 men, Lee himself ordered Magruder to attack. This led to the slaughter of additional thousands in the nine brigades of Huger and McLaws, as each one emerged from the woods separately and was eliminated. The disjointed attacks, spread out over several hours, were marked by what Union General Fitz John Porter called "a reckless disregard of life."[32] He described how the fourteen Rebel brigades successively charged the Union stronghold and "the artillery...mowed them

29. Alexander, *Fighting for the Confederacy*, p. 111.
30. Bevin Alexander, *Lost Victories*, p. 124; Wert, *Longstreet*, p. 146.
31. Bruce, "Lee and Strategy," in Gallagher, *Lee the Soldier*, p. 114.
32. McWhiney and Jamieson, *Attack and Die*, p. 3.

down with shrapnel, grape, and canister; while our infantry, with-holding their fire until the enemy were within short range, scattered the remnants of their columns."[33] The waves of attackers achieved nothing but self-destruction at the hands of Union artillery and infan-try.

Freeman concluded that Lee realized that evening that he had made a mistake in allowing his army's right wing to assault a position of unknown strength. That same evening Lee approached Magruder and asked him why he had undertaken such an attack; Magruder re-sponded, "In obedience to your orders, twice repeated."[34]

In all, Lee had 6,000 men killed or wounded in that single day of slaughter. Fifty percent of the Confederate casualties may have been attributable to artillery.[35] D.H. Hill himself said that Lee's assault at Malvern Hill "...was not war -- it was murder."[36] As a result of this ill-conceived assault, Confederate lines were in complete disarray and could have been swept from the field by a Union assault, which most generals other than McClellan would have launched. Fortunately for Lee, while McClellan was absent at Harrison's Landing and on the James River most of that day, Fitz John Porter was left in charge of the Army of the Potomac without authority to initiate a counter-attack.

As Porter Alexander indicated, Malvern Hill was the first, but certainly not the last, instance in which Lee gave insufficient weight to the Civil War's new weaponry. With increasing frequency throughout the war, the combatants, especially the Yankees, used rifled muskets. They propelled inch-long Minie balls, which were accurate at up to 200 yards and could kill at over half a mile. These weapons were ahead of Lee's tactics. Although Lee was not alone in making this miscalcula-tion, he lost more soldiers in less time than any Confederate general -- losses that the outmanned Confederates simply could not absorb.

The Seven Days' Battle terminated the threat to Richmond but had done so at an unnecessarily high cost. The threat had disappeared after the first day of battle and was known by Lee to be gone after the sec-ond day. Lee's abysmal control of his forces, insistence on continual frontal attacks, and persistent attempts to carry out nearly impossible coordinated attacks resulted in dreadful southern casualties. Of Lee's 95,000 men, 19,700 (21 percent) were killed or wounded; of McClellan's

---

[33]. *Ibid.*

[34]. Freeman, *R.E. Lee*, II, p. 218.

[35]. Griffith, Paddy, *Battle Tactics of the Civil War*, New Haven and London: Yale University Press, 1996) [hereafter Griffith, *Battle Tactics*], p. 170.

[36]. Freeman, *R.E. Lee*, II, p. 218; Sears, *To the Gates*, p. 335; McWhiney and Jamieson, *Attack and Die*, p. 4.

91,000 men, only 9,800 (11 percent) were killed or wounded.[37] As Lee was to learn to his regret, the Confederacy could not afford many such "victories."[38]

Alexander summarized Lee's first series of offensive thrusts as follows:

> Very few of the reports distinguish between the casualties of the different battles, of which there were four, beside a sharp affair of Magruder's at Savage's Station on Sunday the 29th, about which I have never known the particulars except that it was an isolated attack on a strong rear guard by 2 ½ brigades & it was repulsed, as might have been expected. No small force of ours could have hoped for any real success, & all such inadequate attacks were mistakes.
>
> Of the other four actions, three were assaults by main force right where the enemy wanted us to make them. The first, Ellison's Mill [Mechanicsville], was an entire failure & very bloody -- but fortunately was in a small scale. The second, Cold Harbor or Gaines' Mill, was also a bloody failure at first -- being made piecemeal. Finally made in force it was a success. The third, Malvern Hill, was an utter & bloody failure. Ellison's Mill & Malvern Hill could both have been turned [flanked], & Gen. D. H. Hill asserts that the enemy's right at Cold Harbor could have better [sic] assaulted than the centre or left where our attack was made.[39]

Another Confederate General, D.H. Hill, added more criticism of his own Army's efforts: "Owing to our ignorance of the country and lack of reconnaissance of the successive battlefields, throughout this campaign we attacked just when and where the enemy wished us to attack."[40] These Confederate military critics of Lee were not asserting that he should have done nothing, but rather that he should have done things differently. These possibilities included going around McClellan's right flank and cutting off his access to Harrison's Landing on the

---

[37]. Livermore, *Numbers & Losses*, p. 86.

[38]. One northern post-war analyst commented, "That Lee defeated McClellan is clear enough, but can it be claimed in any sense, except technically, the Army of the Potomac was defeated by him during these seven bloody days, a continuous battle in six separate but related actions, in four of which parts of his army were repulsed by parts of the opposing army, and on the sole occasion when all of the forces of each were opposed, the Army of Northern Virginia met with a decisive defeat?" Bruce, "Lee and Strategy," in Gallagher, *Lee the Soldier*, p. 114.

[39]. Alexander, *Fighting for the Confederacy*, p. 120.

[40]. Freeman, *R.E. Lee*, II, p. 232.

James River. What they did oppose were uncoordinated frontal assaults. Of this week-long struggle, Freeman said, "Lee displayed no tactical genius in combating a fine, well-led Federal army."[41]

As a result of Lee's aggressively offensive strategy and tactics during the Seven Days' Battles, the out-manned Confederates suffered 20,000 killed, wounded and missing to the Union's 10,000. Lincoln perceptively noted, "In men and material, the enemy suffered more than we, in that series of conflicts; while it is certain that he is less able to bear it."[42] The overall Livermore hit ratios for those battles were telling: the Union ratio was a positive 107:216, and the Confederate ratio was a very negative 207:102.[43] Distilled to their essence, these figures show that McClellan had lost one in ten while Lee was losing one in five. Victories at that cost would lose the war -- and they did.[44]

Throughout the Seven Days' Battle, Lee's strategy and tactics were excessively aggressive. His strategy was totally offensive. Incredibly, Lee watched thousands of his fine troops slaughtered while charging usually fortified Union forces but did not seem to realize the foolhardiness of such tactics. Lee's Seven Days' battle-plans were overly complex; he frequently issued vague and discretionary orders to his generals, and then he failed to supervise their execution through adequate on-the-field command and control.[45] He repeated these mistakes on several later occasions and thereby squandered the Confederacy's chances of winning the war.

---

[41]. *Ibid.*, p. 241.

[42]. Jones, Archer, "Military Means, Political Ends: Strategy," [hereafter Jones, "Military Means"] in Boritt, Gabor S. (ed.), *Why the Confederacy Lost* [hereafter Boritt, *Why the Confederacy Lost*] (New York and Oxford: Oxford University Press, 1992), p. 55.

[43]. Livermore, *Numbers & Losses*, p. 86.

[44]. Military historian Bevin Alexander said, "With the direct-assault kind of war Robert E. Lee unveiled in the Seven Days, the South might win battles, but it would bleed to death long before it could achieve victory." Bevin Alexander, *Lost Victories*, p. 129.

[45]. Freeman said that, at the Seven Days' Battle, "Lee trusted too much to his subordinates, some of whom failed him almost completely..." Freeman, *R.E. Lee*, II, p. 241.

Chapter 4

Mid-Summer 1862:
Costly Victory at Second Bull Run

July 2, 1862, marked the beginning of a new phase of the war. It was then clear that, at least under the pusillanimous McClellan, the North was not about to capture Richmond, let alone put a quick end to the war. On that day, Little Mac's army began arriving at Harrison's Landing on the James River. From there, its pouting commanding general, would eventually be sending it back north. Also on July 2, Lincoln, realizing that he would have to make greater use of the Union's numerical superiority, issued a call for an additional 300,000 men to enlist for three-year terms.

While fortifying his do-nothing position at Harrison's Landing, McClellan, on July 7, wrote one of his usual complaining and requisitioning letters to Secretary of War Stanton. He complained that the President had caused many of his problems by keeping too many troops defending Washington. He made his usual request for more troops because "...the rebel army is in our front, with the purpose of overwhelming us by attacking our positions, or reducing us by blocking our river communication. I cannot but regard our position as critical."[1] Little Mac was unaware that Lee had started withdrawing his troops back toward Richmond -- a movement hidden from McClellan for days by a cavalry screen. On July 13, Lincoln urged McClellan to resume the assault on Richmond, but all he got was another request for reinforcements.

The scene of battle was about to move north. On July 10, John Pope, the bombastic, newly-appointed Federal Army of Virginia Commander, announced his intention to deal harshly with Confederate sympathizers. The next day, Lincoln, having lost confidence in McClellan, named Major General Henry "Old Brains" Halleck General-in-Chief of the Federal Armies.

---

[1]. Sears, Stephen W., *George B. McClellan: The Young Napoleon* (New York: Ticknor & Fields, 1988), p. 223.

On July 12, Lee learned that Pope had occupied Culpeper, thereby threatening the Virginia Central Railroad connection between Richmond and its Shenandoah Valley breadbasket. Therefore, the next day Lee dispatched Jackson's two divisions to the critical railroad junction town of Gordonsville. Jackson arrived there on July 19. With this movement, Lee began moving toward a two-corps organization similar to that which Johnston earlier had used for better control of the army.

On the same day, July 14, that the U.S. Congress established the State of West Virginia, the boastful Pope moved southward toward Gordonsville with his Army of Virginia. His army consisted of the corps of three, barely-competent major generals: Franz Sigel, Banks and McDowell. By the 21st, they were spread forty miles west to east from Sperryville, at the foot of the Blue Ridge Mountains, all the way across the Piedmont region to Fredericksburg. Pope ordered Banks' cavalry to seize Gordonsville, but Lee had precluded that maneuver with his Jackson gambit.

Two significant political events occurred on July 22. Lincoln advised his Cabinet that he had drafted an Emancipation Proclamation to free slaves in Confederate-controlled areas. He admitted that he could not publicly announce it until the North had some battlefield success; otherwise, it would appear to be an act of desperation. That day also saw the signing of an agreement for an exchange of prisoners between the warring sides; Lincoln and his generals had not yet realized how significantly these exchanges primarily aided the manpower-deficient Confederacy.

Lee was concerned about protecting Richmond and points to the north of Pope. However, he also wanted to take advantage of the division of the Union forces during McClellan's tortoise-like retreat from the Peninsula back to northern Virginia. Lee did an excellent job speculating on McClellan's inactivity, the decreasing threat he posed to Richmond, and his eventual movement back north via the Chesapeake Bay.

In light of the reduced threat to Richmond and the increased threat posed by Pope near Gordonsville, Lee sent A.P. Hill's Division toward Gordonsville on July 27th. Hill joined Jackson there on the 29th. Hoping to head-off the type of problem Jackson had previously had with his subordinates, Lee, on the 27th had written to Jackson, "A.P. Hill you will find I think a good officer with whom you can consult and by advising with your division commanders as to your movements much trouble will be saved by you in arranging details, as they can act more intelligently."[2] Lee's advice went unheeded, and Jackson consulted with no one but Lee until Jackson's death the following year.

Jackson's and Hill's respective departures had left 69,000 and then 56,000 Confederate troops in the Richmond area to keep an eye on McClellan. On July 31, McClellan's army at Harrison's Landing was bombarded by a thousand of D.H. Hill's artillery shells from the south side of the James River. Although the Union soldiers suffered only twenty-five casualties, they were reminded of the continuing Confederate presence near Richmond.

The next day, Lee responded to pompous and ill-advised proclamations of General Pope, who threatened to execute civilians who aided the Confederacy. Lee issued General Order No. 54 stating that Pope and his commissioned officers would not be treated as prisoners of war if captured and that an equal number would be hanged as were executed under Pope's orders.

Developments in early August indicated that action and control on the Union side were shifting from McClellan' army north to Pope's. On August 2, Pope's men crossed the Rapidan and seized Orange Court House, a key, central Virginia, crossroads town. The next day new General-in-Chief Halleck ordered McClellan to bring his Army of the Potomac back to Alexandria. McClellan ineffectively protested that his Army was more useful threatening Richmond than defending Washington. He, of course, could not resist requesting more troops.

Because of the failure of his July call for three-year volunteers, President Lincoln, on August 4, issued a call for 300,000 nine-month volunteers. But he refused to accept two Indiana regiments of African-Americans; it was too early in the war to openly use Blacks in the army. Later that month, on the 22nd, Lincoln, responding to pro-slavery criticism from Horace Greeley of the *New York Tribune*, said, "If I could save the Union without freeing any slave I would do it, and if I could save the Union by freeing some and leaving others alone I would also do that."[3]

With discretionary orders from Lee, Jackson moved out from Gordonsville on August 7.[4] That night, his troops camped at Orange Court House, from which Pope had withdrawn, and Jackson issued the order of battle for the next day. Overnight he changed the order but failed to inform A.P. Hill. This oversight resulted in Hill's barely moving on August 8 and initiated a serious rift between Jackson and Hill. In

---

[2]. Lee to Thomas J. Jackson, July 27, 1862, Dowdey and Manarin, *Papers*, p. 239.

[3]. Nevins, *Ordeal*, VI, p. 232.

[4]. For details of Lee's Second Manassas campaign, see Hennessy, John J., *Return to Bull Run: The Campaign and Battle of Second Manassas* (New York: Simon & Schuster, 1993).

his over-eagerness to exploit the division of the Union armies and circle Pope's left flank, Jackson advanced carelessly toward Culpeper Court House without scouting the area to his west.

As a result, at Cedar Mountain, Banks' Federal corps hit Jackson's Division hard in the left flank.[5] Two divisions of Banks' soldiers smashed into Jackson's men and almost flanked their quickly-formed line. Three of Jackson's brigades broke and fled. Only a brave stand by Jubal Early's Brigade saved the day until the arrival of A.P. Hill's Division. Banks, however, had made the mistakes of attacking without keeping some troops in reserve and failing to send for reinforcements. After the Confederate line held and Hill came to the rescue, the Rebels counter-attacked and drove the Bluecoats from the field.[6] Although the Confederates held the field after the battle, they had paid dearly for their lack of caution. While the Blue had lost 1,400 killed, wounded, and captured, the Gray had suffered 1,300 casualties.[7] The Confederates could not afford battles in which they traded nearly equal losses with their numerically superior foes.

By August 13, Lee accurately calculated that McClellan's force at Harrison's Landing, only twenty-five miles from Richmond, no longer represented a viable threat. Therefore, he moved Longstreet, with the bulk of Lee's remaining forces, toward Gordonsville to counter the threat posed by Pope. The move was prescient because, on the 16th, McClellan, at long last, began moving out of Harrison's Landing to return to Alexandria for the purpose of backing up Pope.

By the 17th, Lee appeared to have Pope's army trapped between the Rapidan on its southern front and the Rappahannock in its rear. Before Lee could take advantage of Pope's incautious movement, however, Pope retired across the Rappahannock to await reinforcements from McClellan. By the 20th Lee had his 80,000-man army across the Rapidan, controlled the west bank of the Rappahannock, and was desperately attempting to cross the latter river to get between Washington and Pope's temporarily outnumbered forces.

On the night of August 22, Jeb Stuart led the 6th Virginia Cavalry on a successful raid on Pope's headquarters at Catlett's Station. Stuart and his men captured some Union officers and, most significantly, Pope's dispatch book. That book revealed the exact position of Pope's army, his need for reinforcements, and the expected arrival times of those reinforcements.

---

[5]. The authoritative work on this battle is Krick, Robert K., *Stonewall Jackson at Cedar Mountain* (Chapel Hill and London: University of North Carolina Press, 1990).

[6]. Hattaway and Jones, *How the North Won*, p. 223.

[7]. Livermore, *Numbers & Losses*, pp. 87-8.

Massive rainfall the next night made the Rappahannock impassable and wiped out offensives planned by both Lee and Pope. Lee used the information obtained by Stuart to devise his next course of action. Lee intended to hold Pope in place along the Rappahannock while he slipped his army, piecemeal, to the northwest, moved around Pope's right (west) flank, and, finally, got between Pope and Washington. Lee hoped to cut off Pope from his supplies and defeat him with his momentarily stronger force. To accomplish this, Lee relied heavily on Stonewall Jackson, the only one of Lee's generals who usually thrived when given independence and daring assignments. Early on August 25, Jackson moved away from the Rappahannock to the northwest and launched one of his patented flanking marches around the right flank and rear of Pope's Army of Virginia.

On the first day of his march, Jackson moved twenty-five miles between the Blue Ridge and Bull Run mountains all the way to Salem, from where he planned to move through Thoroughfare Gap onto Pope's rear. Pope thought he had things in hand because Jackson's movements were being tracked by Union cavalry. That cavalry reported that Jackson had thirty regiments and significant cavalry; in fact, he had sixty-six regiments and all of Lee's cavalry. Jackson's huge force moved through Thoroughfare Gap on the 26th. Early on the 27th, Stuart seized Bristoe Station on Pope's railroad supply line, and Jackson's men destroyed hundreds of boxcars and huge amounts of Union supplies at Manassas Junction four miles to the northeast. Although Jackson's men were allowed to fill their knapsacks with canned lobster and other delicacies, he ordered the destruction of barrels of whiskey to preserve their fighting capacity. In order to carry out this remarkable end run on Pope's army, Stuart's men had ridden and Jackson's foot infantry had, incredibly, marched over 50 miles in 48 hours.

On the same day as the Manassas Junction debacle, Longstreet, who had been holding Pope in place along the Rappahannock, moved away to the northwest to go to Jackson's assistance. Advised of the disaster to his rear, Pope marched hard toward Manassas in the hope of destroying Jackson before Longstreet could come to his rescue. The resultant clash would be known as the Second Battle of Bull Run (Second Manassas).

After repelling the first Union forces responding to his attack at Bristoe Station and Manassas Junction, Jackson withdrew to a strong defensive position at Groveton, just northwest of the 1861 Bull Run battlefield. Although vulnerable until Longstreet could come to his aid, Jackson revealed his position by attacking a portion of thirty-four passing Union regiments, including the famous Iron Brigade, near dusk on the 28th. In two hours of vicious fighting, both sides suffered heavy casualties until darkness halted the battle.

On the morning of the 29th, Jackson's exhausted 23,000 men had moved to a strong position in an unfinished railroad cut between Groveton and Sudley Springs but faced 50,000 Union attackers. Jackson's three divisions withstood a full day of uncoordinated assaults from ten Union divisions. Jackson sent Stuart in search of the marching Longstreet, and he returned with Lee and Longstreet themselves by mid-morning. Pope had failed to isolate Jackson by blocking Thoroughfare Gap in strength, and Lee, therefore, had little difficulty transiting the gap and merging his forces. However, it was early afternoon before Longstreet's men began arriving and digging in on Jackson's right.

That afternoon, Lee wanted to attack immediately with the troops on hand. Longstreet, however, advised Lee against doing so because they did not know the strength of the opposing forces, they knew that McClellan was reinforcing Pope, and Longstreet believed there were Union forces free to attack his right flank in the event of a Confederate assault. Much to the later chagrin of pro-Lee historian, Douglas Southall Freeman, Lee took Longstreet's advice.[8]

On the morning of the 30th, Lee and his generals watched in puzzlement as Pope's forces did nothing. Starting around noon, the Union forces resumed their assaults on Jackson's position. While Lee and Longstreet waited for the perfect moment to counter-attack, Jackson's line was almost broken. Some of his men ran out of ammunition and repelled their attackers by throwing rocks and using their rifles as clubs. They were greatly assisted by oblique and devastating artillery fire on the Federals from the twenty-two guns of a large artillery battalion under Longstreet.

Finally, at 4 p.m., Longstreet launched a devastating counter-attack; Jackson, much later, sent his forces on the offensive, and, between them, they drove the panicked and disorganized Union troops from the field. In three hours on the offensive, however, Longstreet lost more men than Jackson had lost in three days on the defensive.[9] British Major-General J.F.C. Fuller described Jackson's maneuver around Pope's army as sound strategy and Lee's maneuver [Longstreet's attack] as unsound and "...not strategically remunerative."[10]

Aggressive Confederate pursuit toward Fairfax Court House the next day was hampered by heavy rain. That same day, Lee fell while

---

8. Freeman, *R.E. Lee*, II, p. 235.
9. Hennessy, *Return to Bull Run*, p. 57.
10. Fuller, *Grant and Lee*, p. 165.

trying to grab his spooked horse and broke his right wrist. For the next two weeks he traveled by ambulance. Near evening and in a torrential downpour, the two sides clashed again on September 1 at Ox Hill near Chantilly. Both sides suffered heavy losses in the brief, but bloody, Battle of Chantilly, and the Union forces lost two generals (including the beloved Major General Philip Kearny).

Although Lee's forces clearly had won a major battlefield victory at Second Manassas, once again they paid a dear price. His 49,000 men engaged suffered 9,100 casualties (19 percent), while Pope's forces lost 10,100 out of 75,000 (13 percent). At Chantilly, the Confederate casualties were 800 while the Union suffered 1,400 casualties. Over the seven days of Second Manassas and Chantilly, the Livermore hit ratios slightly favored the Confederates; Pope's hit ratio was a negative 132:120 while Lee's was a favorable, but high, 187:208.[11] Thus, of every 1,000 Confederates, 187 were killed or wounded, and 208 inflicted a casualty on the enemy.

Taking casualties of 19 percent to Pope's 13 percent, however, Lee was continuing his pattern of aggressive attrition through offensive strategy and tactics. He had assumed command on June 1 of an army of 95,000; within exactly three months, that now-outnumbered army had suffered almost 30,000 casualties. Although he had moved the scene of conflict from the environs of Richmond to the outskirts of Washington, Lee's offensives were seriously weakening his army.

---

[11]. *Ibid.*, pp. 88-89.

Chapter 5

September 1862: Disaster at Antietam

So far, Lee's summer may have appeared successful to him. He had driven the Yankees from the Peninsula, swept them from the field at Manassas, and beaten them at Chantilly. Although these tactical victories had taken their toll on his army, Lee decided to take a daring gamble and carry the war to the North. On September 3, Lee wrote to Davis that he planned to move north into Maryland to take advantage of Confederate sympathies there and perhaps to move on to destroy the critical railroad bridge across the Susquehanna River at Harrisburg, Pennsylvania. In his letter, Lee admitted that the proposed effort was risky and had little chance of success: "I am aware that the movement is attended with much risk, yet I do not consider success impossible..."[1] Consistent with his eastern theater focus, Lee suggested to President Davis that Braxton Bragg's Army of Tennessee, outnumbered more than 3 to 1 and struggling to defend eastern Tennessee and Chattanooga, be brought east to protect Richmond while Lee went north.[2]

On September 4, Lee's 53,000 battered troops left Manassas. The next day, they crossed the Potomac into Maryland at White's Ferry, just east of Leesburg, with false expectations that many Marylanders would increase their dwindling numbers.[3] Crossing the Potomac was a fateful step because, eventually, Lee would have to return to Virginia; that return would be interpreted as a retreat and defeat, and Lincoln was desperately waiting for anything that could be construed as a Confed-

---

[1]. Lee to Jefferson Davis, September 3, 1862, Dowdey and Manarin, *Papers*, p. 292, 293.

[2]. *Ibid.* "At the time of Lee's request, Bragg was outnumbered 124,000 to 35,000, and the Union Army of the Ohio was maneuvering within twenty miles of Chattanooga." Connelly, "Lee and the Western Confederacy," p. 124.

[3]. One problem was that those Marylanders who had eagerly enlisted for one year in the Confederate army in early and mid-1861 had been involuntarily extended under the Conscription Act even though they were not from a Confederate state. Bruce, "Lee and Strategy" in Gallagher, *Lee the Soldier*, p. 116.

erate defeat. Then he could announce his Emancipation Proclamation and, thereby, change the nature of the war.[4]

While underway in Maryland on the 8th of September, Lee, optimistically, wrote to Davis that this might be a propitious time for the Confederacy, in a perceived position of strength, to propose to the Union a negotiated settlement that included recognition of the Confederacy's independence.[5] However, the reality of the Maryland incursion sharply contrasted with any hope Lee had for success. By the time Lee reached Frederick, Maryland, his soldiers were but a shadow of the army Lee had inherited only three months before. Lee's aggressiveness had resulted in over 30,000 casualties, and straggling became a significant problem throughout Lee's exhausted forces.[6] On August 20, Jackson had ordered that deserters be shot without the nicety of a court-martial to determine their guilt.[7]

Contributing to the straggling problem were the scarcity of provisions and the resulting sickness of many men when they satisfied their hunger by eating raw corn and green apples.[8] In his September 3 letter to Davis, Lee admitted that the army had its problems: "The army is not properly equipped for an invasion of an enemy's territory. It lacks much of the material of war, is feeble in transportation, the animals being much reduced, and the men are poorly provided with clothes, and in thousands of instances are destitute of shoes."[9]

According to Alexander, divisions had been nearly reduced to brigades, and brigades were only slightly larger than regiments.[10] By September 13, Lee was telling Davis that one-third to one-half of his original number of soldiers had deserted.[11] In addition, the army's leadership had been devastated by months of battle; eight of Jackson's

---

[4]. For detailed accounts of the Antietam (Sharpsburg) campaign, see Sears, Stephen W., *Landscape Turned Red: The Battle of Antietam* (New York: Book-of-the-Month Club, Inc., 1994) [hereafter Sears, Landscape]; Luvaas, Jay and Nelson, Harold W., *The U.S. Army War College Guide to the Battle of Antietam: The Military Campaign of 1862* (Carlisle, Pennsylvania: South Mountain Press, Inc., 1987); Priest, John M., *Antietam: The Soldiers' Battle* (Shippensburg, Pennsylvania: White Mane Publishing Company, Inc., 1989); Freeman, *R.E. Lee*, II, pp. 350-414.

[5]. Lee to Jefferson Davis, September 8, 1862, Dowdey and Manarin, *Papers*, p. 301.

[6]. Piston, *Lee's Tarnished Lieutenant*, pp. 27-8.

[7]. Freeman, Douglas Southall, *Lee's Lieutenants: A Study in Command*, 3 vols. (New York: Charles Scribner's Sons, 1942-4; 1972 reprint) [hereafter Freeman, *Lee's Lieutenants*], II, p. 149.

[8]. *Ibid.*, pp. 150-1.

[9]. Lee to Jefferson Davis, September 3, 1862, Dowdey and Manarin, *Papers*, p. 293.

[10]. Alexander, *Fighting for the Confederacy*, p. 139.

[11]. Lee to Jefferson Davis, September 13, 1862, Dowdey and Manarin, *Papers*, p. 307.

nineteen brigades were led by colonels in place of dead or wounded brigadier generals.

Lee then took a potentially fatal gamble and separated his army into four parts -- against the advice of both Longstreet and Jackson. On September 9, he issued his famous Special Order No. 191, calling for Jackson's large corps to seize Bolivar Heights between the Shenandoah and Potomac Rivers (thereby cutting off Harper's Ferry, located southeast of Bolivar Heights at the junction of those rivers); Brigadier General John George Walker's small Division to occupy Loudon Heights south of those rivers and across from Harper's Ferry; McLaws' Division to close the noose on that town by occupying Maryland Heights northeast of the rivers' junction; and Longstreet's and D.H. Hill's divisions to proceed over South Mountain to Boonsboro, north of Harper's Ferry and west of Frederick, Maryland.[12] Subsequently, Lee (apparently anxious to continue northward) aggravated the situation by taking his headquarters and Longstreet's Division farther northwest to Hagerstown, advancing pickets to Middleburg on the Pennsylvania border, and leaving Harvey Hill with less than 6,000 men, thirteen miles behind at Boonsboro. Longstreet, who opposed Lee's splintering of his army, even cursed in Lee's presence as they traveled to Hagerstown: "General, I wish we could stand still and let the damned Yankees come to us!"[13] By that time Lee had split his army into five vulnerable segments.

A strange occurrence increased this vulnerability. Lee's division of his forces was revealed to McClellan when a copy of Lee's Special Order No. 191, having been used to wrap three cigars, was discovered by a Union enlisted man on the morning of September 13 in a field outside Frederick, Maryland. The order fairly flew up the chain-of-command and reached McClellan by noon. He was obviously elated and openly remarked, in the presence of unfriendly Marylanders' ears, that he now had Lee where he wanted him. Little Mac's foolish revelation of discovery the Order resulted in Jeb Stuart's learning, just after midnight on the 14th, of some unusual event in the Union camp.

Whether or when Lee had learned of McClellan's discovery of his Order and of the fact that Lee's forces were badly divided, Lee was alerted by reports of McClellan's unusually semi-aggressive activity that something significant had happened.[14] Nevertheless, Lee continued to risk his entire Army by remaining in Maryland long enough to

---

[12]. Dowdey and Manarin, *Papers*, pp. 301-3.

[13]. Wert, *Longstreet*, p. 184.

[14]. Gordon, Edward Clifford, "Memorandum of a Conversation with General Robert E. Lee," February 15, 1868, pp. 25-27 in Gallagher, *Lee the Soldier*, pp. 25-6.

bring about a major battle. Lee, inexplicably, either failed to realize that "the gig was up" or hesitated to admit the vulnerable position in which he had placed his army. The possible temporary capture of Harper's Ferry was insufficient reason for Lee to remain in Maryland with the bulk of his Army vulnerable to being trapped north of the Potomac River. Except for the plodding response of McClellan, Lee's forces would have been destroyed in piecemeal fashion.[15]

From Frederick, Little Mac sent two of his seven corps southwest toward Crampton's Gap to trap McLaws against the Potomac. He directed his other five corps northwest toward Turner's and Fox's gaps in South Mountain to deal with the isolated, and now separated, divisions of Hill and Longstreet. After learning from Jeb Stuart of McClellan's atypical movement, Lee ordered Longstreet to move Law's and Hood's brigades from Hagerstown to Turner's Gap to fend off disaster.

The Texas Brigade's march presented Lee with a problem. Its soldiers were angry about the possibility of going into battle without their division commander, John Bell Hood, whom Longstreet had placed in arrest status as the result of a dispute at Manassas over the disposition of seized Federal ambulances. As they neared South Mountain and passed Lee, the Texans repeatedly shouted, "Give us Hood!" Lee replied, "You shall have him, gentlemen," and then sought out Hood.[16] Hood later wrote of that encounter:

> I found General Lee standing by the fence, very near the pike, in company with his chief of staff, Colonel [Robert] Chilton. The latter accosted me, bearing a message from the General, that he desired to speak to me. I dismounted, and stood in his presence, when he said, "General, here I am just upon the eve of entering into battle, and with one of my best officers under arrest. If you will merely say that you regret this occurrence [the Manassas incident], I will release you and restore you to the command of your division."[17]

When Hood tried to explain the injustice of his arrest, a frustrated Lee interrupted him and suspended the arrest for the duration of the battle. After Antietam, the issue was never raised again.[18]

---

[15]. Lee later complained that the lost order's discovery had caused him to miss an opportunity to concentrate his troops and attack McClellan's army. Allan, "Conversations" in Gallagher, *Lee the Soldier*, pp. 7-8.

[16]. Freeman, *R.E. Lee*, II, p. 370; Holsworth, Jerry W., "Uncommon Valor: Hood's Texas Brigade in the Maryland Campaign," *Blue & Gray Magazine*, XIII, Issue 6 (Summer 1996), pp. 6-20, 50-55 [hereafter Holsworth, "Uncommon Valor"], p. 11.

[17]. Holsworth, "Uncommon Valor," p. 11.

[18]. *Ibid.*

Reinforced by Longstreet, Harvey Hill's desperate and valiant all-day holding action at Turner's and Fox's gaps on September 14 kept McClellan's army from destroying Lee's scattered forces one after the other. Although the Rebels were on the defensive and held the higher position, they were spread thinly along a three-mile front accessible by five roads. As a result of Lee's dispersion of his forces, they also were outnumbered (28,000 to 18,000) by the aggressive 6th Corps of Major General Jesse Lee Reno and the dawdling 1st Corps of Major General Joseph Hooker.

Because of the Confederates' on-the-field leadership and bravery and their defensive advantage, they managed to prevent a complete Federal break-through during the daylight hours of the 14th. Their position at nightfall, however, was untenable because they had been flanked at both gaps, had taken heavy casualties and were about to be overrun by the enemy's sheer mass. This situation left Lee with no choice but to retreat. He ordered Hill and Longstreet to move toward Sharpsburg.

Since inadequate forces were in place at South Mountain, the Rebels there lost a high 1,900 (10 percent) killed, wounded and missing, while the attacking Yankees lost a tolerable 1,800 (6 percent). The Union's Livermore hit ratio was a slightly unfavorable, and low, 68:66 while the Confederates' hit ratio was a more unfavorable and higher 105:97.[19] Although about one in ten of Harvey Hill's engaged defenders had been casualties, Lee's losses in the one day at South Mountain were a mere prelude to the devastating casualties his army was to suffer three days later at Antietam.

Because of the Union corps' delays in crossing South Mountain at Turner's and Fox's gaps and in getting to some of McLaws' troops through Crampton's Gap a few miles to the south, Walker and McLaws had enough time to bombard Harper's Ferry from the commanding heights while Jackson moved on the town from the northwest. The trapped 12,500-man garrison, under the cowardly non-leadership of Colonel Dixon S. Miles, put up only a feeble fight and quickly surrendered to Jackson on the morning of September 15. Two thousand Union cavalry had escaped under the cover of darkness.

Meanwhile, Lee oversaw the retreat, on the night of the 14th, of Harvey Hill southwest from South Mountain and Longstreet south from Boonsboro toward Sharpsburg, which brought them both closer to Jackson's troops at Harper's Ferry. At about noon on the 15th, Lee gathered those outnumbered retreating forces of Longstreet and Hill at

19. Livermore, *Numbers & Losses*, pp. 90-1.

the small town of Sharpsburg. There, behind Antietam Creek and with the Potomac River at his back, Lee arrayed his troops and awaited both an attack by the ever-cautious Little Mac and the hoped-for arrival of assistance from the victorious troops at Harper's Ferry. Union troops arrived east of the creek on the afternoon of the 15th and kept arriving for the next 24 hours.

On the night of the 15th, Lee learned of the capture of Harper's Ferry. Instead of declaring the campaign a success and safely returning to Virginia, he stayed in his vulnerable position with his meager two divisions. On that night, McClellan outnumbered Lee by 4 to 1 and was in a position to destroy Lee's Sharpsburg defenders. But Little Mac did not attack -- either that night or early the next morning, when Lee had a mere 18,000 troops.

Although three additional Confederate divisions arrived from Harper's Ferry on the 16th, McClellan was acquiring troops even faster than Lee. By midday, McClellan had accumulated an overwhelming force east of Antietam Creek, was aware that Lee still had a significant part of his army at Harper's Ferry, and continued to be in a position to launch a devastating attack on the depleted forces of Lee. Late that afternoon, the Union commander had 72,000 troops and 300 pieces of artillery with which to attack Lee's 27,000 men and 200 guns spread out along a four-mile front. Little Mac passed up this glorious opportunity to destroy Lee's army, did not attack at all on the 16th, and, instead, went about deliberately making arrangements for an attack the next day. Although Lee, therefore, had over a day to prepare for battle, he did not order his men to entrench.

During the bloodiest single day of the War, September 17, 1862, the blundering McClellan once again saved Lee's army from destruction by committing his overwhelmingly superior 75,000 Union troops in serial fashion from north to south along Antietam Creek. This method of attack enabled Lee, as the day-long battle progressed, to move his outnumbered defenders first to the North and West woods and the Cornfield in the north of the battlefield and later to Bloody Lane and the Mumma Farm in the center of the battlefield to contest a series of separate and uncoordinated Union attacks.[20]

Following hours of pre-dawn artillery exchanges, Hooker's 1st Corps launched a dawn attack from the East Woods against Jackson's three divisions on the Confederate left (north). Like most attacks that day, this one was repulsed and then followed by an enemy counterattack. When Major General Richard H. "Fighting Dick" Anderson's

20. Freeman, *R.E. Lee*, II, pp. 389-96.

counter-attack was failing, the ever-aggressive Hood came to the rescue. Hood's Texan-dominated division charged into the never-to-be-forgotten, thirty-acre Cornfield, was decimated (60 percent killed or wounded in thirty minutes), and compelled to retreat. Harvey Hill led another Rebel counter-attack, and Brigadier General Joseph King Fenno Mansfield's Union 12th Corps drove them back with a counter-attack of their own.

When Jackson tried to impede this Federal movement, he lost 50 percent of one brigade and 30 percent of another in the Cornfield. Hooker's and Mansfield's forces were sweeping the field and approaching the Dunker Church south of the Cornfield. There, they finally were repulsed by the combined forces of Hood, Early, Hill, Walker and McLaws. The early morning Cornfield and woods casualties -- incurred in under three hours -- were horrific: Hooker lost 2,600 of 8,600, Hood lost 1,400 of 2,300, the 1st Texas regiment lost 186 of 226 men in twenty minutes, the Louisiana Tigers lost 323 men in fifteen minutes, the 12th Massachusetts lost 224 of 334 men, and on and on.[21] These were not the results of anyone standing on the defensive. The annihilation consisted of one fearless, perhaps mindless, assault after another by the officers and men of both armies, as they swept back and forth across the Cornfield a total of fifteen times.

It takes little imagination to understand that Lee had stripped the middle and southern segments of his lines to prevent a disaster on the north end of the Antietam battlefield, and that McClellan had achieved an almost-inconceivable numerical superiority on those other unentrenched segments of Lee's lines. Little Mac did nothing about it until the fighting had died down in the north.

From nine to noon, the fighting moved south of the Cornfield to the Dunker Church and the Sunken Road, known ever since as Bloody Lane. The church was the scene of more back-and-forth suicidal charges as both sides took the same type of grotesquely massive casualties as they had just to the north. The Confederates, under Harvey Hill, initially had the better of it for about two hours at Bloody Lane, where they stood on the defensive in the shelter of the depressed road and slaughtered a series of Yankee attackers. Ten thousand Union attackers, two full divisions, were halted as their front ranks were cut down man by man, brigade by brigade, in a frontal assault on out-of-sight defenders. Thousands of Union survivors found safety by lying prone on the ground and waiting for others to break the seemingly impregnable Confederate line.

---

21. Holsworth, "Uncommon Valor," p. 54; Fox, *Regimental Losses*, pp. 36, 556, 565.

By midday, the attackers, spurred on by courageous, if foolhardy, assaults by New York's Irish Brigade, managed to flank Bloody Lane, enfilade the suddenly-helpless defenders, and then overrun the position. Fighting at Bloody Lane had resulted in the wounding and killing of 3,000 Blue attackers and 2,600 Gray defenders.

As the Rebel line was being broken there, Longstreet launched a fortunately timed counter-attack back at the Dunker Church, and more vicious fighting broke out on the Mumma Farm between the church and Bloody Lane. Vicious fighting continued to cut down hundreds more on both sides, but the momentum was clearly with the Union forces. They were about to break through the entire center of the battlefield, isolate Lee's flanks, and virtually end the war in the East. Lee had no more reserves. But Longstreet saved the day by personally leading an advance of the Rebel artillery and a devastating assault on startled New Yorkers in the center of the cauldron. Seeing this repulse, the weak-kneed McClellan called off additional attacks in the center of the field just when another assault would have broken Lee's army.

To the south, where Lee had been removing troops all day to protect his left and center, McClellan was compounding all of his other errors of that fateful day. On that end of the battlefield, the road to Sharpsburg crossed the Rohrbach Bridge, destined to be known as Burnside's Bridge, in mocking tribute to Union Major General Ambrose E. Burnside, who took so long to get his troops across it. Ineffectively superintended and perhaps cut out of the chain of command by Little Mac, Burnside had over 9,000 troops to assault the Confederate right flank of about 3,000 defenders.

Of those 3,000 Confederates, only 400 were assigned to defend the bridge itself.[22] The bridge rests in a valley under a steep hill on the west bank, an ideal defensive position that made crossing very difficult. Even so, given Burnside's overwhelming manpower advantage, there was no excuse for the fatally gross tardiness of the Union attack in that sector, and that tardiness cost the Union a battlefield victory.[23]

Although the artillery fire had started at 3 a.m. and the Union assault to the north at dawn, Burnside received no attack orders from McClellan until 10 a.m. Therefore, Burnside's first assault on the bridge did not occur until shortly after that hour. Unprepared for the intense fire it would receive in attacking across the bridge, the 11th Connecti-

---

22. Sears, *Landscape*, p. 260.

23. For information supporting the view that McClellan intended to use Burnside only as a diversion, belatedly ordered his involvement, and later tried to use Burnside as a scapegoat, see Sears, *Landscape Turned Red*, Appendix II ("Burnside and His Bridge"), pp. 353-7.

cut Regiment was repulsed in that assault. It was another two hours until the 2nd Maryland was bloodily thrown back in a virtually identical attack. Belatedly realizing that other avenues of approach were available, Burnside sent a fourth of his troops to cross Snavely Ford less than a mile south of the bridge.

Shortly after 1 p.m., Burnside's men finally made it across Burnside Bridge. However, an additional two-hour delay unbelievably ensued while Burnside properly positioned his troops and provided them with adequate ammunition. It was not until 3 p.m., therefore, that the bulk of his 9th Corps finally began driving up the hills and threatened Sharpsburg itself. Meanwhile, South of the bridge, the rest of Burnside's Corps fought across Snavely Ford and drove two miles inland on the far southern end of the Antietam battlefield. Burnside's numbers had overcome his slowness, and he finally posed a deadly threat to Lee's right flank.

It looked as though Lee's mistakes in entering Maryland, dividing his forces, and choosing to fight at Sharpsburg were about to cost him his army. Even though McClellan had halted the northern and middle assaults, Lee's forces there were effectively tied down and unable to help the 2,000 Rebels remaining on the right flank or the 2,800 in Sharpsburg itself defend against Burnside's finally swarming 15,000 attackers. The Blue attackers on the south were within a half-mile of Lee's only line of retreat to the Potomac, and all seemed lost.

An hour after A.P. Hill had arrived at 2:30 in advance of his men, Lee observed a dust cloud to the south with a mixture of fear and hope. It meant either complete Union encirclement or the arrival of help from Harper's Ferry. Fortunately for Lee, the cloud of dust signified the 3:30 arrival of A.P. Hill's 3,300 men, exhausted from their seventeen-mile, eight-hour march but excited by the desperate situation they found. Unbelievably, these few soldiers, clad in captured Union uniforms, plowed into the flank of Burnside's 15,000 attackers and drove them from the Sharpsburg heights with the surprise and ferocity of their assault. Lee's army was saved, and the Battle of Antietam was over.[24]

Lee could thank McClellan's incompetence and Burnside's sluggishness, as well as the good fortune of Hill's timely arrival, for sparing the Army of Northern Virginia from destruction. The overly cautious Union commander had compounded his error of making consecutive attacks by holding one-third of his forces in reserve and unused throughout the entire battle (primarily Porter's 5th Corps in the center

---

24. Freeman, *R.E. Lee*, II, pp. 398-402; Waugh, *Class of 1846*, pp. 387-90.

of the battlefield). He also failed to use Major General Darius N. Couch's Division, which he left near Harper's Ferry.[25]

Given the forces at his disposal since the night of the 15th, McClellan's attacks were too late, too short, too uncoordinated, and too weak. McClellan also erred by keeping his cavalry in the center of his lines rather than on the flanks, where they could have speeded up Burnside's crossing of the Antietam and precluded, or at least minimized, the surprise and impact of A.P. Hill's last-minute arrival. All these mistakes enabled the Confederates to barely hold throughout the day and, luckily, to escape defeat. Had McClellan used all of his forces and attacked simultaneously along the entire front, there would have been no Army of Northern Virginia by the time A.P. Hill reached Sharpsburg.

That night, the bloodied and ravaged Confederate army had no sane course of action available except retreat. At their Sharpsburg war council that night, Lee's generals responded to his inquiries and reported their abysmal condition to him. Stephen Lee described Hood's shocking report:

> [Hood] displayed great emotion, seemed completely unmanned, and replied that he had no division. General Lee, with more excitement than I ever witnessed him exhibit, exclaimed, "Great God, General Hood, where is the splendid division you had this morning?" Hood replied, "They are lying on the field where you sent them, sir; but few have straggled. My division has been almost wiped out."[26]

East of Sharpsburg, the Union forces still posed a significant threat. Porter's 20,000-man corps was unsullied, Burnside's Ninth was fairly fresh, and McClellan had reinforcements on the way. The unused Federal reserves at Antietam outnumbered Lee's remaining forces. Instead of retreat, however, Lee discussed with his generals whether they should stand in place or attack!

When his generals urged him to retreat because of their severe losses, he rejected their advice and added, "If McClellan wants to fight in the morning, I will give him battle again."[27] Lee thus chose to remain at Sharpsburg through the 18th. Given the inequality of the armies' numbers and fighting conditions, as well as Lee's inability to retreat under fire during daylight, McClellan committed another egregious error by failing to attack that day and, thus, to end the struggle in the

---

[25]. Waugh, *Class of 1846*, p. 391.
[26]. Holworth, "Uncommon Valor," pp. 54-5.
[27]. Bevin Alexander, *Lost Victories*, p. 253; Fuller, *Grant and Lee*, p. 169.

East in one fell swoop. Little Mac issued incredible orders not to pre-cipitate hostilities because he wanted to await expected reinforcements.

General Alexander provided a terse summary of what he judged to be Lee's greatest military blunder -- his excessive audacity at Antie-tam:

> He gave battle unnecessarily at Sharpsburg Sep. 17th, 1862. The odds against him were so immense that the utmost he could have hoped to do was what he did do--to repel all as-saults & finally to withdraw safely across the Potomac. And he probably only succeeded in this because McClellan kept about 20,000 men, all of Fitz John Porter's corps, entirely out of the fight so that they did not pull a trigger. And Lee's po-sition was such, with a great river at his back, without a bridge & with but one difficult ford, that defeat would have meant the utter destruction of his army. So he fought where he could have avoided it, & where he had nothing to make & everything to lose--which a general should not do.[28]

In summary, even though McClellan had fumbled away his glori-ous opportunity to destroy Lee's entire Army, Lee himself had blun-dered just as badly. First, he went on the offensive with a weakened army into Maryland, from which he would have to retreat. Second, he badly divided his forces. Third, he failed to reunite them quickly or to return to the South when he realized that his divided condition was known and after he already had won a significant victory at Harper's Ferry. Fourth, he selected a battlefield which jeopardized his entire army by having no ready means of retreat. Fifth, instead of entrenching and remaining on the defensive at Sharpsburg, Lee counter-attacked frequently throughout the day, and, in those suicidal charges, the at-tacking forces were decimated. Finally, he stayed at Sharpsburg an ad-ditional day and defied McClellan to attack when such an attack could have destroyed Lee's army.

Each of these errors deserves separate examination. Following Cedar Mountain, Second Manassas, and Chantilly, Lee's army was ex-hausted and badly depleted. His men were in no condition to launch a campaign into the North; they were exhausted and sick. Freeman states, "There can be no sort of doubt that Lee underestimated the ex-haustion of his army after Second Manassas. That is, in reality, the ma-jor criticism of the Maryland operation: he carried worn-out men across

---

28. Alexander, *Fighting for the Confederacy*, p. 92.

the Potomac."[29] Instead of savoring his army's series of victories and rebuilding their strength, Lee took them on a mission which could only result in a damaging retreat back to Virginia.[30]

Against the advice of both Longstreet and Jackson, Lee, inexplicably, divided his small forces so badly that even a general as incompetent on the offensive as McClellan could have overwhelmed them separately and almost did destroy them.[31] Dividing his forces to surround Harper's Ferry from three directions is understandable, but allowing Hill's and Longstreet's divisions to float to the north and then splitting them up, instead of using them to screen the Harper's Ferry operation and, possibly, capture the fleeing 2,000 cavalrymen, is inexplicable. Lee's multiple division of his forces was daring but foolish.[32]

After he was aware of the Union discovery of his order, Lee failed to reunite his forces quickly and to return to Virginia. Even worse, he failed to cross the Potomac at Sharpsburg with D.H. Hill's and Longstreet's divisions on the night of the 15th when he learned of the capture of Harper's Ferry.[33] On this point, historian Archer Jones concluded, "So politically and strategically Lee's Antietam campaign was a fiasco. It was really doomed to fail, but Lee could have mitigated the political damage by ending his raid without a battle."[34] He could have avoided perhaps 10,000 casualties by withdrawing into Virginia after the Battle of South Mountain.[35]

Lee gravely erred in selecting the Sharpsburg battlefield. His army was backed up against the Potomac River and had a marginal avenue of retreat. There was no bridge, and the road to the only ford was barely wide enough for a wagon and would have been totally unusable under fire. In addition, Lee's position was vulnerable to Federal artil-

---

[29]. Freeman, *R.E. Lee,* II, p. 412.

[30]. Bevin Alexander, *Lost Victories,* p. 253-4.

[31]. Piston, *Lee's Tarnished Lieutenant,* pp. 24-5.

[32]. Freeman criticized Lee's division of his forces in the Antietam campaign. Freeman, *R.E. Lee,* II, p. 411.

[33]. Bevin Alexander criticized Lee's failure to promptly leave Maryland: "...when the 1862 invasion of Maryland proved to be abortive, Lee did not retreat quickly into Virginia but allowed himself to be drawn into a direct confrontation at Antietam, which he had no hope of winning... Since the Confederacy was greatly inferior to the North in manpower, any such expenditure of blood should have been made only for great strategic gains. Standing and fighting at Antietam offered no benefits, whereas a withdrawal into Virginia would have retained the South's offensive power." Alexander, *Great Generals,* p. 26.

[34]. Jones, Archer, "Military Means," pp. 43-77 in Boritt, *Why the Confederacy Lost,* pp. 60-61.

[35]. Hartwig, D. Scott, "Robert E. Lee and the Maryland Campaign," pp. 331-55 in Gallagher, *Lee the Soldier,* p. 352.

lery on the hills east of the Antietam and provided little or no opportunity for a counter-attack on the Union flanks.[36] Lee admitted his poor battlefield selection in a September 19 after-action report to Davis: "Since my last letter to you of the 18th, finding the enemy indisposed to make an attack on that day, and our position being a bad one to hold with the river in the rear, I determined to cross the army to the Virginia side."[37]

During the opening portion of the battle, the opposing forces swept back and forth across the Cornfield fifteen times. Instead of staying on the defensive, the unentrenched Gray forces frontally counter-attacked again and again – and, as a result, suffered extremely heavy casualties.[38] At their worst, these tactics cost the 27th North Carolina Regiment 61 percent of its 325 men.[39]

Finally, his army having barely survived the all-day battle on the 17th, Lee jeopardized the very existence of that army by remaining on the field in the same vulnerable, difficult-to-retreat-from position for an additional day. He offered McClellan one more chance to crush the Rebel army with his increasingly superior forces. Although Lee had accurately gauged the timidity of the Union commander, there was nothing to be gained by so jeopardizing his decimated force. The safe, sensible course of action would have been to retreat during the night of the 17th rather than throwing down the gauntlet for one more day.

Through his combination of errors, Lee managed to lose an irreplaceable 27 percent of his veteran fighters in a single day. 11,700 of his 52,000 men were casualties, while Little Mac lost an amazingly similar, but militarily tolerable, 11,700 of his 75,000.[40] These respective casualties of 23 percent and 16 percent demonstrate that this was a battle Lee should never have fought, one he fought poorly, or both. The latter appears to have been the case. The Livermore hit ratios for Antietam were incredibly high for a one-day engagement: 155:156 for the Union and 226:225 for the Confederates.[41] Thus, of every 100 Union soldiers, 16 wounded or killed an enemy and 16 were hit; of every 100 Confederates, 23 wounded or killed an enemy and 23 were hit.

Antietam was an unmitigated disaster for the Confederacy. Its greatest impact may have been that it enabled Lincoln to claim victory and, on September 22, issue his Emancipation Proclamation. That dec-

---

[36]. Bevin Alexander, *Lost Victories*, p. 220.

[37]. Lee to Jefferson Davis, September 19, 1862.

[38]. Hattaway and Jones, *How the North Won*, p. 243.

[39]. Fox, *Regimental Losses*, p. 556; McWhiney and Jamieson, *Attack and Die*, p. 4.

[40]. Livermore, *Numbers & Losses*, pp. 92-3.

[41]. *Ibid.*

laration changed the war from one just to save the Union to one both to save the Union and to end slavery. Lincoln's shrewd maneuver foreclosed European intervention on the Southern side.[42]

Through the Seven Days' Battle, Cedar Mountain, Second Manassas, Chantilly, South Mountain, Harper's Ferry and Antietam, Lee's army had suffered an intolerable 45,000 casualties during his first four months in command.[43] His army was exhausted, and straggling again became a problem. Sent to retrieve absentees from the army, Brigadier General John R. Jones wrote, "It is disgusting and heart-sickening to witness this army of stragglers."[44]

[42]. Beringer, Richard E.; Hattaway, Herman; Jones, Archer; and Still, William N. Jr., *Why the South Lost the Civil War* (Athens: University of Georgia Press, 1986) [hereafter Beringer et al, *Why the South Lost*], pp. 169, 179.

[43]. George Bruce provided a post-war northern perspective: "Confederate writers take especial delight in recording that General Grant lost 39,000 men in getting his army to the James River, when he might have reached the same point by the use of transports with his army intact, but they never mention the fact that Lee in five months in 1862 had lost nearly 60,000 men in four battles, and still found Jackson's part of the army one hundred miles south and the remainder only sixty miles north of their starting-points, Grant, in 1864, moving forward toward final victory; Lee, in 1862, by his general policy, toward a sure defeat." Bruce, "Lee and Strategy," in Gallagher, *Lee the Soldier*, pp. 116-7.

[44]. Sears, *Landscape*, p. 307.

Chapter 6

December 1862:
Fredericksburg, A Lesson Not Learned

Two days after the bloody battle at Antietam, Lee's army began its retreat across the Potomac. At midnight, Brigadier General William N. Pendleton reported to Lee that he had lost all the reserve artillery to the enemy, but A.P. Hill counter-attacked and discovered that only four pieces of artillery had been lost. Still hoping to salvage a major victory from his northern trek, Lee sent his army on a march north toward Williamsport and Hagerstown but had to give up that dream when problems developed back at the Sharpsburg crossing. Lee's decimated army then headed south toward the Shenandoah.[1] Lee was still think-ing offensively, however, as he wrote on September 21, "...It is still my desire to threaten a passage into Maryland, to occupy the enemy on this frontier, and, if my purpose cannot be accomplished, to draw them into the Valley, where I can attack them to advantage."[2]

When McClellan failed to follow Lee into Virginia, Lincoln made a personal visit to McClellan at the Antietam battlefield with the specific purpose of prodding him into action. While there, Lincoln corrected Illinois Senator Ozias M. Hatch when the latter identified the Union army there as the Army of the Potomac. Lincoln explained, "So it is called, but that is a mistake; it is only McClellan's body-guard."[3] De-spite the President's visit and clear intent that McClellan pursue Lee, Little Mac continued for several weeks more to make excuses instead of war.

Lincoln's exasperation with McClellan was reflected in his re-sponse to one of Little Mac's excuses for his inertia: "I have just read your dispatch about sore-tongued and fatigued horses. Will you par-don me for asking what the horses of your army have done since the

---

[1]. Freeman, *R.E. Lee*, II, pp. 406-8; Sears, *Landscape*, pp. 307-8.

[2]. McWhiney and Jamieson, *Attack and Die*, p. 71.

[3]. Sears, *Landscape*, p. 325.

battle of Antietam that fatigues anything?"[4] As October turned into November, McClellan finally crossed the Potomac in "pursuit" of Lee, who was in the process of splitting his army between the Valley and Culpeper Court House. Lincoln told McClellan that he was closer to Richmond than Lee and had the inside track (the chord of the circle) to stay there. When Longstreet marched twice as far as McClellan in half the time and reached Culpeper Court House, that portion of Lee's army was closer to Richmond than McClellan. Then Lincoln, not surprisingly, removed McClellan again and named Burnside commander of the Army of the Potomac.[5] Burnside, who initially refused the November 9 appointment, accepted it the next day in order to prevent the honor from going to Joe Hooker, whom he despised. Lee regretted the change and commented to Longstreet, "We always understood each other so well. I fear they may continue to make these changes till they find someone I don't understand."[6]

As a result of Lee's strategy and tactics, the Confederates, in the fall of 1862, suffered from a severe shortage of soldiers. In addition to the 45,000 casualties, Lee's army was missing 20,000 deserters and stragglers.[7] Only a few days after Antietam, therefore, the Confederate Congress raised the draft age to 45 and, thus, impacted small farm families across the South.[8] Congress also aggravated the slaveholder-freeholder split by exempting one white man on each plantation with 20 or more slaves.[9]

Reacting to his extensive losses of experienced officers, Lee, on November 6, formally reorganized his army into two corps under two newly-promoted lieutenant generals. Longstreet's 1st Corps consisted of 31,000 men in five divisions, and Jackson's 2nd Corps was made up of 34,000 men in four large divisions. On the basis of Lee's recommendations, Longstreet had been made the senior lieutenant general in the Confederacy on October 10, and Jackson had been the junior of six lieutenant generals named the following day.[10]

Lee meanwhile continued to demonstrate his Virginia myopia. That November, he still had a reinforced army of 90,000 to face about 216,000 Union troops in the East, while the western Confederates had only 55,000 soldiers against Union forces of 180,000. Nevertheless, in

4. *Ibid.,* pp. 330-1.
5. Sears, *McClellan,* pp. 334-40.
6. Freeman, *R.E. Lee,* II, p. 428.
7. Piston, *Lee's Tarnished Lieutenant,* p. 28.
8. Hattaway and Jones, *How the North Won,* p. 116.
9. Freeman. *R.E. Lee,* III, p. 254.
10. *Ibid.,* II, pp. 417-8.

December, he suggested that General Braxton Bragg's Army might be moved from Tennessee to Virginia.[11] Lee's actions reflected his concern about a new Union offensive. Realizing that Lincoln wanted action, Burnside initiated a course of action that, ultimately, should have convinced Lee of the foolhardiness of frontal assaults against modern weaponry. Burnside decided to take the direct road to Richmond by bridging across the Rappahannock at Fredericksburg.

On November 17, Burnside's army began arriving at Falmouth, across the Rappahannock from Fredericksburg. Unfortunately for him, the bridging equipment arrived days later. Although Burnside afterwards blamed Washington authorities for this lapse, General Jacob Cox provided another view: "...I could easily see that if his supervision of business had been more rigidly systematic, he would have made sure that he was not to be disappointed in his means of crossing the Rappahannock promptly." With a little initiative and creativity, Burnside could have at least ferried most of his men across before the arrival of Longstreet on the 20th. This possibility was demonstrated three weeks later when Burnside rowed infantry across the river to gain a foothold. The task would not even have been that difficult because stray cows were fording the river when Burnside first arrived. By crossing the river earlier and unopposed, the Union forces could have occupied Fredericksburg and the heights beyond and, thereby, avoided the disaster that was to follow.[12]

Because Burnside stayed north of the river, Lee had sufficient time to move his Army to Fredericksburg and the high ground overlooking the town and the river. The extent of Burnside's error in not promptly crossing the Rappahannock is demonstrated by the fact that Jackson's four divisions did not arrive at Fredericksburg from the Shenandoah Valley until December 3. Lee, who had belatedly realized and responded to the threat at Fredericksburg, then made his suggestion that the Army of Tennessee (again facing a threat to Chattanooga) be brought to Virginia.[13]

Burnside pressed his offensive even though he had badly lost the element of surprise. Realizing that Lincoln had fired McClellan for his timidity and wanted offensive progress, Burnside foolishly initiated and persisted in a suicidal frontal assault on an enemy occupying the

11. Lee to Jefferson Davis, December 6, 1862, Dowdey and Manarin, *Papers*, p. 353.

12. Cox, Jacob Dolson, *Military Reminiscences of the Civil War*, 2 vols. (New York: Charles Scribner's Sons, 1900), I, p. 453; Ambrose, Stephen E., *Halleck: Lincoln's Chief of Staff* (Baton Rouge and London: Louisiana State University Press, 1962, 1990), p. 98.

13. Nevins, *Ordeal*, VI, p. 345; Lee to Jefferson Davis, Dec. 6, 1862, Dowdey and Manarin, *Papers*, p. 353.

high ground directly to his front. The persistence and bravery of the Union soldiers could not overcome the advantages held by the defenders.

On December 11, Burnside's engineers attempted to cross the Rappahannock, but Mississippi sharpshooters, under Brigadier General William Barksdale, kept them from building their pontoon bridges even when the sharpshooters were fired on by Union artillery from the Falmouth hills to the north and east. That night, under cover of fog and darkness, the Yankees, at long last, crossed the river in boats and drove the Confederates from the town itself. On the 12th Burnside's forces established footholds on the southwest bank of the river and prepared to launch their long-delayed assaults. Having postponed his boat crossing for three weeks, Burnside then faced Confederates entrenched along miles of hills overlooking Fredericksburg and the Rappahannock River valley.

Early on December 13 the attacking Union Left Grand Division, specifically the 1st Corps' 3rd Division under Major General George Gordon Meade, achieved initial success because of a flaw in A.P. Hill's alignment which left a gap in the Rebel line. The Union breakthrough, joined by Major General John Gibbon's 2nd Division, was thwarted, and Meade's and Gibbon's men were driven back by the second line of Rebel defenders. Hill's mistake, however, resulted in the Rebels losing 3,500 men, while the Yankees lost 4,000 on the eastern end of the lines.

Meanwhile, a Union disaster was developing in the town. Burnside's plans for a flanking assault had gone awry because of his failure to clearly convey his intentions and due to his subordinate generals' half-hearted efforts. Against the advice of his commanders after the slaughter became obvious, Burnside ordered attack after attack up Marye's Heights. All told, from 11 a.m. to 5 p.m., there were fourteen charges up the hill. The result was the massacre of brigade after brigade of William H. French's, Winfield Scott Hancock's, and Andrew A. Humphreys' divisions as fourteen Confederate guns and six or seven thousand Confederate infantrymen, often four deep, fired from the heights and from a sunken road behind a stone wall, eliminating anything that moved on the plateau.

From a nearby location, Rhode Island Lieutenant Elisha Hunt Rhodes "...could see the long lines of Union troops move up the hill and melt away before the Rebel fire."[14] General Humphreys wrote to his wife,

> I led my division into a desperate fight and tried to take at the point of a bayonet a stone wall behind which a heavy line of the enemy lay. The heights just above were lined with artillery that poured upon us round shot, shell, and shrapnel; the musketry from the stone wall made a continuous sheet of flame. We charged within 50 yards of it each time but the men could not stand it.[15]

There were at least 7,600 Union casualties on the slaughtering ground in front of Marye's Heights.[16]

That night and early the next morning, Lee missed a grand opportunity to annihilate the Union troops massed in Fredericksburg. The Union soldiers were shocked and dispirited, and they were trapped against the river with limited means of retreat. Their artillery, across the river, could provide them no protection at night, in the early morning mist, or during an attack at close quarters. Lee, however, rejected advice to assault his vulnerable foe in the town -- apparently with the hope that the Union forces would resume their attack the next day.[17] Lee, thus, returned the favor McClellan had given him by not attacking when Lee kept his own vulnerable army at Sharpsburg an extra day.[18] Although Burnside may have been relatively stronger at Fredericksburg than Lee had been at Antietam, after the primary day of fighting, Lee would have been attacking downhill against only a portion of a completely demoralized Union force that straddled the Rappahannock River and which could not have utilized its artillery against a close-quarters attack.[19]

---

[14]. Rhodes, Elisha Hunt, *All for the Union: The Civil War Diary and Letters of Elisha Hunt Rhodes*, edited by Robert Hunt Rhodes (New York: Orion Books, 1985) [hereafter Rhodes, *All for the Union*], p. 90.

[15]. Barry, John M., *Rising Tide: The Great Mississippi Flood of 1927 and How It Changed America* (New York: Simon & Schuster, 1997), p. 48.

[16]. Of Fredericksburg, Confederate General Joseph E. Johnston commented, "What luck some people have. Nobody will ever come to attack me in such a place." Johnston to Louis T. Wigfall, December 15, 1862, quoted in McWhiney and Jamieson, *Attack and Die*, p. 159.

[17]. Lee to Samuel Cooper, "Battle Report of Fredericksburg Campaign," April 10, 1863, Dowdey and Manarin, *Papers*, p. 373; Allan, "Coversations," April 15, 1868, in Gallagher, *Lee the Soldier*, p. 13.

[18].Fuller, *Grant and Lee*, pp. 172-4.

[19]. Major-General Fuller said, " [At Fredericksburg], on the morning of December 14, [Lee] erred from over-caution, and as [Captain C.C.] Chesney says: 'Missed an opportunity of further advantage, such as even a great victory has rarely offered; it must be borne

Lee almost got his wish for another Union attack. While the wounded, dead, and a few unscathed survivors spent the night on Marye's Heights, Burnside gave the order for renewed attacks in the morning. However, this notion so enraged the Union Grand Division commanders who had witnessed the day's massacre that they revolted and threatened to resign *en masse*. Burnside took the hint, called off the attack, and ordered a retreat back across the river before Lee could pounce upon the Union army along the Rappahannock. The next month, Burnside resigned from a job he never wanted when Lincoln refused to approve his plan to replace most of his subordinate generals.[20]

It is intriguing to analyze Lee's observation of the events that cold December day at Fredericksburg. Overlooking the decimation of the Union forces charging up Marye's Heights, Lee observed, of the thousands of dead and wounded bodies, "It is well that war is so terrible; we should grow too fond of it."[21] Once again the attackers' casualties far exceeded those of the defenders; while the Union lost 10,900 (11 percent) killed and wounded, the Confederates lost only about 4,700 (6 percent). The Livermore hit ratios were what could be expected when one side repeatedly carried out frontal assaults on the other: the Union's was a devastating 103:44 while the Confederate ratio was a high, but very favorable, 64:150.[22] These figures are reminiscent, but the reverse, of those at the Seven Days' Battle.

Nevertheless, Southern losses were accumulating, and, that same December, the Confederate Congress abolished the use of substitutes for draftees and subjected those who had sent substitutes to the draft themselves.[23]

As 1862 came to a close and the war entered its third year, Lee had reason for concern despite his Fredericksburg victory. In a January, 1863, letter to Secretary of War James A. Seddon, Lee expressed his concern about his loss of manpower and the need for additional troops:

> While the spirit of our soldiers is unabated, their ranks
> have been greatly thinned by the casualties of battle and the
> diseases of the camp.

in mind that his troops were not on this occasion suffering from over-marching, want of food and ammunition.'" *Ibid.*, pp. 127-8.

20. Nevins, *Ordeal*, VI, pp. 366-7.

21. Freeman, *R.E. Lee*, p. 462; Hattaway and Jones, *How the North Won*, p. 308; Wert, *Longstreet*, p. 223.

22 . Livermore, *Numbers & Losses*, p. 96.

23 . McPherson, *Battle Cry of Freedom*, p. 603.

More than once have most promising opportunities been lost for want of men to take advantage of them, and victory itself has been made to put on the appearance of defeat, because our diminished and exhausted troops have been unable to renew a successful struggle against fresh numbers of the enemy. The lives of our soldiers are too precious to be sacrificed in the attainment of successes that inflict no loss upon the enemy beyond the actual loss in battle. Every victory should bring us nearer to the great end which is the object of this war to reach.[24]

This letter reflects Lee's proclivity for offense rather than defense because the latter would involve only the mutual exchange of casualties. His concern about casualties and declining manpower was well-founded. In Lee's first seven months of command, his army had inflicted 50,000 casualties on the enemy, but it had done so at a cost it could not afford: about 45,000 casualties of its own. Given the Union's 4:1 manpower advantage, this was a pace that could not be sustained without fatally weakening the Army of Northern Virginia and, eventually, subjecting it to a war of attrition, regardless of its commander's strategy in subsequent years.

What had Lee learned from the Seven Days' Battle, Second Manassas, Antietam, and Fredericksburg? Had he yet learned the folly of frontal assaults in this first of modern wars? Did he comprehend the new-found power of the defense that resulted from rifled guns and artillery? Did he recognize the similar results that occurred when his troops assaulted Malvern Hill, when Pope tried to drive Jackson out of the unfinished railroad cut at Manassas, when both armies charged the other again and again across the Cornfield at Antietam, or when Burnside ordered fourteen assaults at Marye's Heights? Did Lee, with his steadily declining personnel, understand the strategies and tactics which were, in fact, making this war "so terrible"? The year 1863 would tell.

---

[24] . Lee to James A. Seddon, January 10, 1863, Dowdey and Manarin, *Papers*, p. 389.

Fredericksburg.
...ters firing on the rebel works.

Chapter 7

May 1863: Chancellorsville, The Victory That Wasn't

After Fredericksburg, Burnside attempted, unsuccessfully, to retain command of the Union troops in Virginia. The final blow for him was the abysmal failure of his mid-January 1863 attempt to cross the Rappahannock upstream from Fredericksburg in order to surprise the Confederates. Nature took over. Fierce storms turned the offensive into the famous "Mud March," and the Rappahannock was not even crossed.[1]

On January 25, Lincoln named "Fighting Joe" Hooker to replace Burnside as Commander of the Army of the Potomac. Although Lincoln was aware that Hooker had fomented discontent and schemed to replace Burnside, the President believed he no longer had any choice because Burnside had lost the confidence of his entire army. In his appointment letter to Hooker, Lincoln criticized his anti-Burnside conduct and then went on to challenge Hooker to produce results:

> I have heard, in such way as to believe it, of your recently saying that both the Army and the Government needed a dictator. Of course it was not for this, but in spite of it, that I have given you the command. Only those generals who gain success, can set up dictators. What I now ask of you is military success, and I will risk the dictatorship.[2]

Hooker got off to a great start. He restored the Union troops' morale by straightening out the supply mess, getting them up to six months' back pay, and ensuring that they were provided with abundant food, clothing and other necessities. Hooker reorganized the army and restored both discipline and morale. One way he did this was by authorizing

---

[1]. Nevins, *Ordeal*, VI, pp. 366-7.
[2]. *Ibid.*, VI, pp. 433-4; Hattaway and Jones, *How the North Won*, p. 347.

the use of divisional uniform patches, an idea the late General Kearny had used successfully.

Hooker then went about planning the next Union offensive. By that time, Lincoln and Halleck had decided that the best strategy in the East was to go after Lee's army, not Richmond. Lee's continued aggressiveness in 1863 played into their hands. For his spring offensive, Hooker would have seven infantry corps of over 15,000 each and about 10,000 cavalry for a total force of about 130,000. His opponent, weakened by the interminable battles of 1862, would have a mere six infantry divisions totaling about 50,000 and about 6,000 cavalry.[3] In addition, Lee was hampered by the absence of Longstreet with Hood's and Pickett's divisions, which were on a major foraging expedition between Richmond and Suffolk in southeastern Virginia in order to provide food and forage for Lee's troops. Longstreet originally was defending against the threat posed to Richmond and Petersburg, by Burnside's 9th Corps.

At that critical April, 1863, juncture, Lee demonstrated his one-theater mindset and stoutly resisted the use of any of his army to help in the West. The Union, in March, had moved Burnside's 9th Corps to the West from the vicinity of Longstreet in southeastern Virginia, and Lee was content to leave Longstreet far away from Lee's Fredericksburg position.[4] Lee received a report of Burnside's movement on March 28 and was convinced of the report's validity by April 1.[5] Nevertheless, Lee resisted requests and suggestions by western Confederates, President Davis, Secretary of War James A. Seddon, and Longstreet that Longstreet's corps should be sent to the West to counter the increased Union strength there.[6]

In early April, Confederate western Generals John C. Pemberton and the recovered Joseph E. Johnston mistakenly advised Richmond that Grant, apparently, was moving troops from Mississippi to Tennessee to join Burnside and Rosecrans. They responded by sending 8,000 troops from Alabama and Mississippi to General Braxton Bragg in Tennessee and by requesting reinforcements from Lee.

---

[3]. Freeman, *R.E. Lee*, II, p. 483; Allan, "Conversations," February 19, 1870, in Gallagher, *Lee the Soldier*, p. 17.

[4]. Connolly, Thomas Lawrence, *Autumn of Glory: The Army of Tennessee, 1862-1865* (Baton Rouge and London: Louisiana State University Press, 1971, 1991) [hereafter Connolly, *Autumn of Glory*], p. 94.

[5]. Freeman, *R.E. Lee*, II, p. 501.

[6]. *Ibid.*, pp. 503-4; Connolly, *Autumn of Glory*, p. 104; Woodworth, Steven E., *Davis and Lee at War* (Lawrence: University of Kansas Press, 1995) [hereafter Woodworth, *Davis and Lee*], pp. 219-21.

On April 6, ironically the same day that Lee himself observed that the Union apparently "...had a general plan to deceive us while reinforcing the western armies,"[7] Secretary Seddon requested him to acquiesce in the transfer westward of two or three of Longstreet's brigades.[8] Lee strongly opposed the request and argued, contrary to his usual advocacy of concentration of forces,[9] that separate Confederate forces should launch separate offensives from Mississippi to Maryland.[10] He minimized the threat to Vicksburg by stating, "If the statements which I see in the papers are true, Genl Grant is withdrawing from Vicksburg, and will hardly return to his former position there this summer."[11] Lee wanted to move north and did not want to give up any of his troops; weeks before he had ordered the preparation of maps from the Shenandoah through Harrisburg to Philadelphia.[12]

When Seddon came back with a renewed and expanded request for some of Longstreet's forces, Lee came up with a new set of objections. Lee claimed that the forage Longstreet was gathering was critical to an imminent move north by Lee to test Hooker's strength, to ascertain the distribution of Union troops between the East and West, and to attempt to drive Hooker north of the Potomac. He suggested that Tennessee be strengthened by moving troops from Charleston, Savannah, Mobile, and Vicksburg -- anywhere but from Virginia![13] Learning that Grant actually had not moved forces to Tennessee, and yielding to Lee, Davis and Seddon sent reinforcements to Bragg in Tennessee only from Beauregard in the southeast.

As soon as he was assured that he was not going to lose any troops, Lee's plans for an early northern offensive disappeared and he left Longstreet where he was. Lee remained concerned about his supplies, but he remained optimistic that the northern will to win could be destroyed:

> I do not think our enemies are so confident of success as
> they used to be. If we can baffle them in their various designs

---

[7]. Hattaway and Jones, *How the North Won*, p. 362.

[8]. James A. Seddon to Lee, April 6, 1863.

[9]. Hattaway and Jones, *How the North Won*, p. 362.

[10]. Lee to James A. Seddon, April 9, 1863; Lee to Jefferson Davis, April 16, 1863: Dowdey and Manarin, *Papers*, pp. 429-30, 435. "[Lee's] new theories were rationalizations. Like his emphatic reaction, these were subconsciously designed to forestall the diminution of his army and prevent the derangement of his own plans for the spring campaign." Hattaway and Jones, *How the North Won*, p. 363.

[11]. Lee to General Samuel Cooper, Adjutant and Inspector General, April 16, 1863, Dowdey and Manarin, *Papers*, p. 434.

[12]. Woodworth, *Davis and Lee*, pp. 220-1.

[13]. *Ibid.*, pp. 433-4.

this year & our people are true to our cause & not so devoted to themselves and their own aggrandisement, I think our success will be certain. But it will all come right. This year I hope will establish our supplies on a firm basis. On every other point we are strong. If successful this year, next fall [1864] will be a great change in public opinion in the North. The Republicans will be destroyed & I think the friends of peace will become so strong as that the next administration will go in on that basis. We have only therefore to resist manfully.[14]

Lee's refusal to part with any of his men, however, had left the western Confederates shorthanded in two geographic areas. Johnston and Pemberton would be unable to deal with the imminent movement by Grant on Vicksburg, and the fall of that Mississippi River citadel within three months was not a good omen for the 1864 Presidential election. Just as ominously, Bragg's army in Tennessee also went unreinforced against a stronger opponent; it ran out of meat and was short on rations while it occupied an area from which all crops and livestock were being shipped to Lee.[15]

Back on the eastern front, beginning on April 26, Hooker made a major feint by crossing the Rappahannock with two corps below Fredericksburg, but he made his major effort surreptitiously west of the town. On the 29th three entire corps crossed the Rappahannock far upstream at Kelly's Ford and then pushed southward toward the fords of the Rapidan River. That same evening, they reached the Rapidan, secured Ely's Ford, and crossed Germanna Ford to the west. By April 30, the brilliant and undetected move was completed with the securing of U.S. Ford across the Rappahannock downstream of its merger with the Rapidan, the crossing of that ford by two more corps, and the resultant reuniting of the bulk of Hooker's army at the key Chancellorsville crossroads on the left flank of Lee.[16]

Hooker issued a blustering general order bragging that "...the operations of the last three days have determined that our enemy must either ingloriously fly or come out from behind his defenses and give us battle on our own ground, where certain destruction awaits him."[17] Even Union General George Meade, no friend of Hooker, exclaimed

---

[14]. Lee to his wife, April 19, 1863, Dowdey and Manarin, *Papers*, pp. 437-8.

[15]. Connelly, *Autumn of Glory*, p. 114.

[16]. For details concerning Chancellorsville, see Sears, Stephen W., *Chancellorsville* (Boston and New York: Houghton Mifflin Company, 1996) [hereafter Sears, *Chancellorsville*]; Furgurson, Ernest B., *Chancellorsville 1863: The Souls of the Brave* (New York: Alfred A. Knopf, 1992) [hereafter Furgurson, Chancellorsville]; Freeman, *R.E. Lee*, II, pp. 507-63.

[17]. Sears, *Chancellorsville*, p. 192; Hattaway and Jones, *How the North Won*, p. 379.

that day, "Hurrah for old Joe! We're on Lee's flank and he doesn't know it."[18]

Hooker was now in a position to march south out of the Wilderness and interpose the bulk of his army between Lee and Richmond -- unless Lee hastily retreated toward Richmond or Gordonsville, which is what Hooker expected. At worst, Hooker presumed, Lee would attack the Union forces in a way that Hooker could fight with superior numbers from a strong defensive position.

In deploying his forces, Hooker had made one major error; he had sent his cavalry, under Major General George Stoneman, on a raid far to the south. Hooker intended that Stoneman would cut Lee's supply-line and prevent him from retreating to Richmond. These intentions were not realized because of bad weather, Stoneman's incompetence, and Hooker's confusing orders. Not only was Stoneman's cavalry held in check by part of Jeb Stuart's Rebel cavalry, but this cavalry deployment left Hooker blind as well. Without the eyes of his cavalry, Hooker had no idea of the whereabouts of his opponent. As long as Jackson was alive, this was a fatal mistake.

Having been caught napping by Hooker's fleet, flanking thrust, an unhealthy Lee responded quickly and effectively.[19] On April 30 and May 1, Lee left Jubal Early with a small force to defend Fredericksburg and moved the divisions of Richard Anderson, McLaws, and then of Jackson westward to stop the Yankees from escaping the Wilderness. Despite Hooker's overwhelming superiority of forces, especially at the beginning of the battle, he lost his self-confidence and retreated back into the Wilderness on May 1 at the first sign of opposition.[20]

That opposition came as Jackson arrived from Fredericksburg at the commanding Zoan Church ridge east of the Wilderness. Jackson found Anderson's Division entrenching, but ordered them to attack instead. The combined Confederate divisions drove the Union forces back with aggressive, patchwork attacks along the only two roads and an unfinished railroad running west from Fredericksburg to the Wilderness. Instead of capitalizing on his advantageous position threatening the rear of Fredericksburg and the road to Richmond, Hooker had failed to move east and south and, instead, simply consolidated

---

[18]. Sears, *Chancellorsville*, p. 180.

[19]. In April 1863 Lee had been suffering from a throat and chest infection, probably aggravating his underlying arteriosclerotic health problems. Hattaway and Jones, *How the North Won*, p. 379.

[20]. There has been a continuing dispute whether Hooker, a heavy drinker, lost his self-confidence because he had temporarily stopped drinking or because he had lapsed into drinking again. Sears, *Chancellorsville*, pp. 504-6.

the bulk of his huge army in the Wilderness (minus the 6th Corps opposite Fredericksburg and Stoneman's cavalry).

Unlike Hooker, Lee had retained some cavalry, under the leadership of Jeb Stuart, in the vicinity. This action quickly bore fruit. On the afternoon and evening of May 1, Stuart and Brigadier General Fitzhugh Lee (Robert's nephew) discovered that Hooker had left his right flank, west of Chancellorsville, hanging in the air (that is, not protected by a river, ridge, or other natural feature nor bent back, entrenched and supported).

That exposed flank proved irresistible to Lee and Jackson. That night, Lee discussed the situation with the daring and dependable Jackson. Jackson proposed, and Lee agreed, that a surprise flanking march to the west and north should be made by Jackson to attack that inviting Union right flank the next day. Stonewall proposed that he be given two-thirds of the 45,000 men Lee had brought out of Fredericksburg, and Lee consented.[21] With a mere 15,000 facing the bulk of Hooker's army, Lee distracted Union attention away from Jackson's march and camouflaged his own weakness by brazenly initiating minor assaults along the lines throughout the day. Under Lee's direction, therefore, Anderson's and McLaws' divisions succeeded in distracting Hooker without bringing about a major battle.

This daring gamble, which avoided a frontal attack on the numerically superior Army of the Potomac, proved successful. The now-insecure Hooker ignored repeated reports that Rebel forces were marching around his Army toward that hanging right flank he also had ignored. Shortly before dark, Jackson ascertained that Brigadier General Robert E. Rodes was "ready" and gave him the bland order, "You can go forward then." Major portions of Jackson's 30,000-man corps came crashing down the Orange Turnpike, caused panicked wildlife to flee toward the Union lines, caught unwary Union troops cooking their evening meals, and decimated the right wing of the Union army.

However, there were several flaws in Jackson's march and attack, which rendered it less effective than it otherwise might have been. The 7:30 a.m. starting hour for the march was about three hours later than usual for Jackson. Also, the generally westward march was not conducted quickly enough to ensure its full success. Because of narrow roads and paths, it took twelve hours for the ten-mile march and setup of the attack. Early reports that the exposed flank was on the Orange Plank Road proved false, and additional time and daylight were consumed marching farther north to the Turnpike before turning east to

---

[21]. Freeman, *Lee's Lieutenants*, II, pp. 546-7; Alexander, *Lost Victories*, pp. 304-5.

prepare for the attack. The cumulative delays resulted in the attack starting between 5:15 and 6 p.m. -- so close to sunset that it could not be fully developed and the initial Union surprise and panic could not be totally exploited. After the assault, James Coghill of the 23rd North Carolina wrote, "A yankey Colonel that we took prisoner said that if we had to have kept on we would have captured the whole army..."[22]

The attack itself was hampered by the fact that many of Jackson's men did not get involved. Brigadier General Alfred H. Colquitt, an incompetent Georgia political general, severely reduced the impact of the lead division's five-brigade attack by stopping his own brigade, on Jackson's right flank, and by blocking Brigadier General Stephen D. Ramseur's North Carolina Brigade behind him. Colquitt, thus, took at least 20 percent of the leading edge of the attacking force out of the attack by ignoring Jackson's orders to stop for nothing and, instead, heeding a false warning from a staff member that Union troops were on their right flank.

The rout on the Union right, nevertheless, was a major success, and Major General Oliver O. Howard's 11th Corps fled eastward for more than two miles into a gap left by Major General Daniel Edgar Sickles' 3rd Corps, most of which had moved south to attack Jackson's rear guard in the area of Catherine Furnace. But there would be hell to pay by the Confederates for the time-consuming manner in which the surprise attack had been arranged and then unfolded.

Darkness, confusion, and heroic stands by some Union forces brought the advance to a halt. In particular, General Rodes' front-line division was devastated and stopped by cannon fire from Fairview Plateau. The following division, that of the inexperienced Brigadier General Raleigh E. Colston, became badly intermingled with Rodes' division beginning shortly after the assault started. Colston himself described the chaotic situation: "Brigades, regiments, and companies had become so mixed that they could not be handled, besides which the darkness of evening was so intensified by the shade of the dense woods that nothing could be seen a few yards off. The halt at that time was not a mistake but a necessity." General Rodes later explained why it was necessary to call a halt to the charge at about 7:15: "Such was the confusion and darkness that it was not deemed advisable to make a farther advance."[23] Then the accidental shooting of Jackson by his own men as he sought a route to the Union rear in the moonlit darkness took the heart out of the Confederate momentum. His successor, A.P.

22. Sears, *Chancellorsville*, p. 280.
23. Sears, *Chancellorsville*, p. 287.

Hill, also was injured that evening, and cavalryman Jeb Stuart assumed command of Jackson's corps early the next morning.

Jackson and his moonlit party had been decimated by fire from the 18th North Carolina Infantry when they tried to return to the Rebel lines and were mistaken for Union cavalry. Jackson's left arm was shattered by two bullets, and his right palm was struck by a smooth-bore musket bullet. He endured a painful litter ride to a field hospital, where his medical director amputated his left arm just below the shoulder. When informed of Jackson's condition, Lee said, "...Any victory is dearly bought which deprives us of the services of General Jackson, even for a short time."[24] Days later, Lee added, "He has lost his left arm, but I have lost my right."[25] Eight days later, Jackson died of pneumonia at nearby Guinea Station, and Lee lost the only corps commander who was compatible with his own hands-off style of command.

Jackson's assault also took a heavy toll on Jackson's attackers. Although they routed the shocked infantry at the point of assault, the Rebels met more and more resistance as they advanced down the Turnpike past its intersection with the Orange Plank Road. Particularly devastating to them was the Union artillery (twenty or more guns at Hazel Grove and thirty-four more at Fairview Plateau) that blunted their progress. A Federal artillery officer described the scene:

> It was dusk when [Jackson's] men swarmed out of the woods for a quarter of a mile in our front... They came on in line five and six deep... I gave the command to fire, and the whole line of artillery was discharged at once. It fairly swept them from the earth; before they could recover themselves the line of artillery had been loaded and was ready for the second attack... [against which] I poured in the canister for about twenty minutes, and the affair was over.[26]

Another problem resulting from Jackson's flanking march was that Lee's forces were separated and vulnerable to a counter-attack -- especially the two smaller contingents with Lee south and east of Chancellorsville and with Early back at Fredericksburg. Although the inept Hooker failed to take advantage of this situation, Stuart and Lee were left with no choice but to launch desperate offensives the next morning from the west and south, respectively, toward Chancellorsville so that they could join their forces.

---

[24]. Freeman, *R.E. Lee*, II, p. 533.
[25]. *Ibid.*, p. 560.
[26]. McWhiney and Jamieson, *Attack and Die*, p. 4.

Hooker made their task easier that night by ordering the evacuation of Hazel Grove, the commanding prominence in the middle of the Wilderness, which was an ideal artillery position and the key to the battlefield. On the advice of then-Colonel Porter Alexander, Stuart gave the orders that resulted in the dawn capture of Hazel Grove from its Union remnants. Alexander posted fifty guns on Hazel Grove and devastated Union forces to the north and east. Because of Hooker's failure to use more than half of his forces in the fighting (possibly due, in part, to his having been knocked unconscious by a shell fragment from one of Alexander's guns), the Confederates' attack and effort to merge their divided forces were successful -- although costly in terms of dead and wounded.

Unlike during the surprise attack of the prior afternoon and evening, Lee's men, on that May 3 morning, had to push back prepared Union lines in the defender-friendly confines of the Wilderness in order to merge and incurred heavy losses in doing so.[27] By the end of that morning, Lee's forces east and south of Chancellorsville, aided by ill-conceived Union withdrawals, merged with Stuart's men coming in from the west. Together, they pushed back the tenacious, but poorly-led, Union troops and captured the Chancellorsville intersection. There followed a wild celebration as General Lee rode in on Traveller and accepted the accolades of his gritty fighters. That emotional scene may have been the apex of the Confederacy.

The celebration did not last long, however. No sooner had Lee and Stuart joined their forces when serious problems developed with Early's small, isolated force at Fredericksburg. Lee received word that John Sedgwick's 6th Corps had broken through Early's defenses at Fredericksburg, and Lee then moved east with McLaws' Division and some of Anderson's to block Sedgwick at Salem Church from getting through to Hooker. At that point, Hooker missed a grand opportunity to squeeze Lee's forces between Sedgwick's troops and his own. Instead, Lee blocked and then trapped the slow-moving Sedgwick east of Salem Church, west of Fredericksburg and south of the Rappahannock. Although hemmed in by the passive McLaws on the west, the late-arriving Anderson on the south, and an aggressive Early on the east, Sedgwick defended his position skillfully, killed and wounded many overly aggressive Confederate attackers, and then escaped north across

---

[27]. Krick, Robert K., "Lee's Greatest Victory," *American Heritage*, 41, No. 2 (March 1990), pp. 66, 77. Stuart lost thirty percent of Jackson's remaining troops in bloody attacks on entrenched Union troops. Bevin Alexander, *Lost Victories*, p. 318. The fighting that morning cost the Confederates almost 9,000 dead, wounded and missing. Sears, *Chancellorsville*, p. 365.

the Rappahannock via Scott's Ford on the night of May 4-5.

In E. Porter Alexander's opinion, Lee wasted a whole day setting up his trap for, and initiating his attack on, the out-numbered Sedgwick instead of going after him immediately.[28] This gave Sedgwick time to entrench and, ultimately, to escape. All the while Lee was trying to trap and destroy Sedgwick, the hapless Hooker stood by and did nothing while his forces remaining in the Chancellorsville area outnumbered Lee's there by a four-to-one margin.

Never one to pass up an opportunity to attack, Lee hurried back to Chancellorsville on May 5 after Sedgwick's nighttime retreat in an effort to assault Hooker's forces before they could similarly retreat across the Rappahannock -- at U.S. Ford. General Winfield Scott Hancock was overseeing an orderly and well-defended retreat, and Lee was fortunate not to have had the opportunity to attack. In fact, according to E. Porter Alexander, Lee was saved from disaster by Hooker's May 5-6 retreat back across the river:

> There was still another occasion when I recalled ruefully Ives's prophecy that I would see all the audacity [on Lee's part] I wanted to see, & felt that it was already over fulfilled: but when, to my intense delight, the enemy crossed the river in retreat during the night, & thus saved us from what would have been probably the bloodiest defeat of the war. It was on the 6th of May 1863 at the end of Chancellorsville... Hooker's entire army, some 90,000 infantry, were in the Wilderness, backed against the Rapidan [actually the Rappahannock], & had had nearly three days to fortify a short front, from the river above to the river below. And, in that dense forest of small wood, a timber slashing in front of a line of breastworks could in a few hours make a position absolutely impregnable to assault. But on the afternoon of the 5th Gen. Lee gave orders for a grand assault the next morning by his whole force of about 40,000 infantry, & I was all night getting my artillery in position for it. And how I did thank God when in the morning the enemy were gone![29]

Bitterly disappointed at the failure to launch the ill-conceived offensive that he had hoped would bring a grand victory, Lee erupted when Brigadier General Dorsey Pender reported to him that the Federal entrenchments had been abandoned overnight.[30] He demeaned

---

[28]. Alexander, *Fighting for the Confederacy*, p. 213.
[29]. *Ibid.*, p. 92.
[30]. Hattaway and Jones, *How the North Won*, p. 385.

him by saying, "Why, General Pender! That is the way you young men always do. You allow those people to get away. I tell you what to do, but you don't do it! Go after them! Damage them all you can!"[31]

Chancellorsville, Jackson's last battle, also proved to be Lee's last major "victory." The classic flanking maneuver employed by Jackson was not to be repeated. After Jackson's death there was no one forceful enough (and only Longstreet apparently tried) to convince Lee of the necessity of preserving his most precious resource, his army, by remaining on the defensive whenever possible and by flanking, rather than frontally assaulting, superior enemy forces. There also was no one left capable of converting Lee's discretionary orders into daring success on the battlefield.[32]

Although often regarded as Lee's greatest victory, Chancellorsville was a tribute to the incompetence of Hooker under fire and, most importantly, was a disaster for the South.[33] Hooker had sent his cavalry away from the battle, failed to use much of his infantry, meekly surrendered one strong position after another, and failed to take advantage of his artillery superiority. Nevertheless, after the havoc wreaked by Jackson's flanking maneuver, the Confederates decimated themselves in a series of frontal attacks on Union defenders. As a result, while inflicting 10,700 (11 percent) northern casualties (killed and wounded), the Rebels themselves suffered an intolerably high -- and irreplaceable -- almost 11,100 (19 percent) casualties (killed and wounded) of their own. The total numbers killed and wounded on the two sides were about equal, and even a few more Confederates were killed.[34]

Although each side had relatively balanced Livermore hit ratios, the Confederate numbers were much higher. For each 1,000 engaged, the Union side had suffered 114 hit and had hit 114 of the enemy, while of each 1,000 Confederates, 187 were hit and 194 hit the enemy.[35] As

---

31. Furgurson, *Chancellorsville*, p. 318.
32. On several occasions, Jackson had recommended flanking offensive campaigns into the North, but Lee and Davis rejected his recommendations. Alexander, *Great Generals*, pp. 123-42; Allan, "Conversations," December 17, 1868, in Gallagher, *Lee the Soldier*, p. 15; Alexander, *Lost Victories, passim*.
33. "[Chancellorsville] looked to be a great Confederate victory, but the appearance was deceiving." Alexander, *Lost Victories*, p. 322.
34. Livermore, *Numbers & Losses*, pp. 98-9. Stephen Sears states that the Confederates had 30 more soldiers killed than the Union and only 439 fewer wounded. Sears, *Chancellorsville*, p. 442. Although most later authorities use larger numbers than Livermore for Hooker's forces and those numbers reflect a greater manpower disparity, those larger numbers also reduce the casualty percentage suffered by Hooker's army. See Appendix II herein, "Casualties in the Civil War."
35. Livermore, *Numbers & Losses*, pp. 98-9.

these hit ratios indicate, Lee's forces were much more active than their opponents, were often on the offensive, and thus incurred higher losses. Outnumbered 4 to 1 at the outset of the war and devastated by their 1862 losses, the Confederates could not afford many more battles in which they suffered 19 percent casualties to their foe's mere 11 percent.

His numerical losses were serious enough to cause Lee to change his Army's manner of counting casualties by eliminating "slight injuries," to complain of his numerical inferiority, and to make one of his periodic appeals to President Davis for reinforcements from elsewhere.[36] With both Vicksburg and Chattanooga threatened, Lee opposed sending one of Longstreet's divisions to the West and argued to Secretary of War Seddon that, unless he was reinforced, he would have "...to withdraw into the defences around Richmond... The strength of this army has been reduced by the casualties in the late battles."[37] The next day, Lee wrote Davis: "It would seem therefore that Virginia is to be the theater of action, and this army, if possible, ought to be strengthened... I think that you will agree with me that every effort should be made to reinforce this army in order to oppose the large force which the enemy seems to be concentrating against it."[38]

Chancellorsville demonstrated Lee's propensity for offensive strategy and tactics. It also displayed his Virginia-only focus as he refused to part with Longstreet beforehand and sought reinforcements afterward. While his focus on Virginia had serious ramifications elsewhere, Lee's aggressive strategy and tactics again resulted in irreplaceable losses to his own army.

Perhaps as damaging as Lee's actual losses was the overconfidence that Chancellorsville inspired in Confederate minds -- particularly in the mind of Robert E. Lee.[39] On May 21, Lee wrote to Hood about the men in the Army of Northern Virginia:

> I agree with you in believing that our army would be invincible if it could be properly organized and officered. There never were such men in an army before. They will go anywhere and do anything if properly led.[40]

Every tactical gamble Lee had taken appeared to have been successful, the enemy had been driven from the field and across the Rappahan-

---

[36]. General Order No. 63, May 14, 1863, Fox, *Regimental Losses*, p. 559.
[37]. Lee to James A. Seddon, May 10, 1863, Dowdey and Manarin, *Papers*, p. 482.
[38]. Lee to Jefferson Davis, May 11, 1863, Dowdey and Manarin, *Papers*, pp. 483-4.
[39]. McPherson, *Battle Cry of Freedom*, p. 645; Woodworth, *Davis and Lee*, p. 230.
[40]. Lee to John B. Hood, May 21, 1863, Dowdey and Manarin, *Papers*, p. 490.

nock, and there seemed no task beyond the capability of his brave army. Lee's actions in the succeeding weeks reflected a fatal belief that the Army of Northern Virginia was invincible.[41] His belief, according to E. Porter Alexander, was shared at that time by his army:

> But, like the rest of the army generally, nothing gave me much concern so long as I knew that Gen. Lee was in command. I am sure there can never have been an army with more supreme confidence in its commander than that army had in Gen. Lee. We looked forward to victory under him as confidently as to successive sunrises.[42]

Lee's over-confident army, however, had seen its last major "victory."

---

[41]. Pfanz, Harry W., *Gettysburg: The Second Day* (Chapel Hill and London: The University of North Carolina Press, 1987) [hereafter Pfanz, *The Second Day*], p. 4.

[42]. Alexander, *Fighting for the Confederacy*, p. 222.

Confederate General George Edward Pickett. After the Union army turned back Pickett's charge, Robert E. Lee ordered him to rally his division for a renewed assault. The 38-year-old general responded, "I have no division now." After the war, Pickett recalled bitterly how Lee had his division "slaughtered at Gettysburg." (LC)

Chapter 8

July 1863:
Suicide at Gettysburg

Lee, with Jackson no longer at his side, next made the fateful decision to invade the North -- a decision that carried him to Gettysburg and destroyed the possibility of a Confederate military (but not necessarily a political) victory. He did so only after rejecting pleas that he send part of his army to rescue the 30,000 troops being bottled up near Vicksburg, Mississippi, by Ulysses S. Grant. Secretary of War Seddon and Longstreet recommended to President Davis either that course of action or a reinforcement of Bragg for an assault on Middle Tennessee. They could have argued that Chancellorsville demonstrated that Lee could survive and even win without Longstreet.[1]

Between May 14 and 17, while Grant took Jackson, Mississippi, and moved toward Vicksburg, the Confederacy's leadership met in Richmond to debate the issue of whether or not to send some of Lee's troops to trap Grant between Jackson, Mississippi, and John Pemberton's 30,000-man army in Vicksburg. Using all the political capital earned by his Chancellorsville "victory," Lee was able to convince Davis that Richmond would be threatened if Lee's army was reduced in strength and that the best defense of Richmond would be an offensive campaign into the North. Lee demonstrated his lack of a national strategic vision by arguing that this issue was a "...question between Virginia and the Mississippi." He also argued that the oppressive Mississippi climate would cause Grant to withdraw from the Vicksburg area in June.[2]

---

[1]. McPherson, *Battle Cry of Freedom*, pp. 646-7.

[2]. Lee's arguments are reflected in his letters of April and May 1863. Lee to James A. Seddon, April 9, 1863; Lee to Samuel Cooper, April 16, 1863; Lee to Jefferson Davis, April 16, 1863; Lee to James A. Seddon, May 10, 1863; Lee to Jefferson Davis, May 11, 1863; Dowdey and Manarin, *Papers*, pp. 430-1, 433-4, 434-5, 482, 483-4. See Connelly, Thomas Lawrence and Archer Jones, *The Politics of Command: Factions and Ideas in Confederate Strategy* (Baton Rouge: Louisiana State University Press, 1973) [hereafter Connelly and Jones, *Politics of Command*], p. 126-8.

Lee prevailed, and, on May 26, the Confederate Cabinet authorized him to launch a northern offensive in the East. As Lee moved north, he unrealistically wrote to Davis that his eastern offensive might even result in the Union recalling some of its troops from the West. Lee hedged his bet by coupling this statement with a request that troops be transferred to Virginia from the Carolinas to protect Richmond, threaten Washington, and aid his advance.[3] Although Longstreet acquiesced in Lee's strategic offensive, he spent a great deal of time trying to convince Lee to go on the tactical defensive once in the North in an effort to repeat the victory at Fredericksburg. Confederate General Wade Hampton later complained that he thought the Pennsylvania campaign would enable the Confederates to choose a battlefield but that, instead, "...we let Meade choose his position & we then attacked."[4]

There is evidence in Lee's correspondence that he went north with mixed intentions. These are reflected in two June 25 letters Lee wrote to Davis. In the first, he said, "I think I can throw Genl Hooker's army across the Potomac and draw troops from the south, embarrassing their plan of campaign in a measure, if I can do nothing more and have to return."[5] Later that day, he seemed to reflect Longstreet's view: "It seems to me that we cannot afford to keep our troops awaiting possible movements of the enemy, but that our true policy is, as far as we can, so to employ our own forces as to give occupation to his at points of our own selection."[6]

General E. Porter Alexander later stated that sending troops to the West would have been a better use of them, would have taken advantage of the South's interior lines, and was successful when used that

---

3. Lee to Jefferson Davis, June 23, 1863, Dowdey and Manarin, *Papers*, pp. 527-8; Hattaway and Jones, *How the North Won*, pp. 401-2, 404. Steven Woodworth noted that, "Calling for Beauregard a month earlier, when the northern invasion itself was still being debated by the cabinet, would have made fatally obvious to the cautious president that what Lee had in mind was an all-out end-the-war gamble." Woodworth, *Davis and Lee*, pp. 238-9.

4. Hattaway and Jones, *How the North Won*, p. 414.

5. Lee to Jefferson Davis, June 25, 1863, Dowdey and Manarin, *Papers*, pp. 530, 531.

6. Lee to Jefferson Davis, June 25, 1863, Dowdey and Manarin, *Papers*, p. 532. Bruce criticized Lee's post-battle rationale that he wanted to draw Hooker away from the Rappahannock and maneuver to gain a battlefield victory: "This discloses a piece of strategy with no definite objective, but one resting on a contingency. There is certainly something quixotic in the idea of moving an army two hundred miles for the purpose of finding a battlefield, leaving his base of supplies one hundred miles or more at the end of the railroad at Winchester, when able to carry along only ammunition enough for a single battle, as was necessarily the case." Bruce, "Lee and Strategy" in Gallagher, *Lee the Soldier*, p. 117.

autumn (at Chickamauga) under less favorable circumstances.[7] Lee's failure to send troops to either Vicksburg or middle Tennessee, in order to maintain his own army at full strength, was a significant factor in the fall of Vicksburg, the loss of the Mississippi River (a maritime highway and line of supply) to Union control, a retreat by Bragg out of middle Tennessee and northern Alabama after he had been forced to send troops to aid Vicksburg, the exposure of Chattanooga to Union capture, and the continuing Union success in the West that, ultimately, would spread through Georgia to Lee's own back door. As Archer Jones explained, "This opening of the Mississippi had a profound effect by spreading hope in the North for an early victory and in the South widespread pessimism."[8]

The Confederate Army of Tennessee had been considerably weakened that spring and summer because the Confederate commissary in Atlanta shipped massive foodstuffs to Lee and virtually nothing to Bragg.[9] Not only did Lee refuse to send troops to the West, but he implored Bragg to invade Ohio to complement his own planned incursion into Pennsylvania.[10] He did this at a time when Bragg had only 50,000 troops in Tennessee which were being used either to hold Tennessee or to send assistance to Vicksburg. At the time, Union strength in the West was 214,000 men.[11]

Gettysburg -- the finale to Confederate military prospects in the East -- exposed Lee at his worst. As was the case when he went north in 1862, an embarrassing retreat and perceived defeat were inevitable.[12] General Alexander later expressed his concern that Lee's nearest ammunition supply railhead was at Staunton, Virginia, 150 wagon-miles

---

[7]. Alexander, *Fighting for the Confederacy*, pp. 219-20.

[8]. Jones, "Military Means," in Boritt, *Why the Confederacy Lost*, p. 67.

[9]. Connelly, *Autumn of Glory*, p. 114.

[10]. Connelly, "Lee and the Western Confederacy," p. 124.

[11]. *Ibid.* "Lee's Pennsylvania campaign demanded that the Confederacy not use eastern reserves to attempt to lift the Vicksburg siege; Bragg, weakened to aid Johnston [near Vicksburg], was driven from Middle Tennessee by Rosecrans's brilliant Tullahoma campaign; and Johnston's fragment was too small to operate effectively against the heavily reinforced Grant." Hattaway and Jones, *How the North Won*, p. 415.

[12]. Beringer et al, *Why the South Lost*, pp. 264, 300; Jones, Archer, *Civil War Command & Strategy* (New York: The Free Press, 1992) [hereafter Jones, Command & Strategy], p. 168; "If on the other hand [Lee] fought a battle in Pennsylvania, he could choose his position and compel the Union army to fight another battle of Fredericksburg [what Longstreet recommended and Lee did not do]. But again Lee overlooked the political effect of fighting. Even a victorious defensive battle would look like a defeat because of the inevitable retreat of a raiding army forced to concentrate and unable to forage." Jones, "Military Means," in Boritt, *Why The Confederacy Lost*, p. 68.

from Gettysburg.[13] Just as in 1862, Lee was moving north with a badly-weakened army but was blinded by its prior tactical success earlier in the year.[14] In addition, Lee spread his forces all around south-central Pennsylvania without knowing the location of the Army of the Potomac.

In going north again, Lee was demonstrating his flawed philosophy that the best defense was a good offense.[15] He hoped to draw Hooker's army out of Virginia and have the two armies live off the Pennsylvania countryside during the summer and early fall. He succeeded in taking everyone north, but his stay was shorter than he had hoped, and his ultimate retreat to the Rappahannock line gave the appearance of defeat to those not mesmerized by the myth of his invincibility. Gettysburg was Lee's final, major, strategically, offensive campaign.[16]

Following Chancellorsville and Jackson's death, Lee reorganized his 75,000-man army. From two infantry corps of four divisions each, he created three corps, each having three divisions. The 1st Corps was commanded by Longstreet, the 2nd by Ewell, and the 3rd by A.P. Hill. Neither Ewell nor Hill had worked directly under Lee's command; neither of them was a Stonewall Jackson. Lee's offensive strategy and tactics had adversely affected the entire command structure of his army.[17] Lee's failure to adjust his style, expectations, and orders to the poorer and less-experienced generals in his army, especially after Chancellorsville, would prove to be troublesome and even disastrous.

Jeb Stuart commanded the cavalry division, and his swash-buckling style led to serious problems soon after Lee's army started north on June 3. On the eve of this departure on a major invasion of the North, Stuart's cavalrymen seemed less interested than usual. One Confederate captain later explained that the troops were "...worried

---

[13]. Alexander, *Fighting for the Confederacy*, pp. 110, 222.

[14]. "Rather than a menace, Lincoln perceived Lee's raid, like the previous advance to Antietam, as an opportunity to strike the enemy when vulnerable and far from his base, 'the best opportunity' he said, 'we have had since the war began.'" Hattaway and Jones, *How the North Won*, p. 400.

[15]. In 1868 Lee allegedly told William Allan that his intentions in moving north were defensive: "First [Lee] did not intend to give general battle in Pa. if he could avoid it--the South was too weak to carry on a war of invasion, and his offensive movements against the North were never intended except as parts of a defensive system." Allan, "Conversations" in Gallagher, *Lee the Soldier*, p. 13. Lee's actions in 1862 and 1863 seem inconsistent with that description.

[16]. Perhaps the best study of Lee's Gettysburg campaign is Coddington, Edwin B., *The Gettysburg Campaign: A Study in Command* (New York: Charles Scribner's Sons, 1984) [hereafter Coddington, *Gettysburg Campaign*].

[17]. Weigley, *American Way of War*, p. 116.

out by the military foppery and display (which was Stuart's greatest weakness)."[18]

Lee's lax oversight of Stuart and the cavalry arm of his Army led to one near-disaster and to one real disaster. Stuart's cavalry was supposed to have been protecting Lee's right flank and hiding his northward movement from Yankee eyes. On June 5, Stuart's approximately 9,500 officers and men held a grand parade at Brandy Station close by the Orange and Alexandria Railroad -- to the joy of the local ladies and to the disgust of the Confederate infantry.[19] The only disappointment was that the Commanding General could not be there. But Stuart received another opportunity to strut his forces when Lee arrived on the 7th and requested another review the next day. Thus, the cavalry's spectacle was repeated on June 8th, one day before the date Lee had ordered them to move across the Rappahannock to cover the continuing northward march of Ewell and Longstreet.[20] Lee himself was pleased; he wrote to his wife, "...I reviewed the cavalry in this section yesterday. It was a splendid sight. The men & horses looked well. They had recuperated since last fall. Stuart was in all his glory."[21]

Early the next morning (June 9), the Confederates, instead of moving out themselves, were caught off-guard by a dawn attack launched by Brigadier General Alfred Pleasonton's Union calvary. Eleven thousand Union troopers crossed the Rappahannock at Beverly's Ford and, a few miles south, at Kelly's Ford; they launched attacks on Stuart's scattered forces. They got all the way to Brandy Station and Stuart's headquarters at nearby Fleetwood House before being repulsed by superior numbers of Confederate cavalry under Brigadier Generals Rooney Lee (Robert E. Lee's son) and William E. "Grumble" Jones, with their horse artillery, and, ultimately, Rebel infantry. Stuart almost lost his artillery, and an all-day battle swirled around Fleetwood Hill, which changed hands four times. Union losses were about 900 to the Rebels' 500, but the Northern horsemen achieved their goal of pinpointing the location of the bulk of the Army of Northern Virginia while demonstrating, for the first time, their ability to initiate and sustain a credible offensive.

Thus, Stuart's grand parades for Lee had been capped at Brandy Station by an early morning Union cavalry attack which had caught the

---

[18]. Gallagher, Gary W., "Brandy Station: The Civil War's Bloodiest Arena of Mounted Combat," *Blue & Gray Magazine*, VIII, Issue 1 (Oct. 1990), pp. 8-22, 44-53; p. 13.

[19]. Blackford, William Willis, *War Years with Jeb Stuart* (Baton Rouge and London: Louisiana State University Press, 1945, 1993), pp. 211-2.

[20]. *Ibid.*, pp. 212-3.

[21]. Lee to his wife, June 9, 1863, Dowdey and Manarin, *Papers*, pp. 506-7.

Rebels unprepared and which had been repulsed only by the bravery of the Southerners' horse artillery, their superior numbers, and the advantage of being on the defensive. The Battle of Brandy Station was a tactical draw but a Union strategic victory, and it marked the end of the dominance of the Confederate cavalry over their Union counterparts. Lee's son, Rooney, was gravely wounded at Brandy Station and then was kidnapped by Union troops later that month.

Embarrassed by his lack of preparedness and near-defeat at Brandy Station, Stuart sought to redeem himself later in June by setting off on another grand swing around the Union army. Lee, instead of reining in the flamboyant Jeb, provided Stuart with such ambiguous orders that Lee's invasion of Pennsylvania and most of the battle at Gettysburg were carried out without knowledge of his adversaries' whereabouts. Amazingly, Lee repeated the same error Hooker had just committed when he stripped himself of cavalry for the entire battle at Chancellorsville. Lee allowed Stuart to depart with half his cavalry and to take along his best subordinate commanders, Major General Wade Hampton and Brigadier General Fitzhugh Lee, while leaving the weak Brigadier General Beverly Robertson to screen and scout for the army commander.

How could this have happened? Simply, Stuart had a series of orders to choose from and decided upon the most glorious opportunity offered to him. On June 22, with Ewell already in Pennsylvania and Stuart still in Virginia, Stuart received the following orders from Lee:

> If you find that [Hooker] is moving northward, and that two brigades can guard the Blue Ridge & take care of your rear, you can move with the other three into Maryland & take position on General Ewell's right, place yourself in communication with him, guard his flank, keep him informed of the enemy's movements, & collect all the supplies you can for the use of the army.[22]

Lee sent those orders, with an accompanying note, to Longstreet, who then forwarded the orders to Stuart with a cover letter stating:

> [Lee] speaks of your leaving, via Hopewell Gap, in the Bull Run Mountains and passing by the rear of the enemy. If you can get through by that route, I think you will be less likely to indicate what your plans are than if you should cross by passing to our rear... I think that your passage of the Potomac by our rear at the present moment will, in a measure,

22. Lee to J.E.B. Stuart, June 22, 1863, Dowdey and Manarin, *Papers*, p. 523.

disclose our plans. You had better not leave us, therefore, unless you can take the proposed route in rear of the enemy.[23]

The very next day, in Rectortown, Maryland, Stuart received another set of orders, dated June 23, from Lee:

> If Genl Hooker's army remains inactive you can leave two brigades to watch him & withdraw the three others, but should he not appear to be moving northward, I think you had better withdraw this side of the mountain tomorrow night, cross [the Potomac] at Shepherdstown next day, & move over to Fredericktown.
>
> You will however be able to judge whether you can pass around their army without hinderance, doing them all the damage you can, & cross the river east of the mountains. In either case, after crossing the river, you must move on & feel the right of Ewell's troops, collecting information, provisions, &c.[24]

Utilizing the confusing discretion Lee had provided to him, Stuart engaged in a meaningless frolic-and-detour and did not rejoin Lee until late the second day at Gettysburg. Stuart decided to pass behind the Union army and cross the Potomac east of the Blue Ridge Mountains after effectively screening Lee's northward movement in successful cavalry actions at Aldie, Middleburg, and Upperville. Thus, on June 24, he left Salem, Virginia, moved south of Manassas Junction, crossed the Occoquan and Potomac Rivers, moved eastward through Rockville and north through Westminster in Maryland, before finally entering Pennsylvania near Hanover. Although then only a few miles east of Gettysburg, Stuart had no idea where Lee was and, therefore, headed north to Carlisle instead of west to Gettysburg. All the while, Stuart was slowed down by a captured wagon train which he regarded as precious booty.

As a result of this eight-day "ego trip," Stuart did not join Lee at Gettysburg until the evening of July 2 -- too late to be of any assistance. Lee had to learn, on June 28, from a spy of Longstreet's, of George Meade's appointment to succeed Hooker and of Meade's army's northward movement across the Potomac. Lee had no idea which Union corps were going to arrive when at Gettysburg, and, on the critical second day of July, he had to base his plan of battle on skimpy and incorrect information concerning Union strength in the area of the Round

---

[23]. James Longstreet to J.E.B. Stuart, June 23, 1863, quoted in Freeman, *R.E. Lee*, III, p. 44.

[24]. Lee to J.E.B. Stuart, June 23, 1863, Dowdey and Manarin, *Papers*, p. 526.

Tops south of Gettysburg. Although Lee rebuked Stuart upon his tardy arrival at Gettysburg by saying, "Well, General Stuart, you are here at last,"[25] Lee had only himself to blame for letting his strong-willed cavalry commander get away from his army.[26]

Lee's vague orders to Stuart presaged a series of such orders which plagued the Confederates throughout the entire Gettysburg campaign. Some defenders of Lee have attempted to justify Lee's ambiguous orders as an essential part of his aggressive tactics and strategy. If so, dangerously vague orders may also be seen as another disadvantage of the offensive style of warfare that lost the war.

While Stuart campaigned east of the Blue Ridge, Lee was having success to the west. Ewell's 2nd Corps led the northward sweep and routed the 9,000 Yankee defenders of Winchester, Virginia, on June 14 and 15. Word of the rout reached Richmond the next day, when Confederate Chief of Ordnance Josiah Gorgas ominously noted Lee's movement in his journal: "What the movement means it is difficult to divine. I trust we are not to have the Maryland campaign over again."[27]

After Winchester, Ewell, A.P. Hill, and Longstreet moved their respective corps, in that order, through Sharpsburg and Hagerstown, Maryland, and across the Mason-Dixon Line into the Cumberland Valley of Pennsylvania. Ewell moved his leading corps through Chambersburg and then eastward through the mountains to York and Carlisle.

In the midst of this movement, Lee finally revealed to Davis the scope of his planned offensive by belatedly requesting back-up diversionary reinforcements. On June 23, and twice on June 25, he wrote to Davis that an army should be raised in the Southeast under General Beauregard and moved to Culpeper Court House to threaten Washington.[28] In one of the June 25 letters, he explained that his own northward movement "...has aroused the Federal Government and people to great exertions and it is incumbent upon us to call forth all our ener-

---

[25]. Freeman, *Lee's Lieutenants*, III, p. 139.

[26]. In addition, Lee had skilled cavalry with him, including the Sixth, Seventh, Eleventh and Thirty-fifth Virginia cavalry regiments (heroes of Fleetwood Hill at Brandy Station), that he could have used for scouting purposes, but did not. Nevertheless, after the war, Lee blamed Stuart for disobeying orders, keeping Lee uninformed and thereby forcing the fighting at Gettysburg. Allan, "Conversations," April 15, 1868 and February 19, 1870, in Gallagher, *Lee the Soldier*, pp. 13-4, 17.

[27]. Wiggins, Sarah Woolfolk (ed.), *The Journals of Josiah Gorgas 1857-1878* (Tuscaloosa and London: The University of Alabama Press, 1955) [hereafter Gorgas, *Journals*], p. 70.

[28]. Lee to Jefferson Davis, June 23 and 25, 1863, Dowdey and Manarin, *Papers*, pp. 527-8, 530-1, 532-3.

gies."[29] Lee's unrealistic, but typical, suggestion to reinforce Virginia overlooked the facts that Pemberton was trapped in Vicksburg and that Beauregard already had sent reinforcements to the West.

By June 28, Ewell was in position to move on the Pennsylvania capital of Harrisburg. Meanwhile Lee, unaware of the whereabouts of the Union army, was with Hill and Longstreet back at Chambersburg. That night, Lee learned from Thomas Harrison, one of Longstreet's spies, that Major General George Gordon Meade had replaced the hapless Hooker as commander of the 95,000-man Army of the Potomac and that his army had moved north to Frederick, Maryland. Lee decided to take them on by moving his entire army east of the mountains. Realizing the necessity of concentrating his numerically-inferior force but not sure where the enemy was, Lee sent orders to Ewell to head back toward either Cashtown or Gettysburg.[30]

Day one of Gettysburg (July 1, 1863) included a near-disaster, a fortuitous success, and a missed opportunity for Lee's army. On the prior day, the Confederates had discovered a division of Federal cavalry under Brigadier General John Buford at Gettysburg when they headed there in hopes of obtaining shoes from local factories. Thus, the next morning a stronger Confederate force, the divisions of Major Generals Henry Heth and Dorsey Pender of Hill's Corps, headed east from Cashtown toward Gettysburg to deal with Buford.

Because of Stuart's absence and Lee's consequent ignorance concerning the whereabouts of General Meade's forces, Heth's and Pender's infantry divisions found more than they had bargained for. Initially they were handicapped by the fact that at least two-thirds of Lee's army was going to have to use a single route, the Chambersburg Pike or Cashtown Road, to get to Gettysburg. Heth, under somewhat puzzling orders from Lee not to bring on a general engagement, pushed ahead with two brigades. Why was Heth sent against a position known to be held by Union forces if he was not to bring on a general engagement? Was he to stand in place when he encountered resistance and back up two-thirds of Lee's army on a single road?

On June 30, Buford had astutely recognized the tactical value of the high ground south of Gettysburg and decided to save it for the main Union army once it arrived. Instead of putting his own cavalrymen on those hills, therefore, he deployed them during the night west and north of the town so they could delay the Confederates until Union infantry arrived. He sent word to his superior, General Pleasonton, the

[29]. Lee to Jefferson Davis, June 25, 1863, Dowdey and Manarin, *Papers*, p. 531.
[30]. Pfanz, *The Second Day*, p. 20.

Army of the Potomac's cavalry commander, that A.P. Hill's corps was massed back of Cashtown nine miles west and that Hill's pickets, composed of infantry and artillery, were in sight. He also passed along rumors that Ewell was coming south over the mountains from Carlisle.[31]

In a fierce struggle that began at 5:30 a.m. on July 1, Buford's cavalry stubbornly resisted the 7,500-man advance of Brigadier Generals James J. Archer's and Joseph R. Davis' brigades of Heth's Division. With the firing of the first shot, Buford had sent word of the fighting to Major General John Fulton Reynolds, commander of the 1st Corps. Reynolds, then eight miles away at Emmitsburg, Maryland, ordered his 9,500 men to shed their baggage and speedily march to Gettysburg.

Buford sent skirmishers west on the Chambersburg Pike to Herr's and Belmont School House ridges west of his McPherson's Ridge campsite. Their determined resistance, aided by Spencers and other repeating rifles, forced the Confederates to spend more than a precious hour deploying into a battle line. While this was going on, Reynolds arrived and conferred with Buford about the critical situation. Reynolds then went back to hasten his infantry to the front, sent word to Oliver O. Howard to speed his 11th Corps to Gettysburg, and sent a message to Meade advising him that Gettysburg was to be the collision point of the East's two armies.

Heth, enjoying momentary superiority, ordered his two brigades forward. Buford's skirmishers grudgingly gave up the forward ridges and a small stream called Willoughby Run. They gradually fell back to McPherson's Farm on McPherson's Ridge only a mile west of Gettysburg. Buford sent a message to Meade describing the battle, stating that A.P. Hill's entire corps was moving on Gettysburg, and advising that Confederate troops had been discovered approaching Gettysburg from the north.[32]

The nature of the battle changed when Reynolds' men, led by the Iron Brigade, began arriving at the scene shortly after 10 a.m. That proud brigade was the 1st Brigade of the 1st Division of the 1st Corps of the Army of the Potomac and was composed of stalwart, black-hatted troops from the Upper Midwest. Reynolds was instantly killed

---

[31]. Luvaas, Jay and Nelson, Harold W. (ed.), *The U.S. Army War College Guide to the Battle of Gettysburg* (Carlisle, Pennsylvania: South Mountain Press, Inc., 1986), p. 5; Krolick, Marshall D., "Gettysburg: The First Day, July 1, 1863," *Blue & Gray Magazine*, V, Issue 2 (Nov. 1987), pp. 8-20 [hereafter Krolick, "The First Day"], pp. 14-15. On Buford's critical role on June 30 and July 1 at Gettysburg, see Longacre, Edward, *General John Buford: A Military Biography* (Conshohocken, Pennsylvania: Combined Books, 1995), pp. 179-203; Krolick, "The First Day."

[32]. Krolick, "The First Day," p. 15.

by a Rebel sharpshooter while directing his troops in an assault on Archer's brigade. Nevertheless, this Union counter-attack was devastating and resulted in the killing, wounding, or capturing of much of that brigade, including the apprehension of General Archer himself. The blue-clad forces drove the Confederates back toward Herr's Ridge. Buford's brilliant delaying tactics had saved the day and, perhaps, the entire battle; and Reynolds had arrived in the nick of time to repel the first serious Confederate assault at Gettysburg.

Back at Cashtown, Lee had heard the sounds of battle and started toward Gettysburg. The impact of Stuart's absence was reflected in Lee's comment as he headed toward the fateful battlefield: "I cannot think what has become of Stuart; I ought to have heard from him long before now... In the absence of reports from him, I am in ignorance of what we have in front of us here. It may be the whole Federal army, or it may be only a detachment. If it is the whole Federal force, we must fight a battle here . . ."[33]

As the Union forces gained strength, so did Lee's. Down Mummasberg Road from the northwest came Rodes' 8,000-man division of Ewell's 2nd Corps, which had been as far north as Carlisle. They arrived about 11 a.m., the same time as forward elements of Howard's 11th Corps arrived to impede their advance. Because of Reynolds' death, Howard had assumed overall command of the Union forces and Major General Carl Schurz had taken command of the 11th Corps. At about noon Rodes' artillery began shelling the Union lines, and by 2 p.m., his infantry launched an assault on Schurz' troops north of town. At about the same time, Meade learned of Reynolds' death and dispatched Winfield S. Hancock from Taneytown to go to Gettysburg to take command (even though the unreliable Howard was senior to him).

Rodes' five-brigade attack from the northwest was uncoordinated and ineffective. Brigadier General Alfred Iverson, Jr.'s Brigade was slaughtered and then pinned down by Union troops who may have fired 100,000 shots at them from behind a stone wall. Iverson lost more than 900 of his 1,400 men, and that 66 percent casualty rate was the highest for any Rebel brigade at Gettysburg.[34] Rodes failed to break through the 11th Corps' lines, and the Confederate situation looked bleak. Good fortune, however, arrived at around 3 p.m. in the person of Jubal Early and his 5,500-man division (also of Ewell's Corps).

---

[33]. Coddington, *Gettysburg Campaign*, p. 281.

[34]. Kross, Gary, "That One Error Fills Him with Faults: Gen. Alfred Iverson and His Brigade at Gettysburg," *Blue & Gray Magazine*, XII, Issue 3 (February 1995), pp. 22, 52-3.

Moving from Carlisle toward Cashtown, Early had heard the battle and headed south on roads approaching Gettysburg from the north and north-northeast. These approaches brought Early's division in on Schurz' right and, more importantly, east of Schurz' exposed right flank.

Although the arrival of Rodes' and Early's divisions of Ewell's 2nd Corps prevented a disastrous defeat of A.P. Hill's men coming down the bottle-necked Chambersburg Pike, their earlier arrival would have been even better. Because of Stuart's absence and Lee's subsequent ignorance of the Union army's precise location, Lee had ordered Ewell to march from Carlisle to either Cashtown or Gettysburg. Ewell's choice of Cashtown resulted in a several-hour delay in his corps' arrival at Gettysburg. Had Ewell been ordered to march directly to Gettysburg, his men should have been able to drive out Buford's and Reynolds' troops, reduce Hill's and their own casualties, and occupy the high ground above the town before the arrival of Union reinforcements.

But this was not the end of the problems that resulted from Lee's ignorance of the Union army's whereabouts. Lee, still at Cashtown as the morning fighting erupted in Gettysburg, was advised by a messenger from Ewell, Major G. Campbell Brown, that Ewell was heading south toward the sounds of battle. Lee asked about Stuart, ordered Ewell to send scouting parties to look for Stuart, and then, incredibly, told Major Brown that he (Lee) did not want a major engagement brought on.[35]

Even worse, Lee then used the critical Chambersburg Pike to send Ewell's other division (under Major General Edward "Old Allegheny" Johnson) and Ewell's entire ten-mile-plus train of wagons eastward toward Gettysburg. That division and Ewell's train were on the same road as Hill's and Longstreet's Corps because of Lee's Cashtown-or-Gettysburg orders to Ewell. Lee's use of the Chambersburg Pike for a crucial ten-hour period to move Ewell's wagon-train, estimated at fourteen miles long by McLaws, compounded the bottle-neck on that road. Meade, on the other hand, had his army marching full-bore for Gettysburg on several roads with its trains behind.[36] Lee's action delayed the arrival near Gettysburg of Longstreet's leading divisions, those of McLaws and Hood, until midnight and later.[37] Incredibly, Lee

---

[35]. Pfanz, *The Second Day*, p. 22.

[36]. *Ibid.*, p. 23.

[37]. Pfanz made this Lee-Meade comparison and also concluded, "Obviously [Lee] did not expect a battle that would limit his army's ability to maneuver as early as 1 July or he

had bottle-necked seven of his nine divisions on a single road and, thereby, retarded their arrival for both the first and second days of battle at Gettysburg.[38]

Nevertheless, as a result of Early's fortuitous afternoon arrival on the field, when Lee arrived on Herr's Ridge from Cashtown, he observed the pleasing panorama of Schurz' line crumbling and those Union troops starting to retreat. Lee hastily sent Heth's badly beaten-up division and Dorsey Pender's fresh brigade into the fray west of town at around 3:30. Initially, Lee did not hesitate to take advantage of his momentary numerical and positional superiority and the opportunity to destroy two Union corps before Meade had his whole army up.

Between 3 and 5 o'clock in the afternoon on Day 1, it looked like Gettysburg was going to be a great victory for Lee. Ewell's two-division attack from the north forced Howard's flanked corps, under Schurz' command, to flee south in disarray into Gettysburg and through the town to Cemetery Hill and Culp's Hill. When Schurz' soldiers disappeared from their right flank, the exhausted Union 1st Corps troops, who had been defending the Chambersburg Pike approach west of town for several hours, had no choice but to retreat to Seminary Ridge by 4 o'clock and, ultimately, to Cemetery Hill.

Hancock arrived at Cemetery Hill before 4 o'clock in time to see the massive retreat of two Union corps. He sent some troops to the unoccupied Culp's Hill, and started the men entrenching. At around 5 o'clock, Slocum began arriving with his 8,500-man 12th Corps, but it deployed along Cemetery Ridge south of the high ground. Therefore, an immediate attack by all of Lee's forces had an excellent chance of dislodging the minimal Union forces from their position on the heights (Cemetery and Culp's Hills). The likelihood of their success was demonstrated by Ewell's near-success on those same hills 24 hours later.

Even though Stonewall Jackson was dead, Lee persisted in issuing ambiguous orders that only Jackson could have turned into victories. Lee, with at least a 35,000 to 21,000 manpower superiority through the late afternoon and evening, did not aggressively take charge of the field nor order any of Hill's troops to their front and left to join or support an attack by Ewell on the two hills. Ewell and Early were on their own. At that point, Ewell should have had over 10,000 men still able to attack -- especially 5,000 relatively fresh men in four brigades of Early's division. Early's men were actively pursuing the Union troops through

would not have given hundreds of wagons precedence over much needed infantry."
Ibid., p. 22.
[38]. Wert, *Longstreet*, p. 255.

the town and could have continued up the hills while panic reigned. Instead, Early halted the pursuit because of a report from William ("Extra Billy") Smith's Brigade of Union troops coming in from the east; worse, Early sent another brigade (Gordon's) off to that quarter, and both brigades were left off to the east until the next day.[39]

Early then went looking for Ewell. Receiving Early's report and conflicting information concerning Union strength on Culp's Hill, Ewell decided not to assault.

With Union troops in chaotic retreat through the town, Lee committed two egregious errors. First, he failed to take firm control of all troops he had on hand and deploy them for a maximum-strength attack on the 80-foot-high Cemetery Hill and the 100-foot-high Culp's Hill, the dominant heights in the immediate vicinity of the town. He ignored all troops other than Ewell's, particularly A.P. Hill's, and, thus, failed to take advantage of his numerical superiority.

Second, at 4:30 he issued a merely discretionary order, via Major Walter Taylor, to the stalled Ewell to take the high ground. Given the critical nature of the situation, Lee's orders to Ewell were appalling: Ewell was to take the heights "...if he found it practicable, but to avoid a general engagement until the arrival of the other divisions of the army," which were being hurried to Gettysburg.[40] This order seems inexplicable because there had been a general engagement since about dawn that day, the remaining Confederate forces were caught in a Chambersburg Pike traffic jam, and the Union presence could only increase. In the absence of a mandatory order to immediately take those critical positions, Ewell, not surprisingly, failed to move on Culp's Hill and Cemetery Hill before the out-numbered and disorganized Union forces there had dug in and been reinforced.

Even the arrival at dusk of Ewell's third division, that of "Old Allegheny" Johnson, was not sufficient to encourage the reticent Ewell, unmoved by Lee's weak order, to take the high ground -- at the very least the dominant heights of Culp's Hill. Virtually all of Ewell's generals urged an assault on the high ground; they included Early, who had passed up the earlier opportunity to do so when he alone would have been responsible.[41] Major General Isaac R. Trimble asked for a single regiment to take the two hills and stalked away in disgust when Ewell

---

[39]. Pfanz, Harry W., *Gettysburg--Culp's Hill and Cemetery Hill* (Chapel Hill and London: The University of North Carolina Press, 1993) [hereafter Pfanz, *Culp's and Cemetery Hills*], pp. 67-9.

[40]. *Ibid.*, p. 72; Coddington, *Gettysburg Campaign*, p. 315.

[41]. Wert, *Lee's Tarnished Lieutenant*, p. 49.

declined to attack.[42] At the same time, Lee deliberately and inexplicably held the nearby, unbloodied troops of Major General Richard H. Anderson's division in Hill's corps in reserve apparently because Lee's whole army was not yet concentrated and he lacked information on the enemy's strength.[43] For these reasons, leading Gettysburg historian Edwin B. Coddington concluded, "Responsibility for the failure of the Confederates to make an all-out assault on Cemetery Hill on July 1 must rest with Lee."[44] That was the only time on July 1 that either 'side did not immediately use (usually successfully) all the forces it had managed to get to Gettysburg.

Lee's, Ewell's and Early's hesitation proved disastrous. Lee's failure to take full advantage of his temporary superiority and to issue a definitive attack order to Ewell left his enemy in control of the high ground for the final two days of the battle. As a result, Union forces retained the commanding heights which Buford, Reynolds, and Hancock had successively determined to protect and hold because they were the key to battlefield control at Gettysburg.

Lee's reticence to command an all-out assault on the first day at Gettysburg appears to have been due to his desire to have his entire Army there before undertaking a "general engagement." This approach seems strange in light of the facts that even a greater proportion of the Union army was absent, that, on the afternoon of July 1, Lee outnumbered his adversary, and that every passing hour allowed the Yankees to move toward numerical and positional parity and then superiority.

On the morning of July 2, Lee expressed his disappointment concerning the events of the previous late afternoon: "We did not or could not pursue our advantage of yesterday and now the enemy are in a good position."[45] This amounted to a rebuke of Ewell, but Lee must have known that he bore at least as much responsibility as Ewell for the Army's failure to seize the commanding heights on that vital first day at Gettysburg. With Confederate losses (killed, wounded and missing) at 6,500 and Union losses at 9,000, Lee had won an engagement but had missed an opportunity to win the Battle of Gettysburg.

By the next morning, the situation had seriously changed. Hancock's 13,000-man 2nd Corps and Major General Dan Sickles' 12,000-

42. Freeman, *Lee's Lieutenants*, III, pp. 94-5.

43. Coddington, *Gettysburg Campaign*, pp. 316-7; Gallagher, "'If the Enemy Is There, We Must Attack Him': R.E. Lee and the Second Day at Gettysburg," pp. 497-521, in Gallagher, *Lee the Soldier*, p. 508.

44. Coddington, *Gettysburg Campaign*, p. 320. William Garrett Piston concluded likewise. Piston, *Lee's Tarnished Lieutenant*, p. 49.

45. Freeman, *R.E. Lee*, III, p. 91; Pfanz, *The Second Day*, p. 111.

man 3rd Corps arrived by early morning. Thus, instead of three corps with 21,000 men on the battlefield, the Union now had five corps and 46,000 men. Two more corps (the 5th and 6th Corps) with 28,000 more men were forced-marched about thirty and thirty-six miles, respectively, to get there that day. Instead of scrambling to find any kind of position as they had done on the prior day, the northerners had established a strong line running from near Little Round Top (two miles south of town) north along Taneytown Road and Cemetery Ridge to Cemetery Hill and then curving east to Culp's Hill and southeast parallel to the Baltimore Pike. The Yankees now had superior numbers, an imposing defensive position and the advantage of interior lines (which permitted them to quickly move soldiers to threatened points in their lines). Meade's army had 27,000 men per mile along a three-mile inverted-fishook line, Lee's army had 10,000 men per mile along a five-mile semi-circle.[46] That disparity augured ill for Lee's army.

On July 2, Lee erred again -- in several ways. Without Stuart's cavalry to advise him accurately on the enemy's positions, Lee ordered skimpy and, consequently, inadequate reconnaissance of the Union left. Somehow, these small scouting parties failed to detect Federal forces on the south end of Cemetery Ridge and on, and in front of, the Round Tops. As a result, he erroneously believed that the prominent hills, Little Round Top and the more southern Big Round Top, and the areas around them were not occupied by Union troops.[47]

Lee ordered Longstreet, with his two delayed and exhausted divisions, to undertake a several-mile march and then to attack the left flank of the Union forces. In doing so, Lee ignored Longstreet's astute advice to move south of Gettysburg, seek a strong defensive position and await a Union attack.[48] Longstreet had learned the Civil War's major lesson: frontally-attacking armies paid a high price.

Late the prior afternoon, Longstreet and Lee had watched the retreat of the Yankee forces to the high ground immediately south of Gettysburg and discussed what to do the following day. Longstreet wanted to turn the Union left flank, establish a strong position and await an attack.[49] Ironically, at about that same hour, Union General Hancock was sending a message to Meade that the Union's strong position would be difficult to take but could be turned.[50] Lee's response to Longstreet, however, was, "If the enemy is there tomorrow, we must

---

46. Hattaway and Jones, *How the North Won*, p. 406.

47. Coddington, *Gettysburg Campaign*, pp. 372-4.

48. *Ibid.*, pp. 360-3.

49. *Ibid.*

50. *Ibid.*, p. 324.

attack him."[51] Longstreet argued that the Union forces would be compelled to attack any Confederate force placed between them and Washington and that bringing on this Fredericksburg-type situation was consistent with a strategically offensive and tactically defensive campaign, which is what Longstreet thought had been agreed upon. Perhaps desperate for a convincing victory to justify his gamble on the invasion of the North and concerned about his medium-term supply situation, Lee insisted upon an attack.

Their climactic dialogue on this subject went about as follows:

> Lee: They are in position, and I am going to whip them or they are going to whip me. If the enemy is there tomorrow, we must attack him.

> Longstreet: If he is there tomorrow, it will be because he wants you to attack -- a good reason, in my judgment, for not doing so.[52]

In his Gettysburg Battle Report, Lee later justified his deliberate offensives of July 2nd and 3rd on the grounds that retreat would have been difficult and awaiting attack was impractical because of foraging difficulties.[53] General E. Porter Alexander had the following thoughts about Lee's rationale:

> Now when it is remembered that we stayed for three days longer on that very ground, two of them days of desperate battle, ending in the discouragement of a bloody repulse, & then successfully withdrew all our trains & most of the wounded through the mountains; and, finding the Potomac too high to ford, protected them all & foraged successfully for over a week in a very restricted territory along the river, until we could build a bridge, it does not seem improbable that we could have faced Meade safely on the 2nd at Gettysburg without assaulting him in his wonderfully strong position. We had the prestige of victory with us, having chased him off the field & through the town. We had a fine defensive position on Seminary Ridge ready at our hand to occupy. It was not such a really *wonderful* position as the enemy happened to fall into, but it was no bad one, & it could never have been

---

[51]. *Ibid.*, p. 361; Pfanz, *The Second Day*, p. 26.

[52]. Pfanz states that the exact dialogue will never be known. Pfanz, *The Second Day*, pp. 26-7.

[53]. Lee to Samuel Cooper, Battle Report of Gettysburg Campaign, January 20, 1864, Dowdey and Manarin, *Papers*, p. 376.

successfully assaulted... We could even have fallen back to Cashtown & held the mountain passes with all the prestige of victory, & popular sentiment would have forced Meade to take the aggressive.[54]

Not only were there problems with Lee's offensive strategy on July 2, but his execution of it proved disastrous. Lee again failed to give clear and forceful orders to Ewell's corps, and the result was an abysmal lack of coordination between the Confederates' attacking left and right flanks. Lee's plan called for Ewell to demonstrate against the Union right and to attack if an opportunity developed and for Longstreet to attack the Union left. Even though Ewell's timidity had clearly been demonstrated the previous day, Lee failed to adequately oversee his efforts on the 2nd. As a result, the day passed with no assault by the Confederate left wing to divert attention from Longstreet's attack on the Confederate right.[55]

Likewise, Lee failed to see, personally or through staff, the execution of his orders on the right flank. No one ascertained the precise, secure route that Hood's and McLaws' divisions of Longstreet's corps needed to take to reach their attack positions. This lack of oversight compounded Longstreet's difficulties in proceeding to the southern Union flank without being observed by the Yankees. Lee's subordinate, E. Porter Alexander, commented on this particular situation:

> That is just one illustration of how time may be lost in handling troops, and of the need of an abundance of competent staff officers by the generals in command. Scarcely any of our generals had half of what they needed to keep a constant & close supervision on the execution of important orders. An army is like a great machine, and in putting it into battle it is not enough for its commander to merely issue the necessary orders. He should have a staff ample to supervise the execution of each step, & to promptly report any difficulty or misunderstanding. There is no telling the value of the hours which were lost by that division that morning.[56]

Some of the post-war defenders of Lee and critics of Longstreet, such as Jubal Early[57] and William Pendleton,[58] contended that Lee had

---

[54]. Alexander, *Fighting for the Confederacy*, pp. 233-4.
[55]. Lee to Samuel Cooper, Battle Report of Gettysburg Campaign, January 20, 1864, Dowdey and Manarin, *Papers*, p. 577.
[56]. Alexander, *Fighting for the Confederacy*, p. 236.
[57]. Piston, *Lee's Tarnished Lieutenant*, p. 118.
[58]. Coddington, *Gettysburg Campaign*, p. 270.

ordered Longstreet to attack at dawn. There is no credible evidence to support this contention. Alexander commented that this position was not believable, that Lee would have ordered Longstreet's troops into position during the night if he had desired a dawn attack, and that the enemy's position was never thoroughly determined until morning.[59] Lee, having personally delayed Longstreet's divisions for ten hours the prior afternoon and having caused them to arrive near Gettysburg in the wee hours of July 2, was well aware of their inability to initiate an early morning assault in a position miles away from their bivouac. Because of Chambersburg Pike congestion, Longstreet's two primary divisions to be used in the attack had arrived near Gettysburg at midnight (McLaws' Division) and dawn (Hood's Division).

In fact, Lee ordered a scouting expedition around dawn and was not in a position to order an attack until he had specific information, based on daylight observations, on whom should be attacked where.[60] At about 11 a.m., Lee finally issued his only specific attack order of the day, directing Longstreet to proceed south to get into position to attack.[61]

In addition, Lee specifically consented to Longstreet's request that his attack be delayed until Brigadier General Evander Law's Brigade of Hood's Division could be brought up.[62] Law, another victim of the Chambersburg Pike bottle-neck, had set out at about 3 a.m. and had arrived on scene at around noon. In light of his actions and knowledge, Lee could not have expected an attack before mid-afternoon. Even Douglas Southall Freeman, who severely criticized Longstreet for delaying the attack, contended that Lee virtually surrendered control to Longstreet and concluded, "It is scarcely too much to say that on July 2 the Army of Northern Virginia was without a commander."[63] As commanding general of that army and on-scene commander of the battle, Lee was responsible for where and when Longstreet attacked.

As Longstreet proceeded on his southward march toward the Union left, he received reliable scouting reports that the Union left flank was "hanging in the air" and could be rolled up. Twice he passed

[59]. Alexander, *Fighting for the Confederacy*, p. 237.

[60]. Pfanz, *The Second Day*, p. 106. Pfanz also says there were other early morning probes of the Union left by Colonel Armistead H. Long and General William N. Pendleton, the latter a major pro-Lee, anti-Longstreet commentator in the post-war decades. *Ibid.*, pp. 105-6.

[61]. Coddington, *Gettysburg Campaign*, p. 378; Freeman, *R.E. Lee*, III, p. 93; Freeman, *Lee's Lieutenants*, III, p. 115.

[62]. Alexander, *Fighting for the Confederacy*, p. 278; Coddington, *Gettysburg Campaign*, p. 378.

[63]. Freeman, *R.E. Lee*, III, p. 150.

this information on to Lee and requested permission to launch a flanking attack. Lee declined, however, and repeated his order to attack -- probably under the erroneous impression that he still was ordering a less sweeping flanking attack. McLaws' and Hood's divisions had difficulty finding their way on unfamiliar roads to their designated attack positions and even had to turn back and retrace their steps when they discovered that a point on the line of march was visible from a Union signal station on Big Round Top. They were being guided by Captain Samuel L. Johnston of Lee's staff, and Lee himself rode part of the way south with Longstreet.[64] Lee oversaw and approved Longstreet's troop dispositions.[65]

Beginning their attack after 4 p.m., Longstreet's forces fought bravely in the Wheatfield, at the Peach Orchard, and at the Devil's Den and almost succeeded in capturing both Big Round Top and Little Round Top. The near-success at all those locations indicates what a brilliant victory might have been achieved if Lee had turned Longstreet's men loose for a flanking attack instead of squandering them in frontal assaults along the Union lines on Cemetery Ridge. Stonewall Jackson was dead, and the Lee-Jackson charismatic relationship, which had been present at Second Manassas and Chancellorsville, had no worthy successor.

Nevertheless, the attack on the afternoon of July 2 still had prospects for success had it been properly planned, executed, and supervised. Union General Sickles had presented Lee with a grand opportunity by advancing his 3rd Corps, contrary to the orders he had received from Hancock, into a vulnerable position in the Peach Orchard along Emmitsburg Road well in front of the intended Union line along Cemetery Ridge. Instead of simultaneously attacking the north-to-south Union line along their entire front, however, the Confederates attacked in piecemeal fashion. Hood's Division first attacked the Union left flank for an extended period of time before McLaws' Division was ordered to attack Sickles' center and right. This staggered, or en echelon, attack enabled the Union defenders to respond to each successively threatened position.

When Hood, McLaws and their brigadiers had first gotten into position, they had been surprised to find large Union troop concentrations in areas they had been informed were devoid of enemy forces. Both Hood and McLaws sought Longstreet's permission to avoid the desperate frontal assault they envisioned, but Longstreet, having failed

64. Coddington, *Gettysburg Campaign*, pp. 378-81; Freeman, *R.E. Lee*, III, pp. 95-7.
65. Piston, *Lee's Tarnished Lieutenant*, pp. 55-8.

numerous times to change Lee's mind over the previous twenty-four hours, directed that Lee's attack order be carried out.[66] In addition, Lee personally refused Hood's final request to send a brigade around the Union flank on the Round Tops.[67]

Each of the individual Confederate attacks was successful in driving back the enemy and capturing territory, but their overall impact was greatly reduced by uncoordinated timing. The attacks did not begin until 4:30 p.m. First, Hood's men attacked on the far south of the battlefield, crossed and followed Plum Run, captured Devil's Den below the Round Tops, and would have captured Little Round Top but for the brilliant courage of Colonel Joshua Chamberlain and his 385-man 20th Maine Regiment. Hood's attack was underway before McLaws (Joseph B. Kershaw's and Barksdale's brigades) moved against Sickles' over-extended position to Hood's north. Later, Paul J. Semmes' and William T. Wofford's brigades of McLaws' Division belatedly entered the fray, their tardiness due to poor coordination by McLaws. In fierce fighting, the Confederates drove Sickles' corps from the Peach Orchard, engaged in bitter combat for control of the adjoining Wheatfield, and, finally, drove the defenders back to the northern base of Little Round Top.

To their north, Dick Anderson's Division of A.P. Hill's 3rd Corps participated very ineffectively in the late stages of the attack. Brigadier General Carnot Posey's Brigade advanced haphazardly, and Brigadier General William Mahone's Brigade never moved off Seminary Ridge. Throughout the day, Hill's Corps and much of Anderson's Division acted as though they were unaware of Lee's plans or any role for them in the struggle. Apparently Lee had intended for them to join in the sequential attacks beginning at the southern end of his line but took no actions to get them properly aligned or to bring all of them into the fray as the afternoon turned to evening.[68]

On the Union side, Hancock took advantage of the disjointed Confederate attack and sent reinforcements to each successively attacked position. The 2nd Corps went to the Round Tops and to Sickles' left, and the 5th Corps reinforced Sickles. The 6th Corps, which arrived at 2 p.m. after marching thirty-four miles in seventeen hours, and the 12th Corps backed up the others, and stopped the Confederates before they could get to Cemetery Ridge.

---

66. Coddington, *Gettysburg Campaign*, p. 382.

67. *Ibid.*, pp. 55-8.

68. Freeman, *R.E. Lee*, III, pp. 100-1.

As a result of all these developments, by the time Sickles' line finally was broken and the Wheatfield secured, darkness was beginning to fall and additional Union troops had moved into position to back up Sickles and hold Cemetery Ridge. At one critical juncture, the Rebels broke the Union's Wheatfield lines and were about to advance onto Cemetery Ridge. Hancock sent in the 262-man 1st Minnesota Regiment to push them back at all costs, and that Regiment stormed in and broke the attack at a cost of 50 killed and 175 wounded. The failed, Day 2 Confederate attack in echelon cost the Union 6,000 killed and wounded and the Rebels 6,500 and was reminiscent of similar failures by Lee's army during the Seven Days' campaign.

Where was Lee while this major, uncoordinated, and costly attack was falling apart? He was overlooking the battle from the cupola and elsewhere at the Lutheran Seminary on Seminary Ridge, part of the time with Generals A.P. Hill and Heth. He neither sent nor received more than a message or two and, apparently, sent only one order during the battle.[69] He had given his orders many hours before when conditions were radically different, but he merely stood by and watched the bloody assaults falter and fail. In a prelude to the more famous events of the next day, Lee allowed one third of his force to attack while the others remained in place.[70] In sharp contrast, George Meade actively moved his forces all over the battlefield to meet each new attack, took corrective actions when he discovered Sickles' disastrous abandonment of his assigned position, and used this "hands-on" approach throughout the entire battle to prevent a Rebel break-through along his critical Cemetery Ridge line.[71]

Between dusk and 10 p.m. on the evening of July 2, Ewell's forces finally attacked Cemetery Hill on the Union right flank. They were twenty-four hours too late for a likely success and several hours too late to coordinate with Longstreet. Nevertheless, the brave men of two

---

[69]. Lee's inaction prompted Arthur J.L. Fremantle, a British military observer at Gettysburg, to comment, "It is evidently his system to arrange the plan thoroughly with the three corps commanders, and then leave to them the duty of modifying and carrying it out to the best of their abilities." Piston, "Cross Purposes" in Gallagher, *Third Day*, pp. 31, 43.

[70]. Piston, *Lee's Tarnished Lieutenant*, p. 58.

[71]. Bruce points to Lee's failure, on both July 2 and 3, to launch properly coordinated attacks: "For two days, Gettysburg presents the spectacle of two desperately fought and bloody battles by less than one third of [Lee's] army on each occasion, the other two thirds looking on, for the conflict was visible from nearly every point on the Confederate lines. Does not all this present another question to solve [than] whether a corps commander was quick or slow? Was the commander-in-chief justified in assigning such a task to such a force?" Bruce, "Lee and Strategy" in Gallagher, *Lee the Soldier*, p. 122.

brigades (Colonel Isaac E. Avery's [Brigadier General Robert F. Hoke's] 6th North Carolina and Brigadier General Harry T. Hays' Louisiana Tigers) fought their way to the top of Cemetery Hill. The failures of high command to provide support, however, compelled them to retreat. Ewell failed to commit his artillery to support the assault, while Early never committed the reserve brigade of Brigadier General John Brown Gordon to the battle.[72]

Furthermore, like the attack to the south several hours before, the entire attack on Cemetery Hill was planned in echelon -- Johnson to attack first, followed by Early and then Rodes. The reality was an ineffective assault by one brigade after another and the failure of many brigades to engage at all. In fact, Avery's and Hays' brigades had completed their successful attacks and had been compelled to withdraw before Rodes launched his forces from the town itself. In summary, the timing was atrocious, the strategy was poor, and the execution was worse. The result was a failure to secure and hold Cemetery Hill, which dominated the north end of the battlefield.[73] Early on the morning of July 2, Confederate Major General Edward Johnson assaulted Culp's Hill with even less success.[74]

In fact, as E. Porter Alexander points out, Lee wasted Ewell's 2nd Corps by leaving it in an isolated and harmless position northeast of the primary struggles on the second and third days of Gettysburg:

> Ewell's troops were all placed beyond, or N.E. of Gettysburg, bent around toward the point of the fish hook of the enemy's position. It was an awkward place, far from our line of retreat in case of disaster, & not convenient either for reinforcing others or being reinforced. And...this part of the enemy's position was in itself the strongest & it was practically almost unassailable. On the night of the 1st Gen. Lee ordered him withdrawn & brought around to our right of the town. Gen. Ewell had seen some ground he thought he could take & asked permission to stay & to take it. Gen. Lee consented, but it turned out early next morning that the position could not be taken. Yet the orders to come out from the awkward place he was in--where there was no reasonable probability of his accomplishing any good on the enemy's line in his front & where his artillery was of no service--were never renewed & he stayed there till the last. The ground is there

72. Freeman, *R.E. Lee*, III, pp. 101-2; Pfanz, *Culp's & Cemetery Hills*, pp. 235-83.

73. *Ibid.*

74. Pfanz, *Culp's and Cemetery Hills*, pp. 284-327.

still for any military engineer to pronounce whether or not Ewell's corps & all its artillery was not practically paralysed & useless by its position during the last two days of the battle.[75]

In conclusion, the second day of Gettysburg was a disaster for which the Commanding General of the Army of Northern Virginia must be held accountable. Over the objection of the corps and division commanders involved, Lee ordered Longstreet's 1st Corps to launch a frontal, in echelon assault on strong Union positions. Lee stood idly by while A.P. Hill's 3rd Corps in the center of the Confederate lines and directly in front of Lee, did little to assist Longstreet.[76] Finally, Lee neither moved Ewell's 2nd Corps to an effective supporting attack position nor ensured that it attacked the Union right flank at the same time Longstreet was attacking the Union left.

Lee's performance the next day was even worse. Frustrated by his two successive days of failure, he compounded his errors on the third and final day of Gettysburg.[77] His original plan for that day again involved simultaneous attacks by Ewell on the Confederate left and Longstreet on the Rebels' right. This plan was thwarted when Meade ordered a Union attack on Ewell's forces, which had occupied Union trenches the prior evening. The result was a five-hour, early morning battle at the north end of the battlefield, as Johnson's Division of Ewell's Corps unsuccessfully tried again and again to capture Culp's Hill. Federal forces still held that critical position as dawn broke on the fateful third of July.[78]

With Ewell engaged, Lee changed his mind and decided to attack the center of the Union line. The prior evening, Union Major General John Newton, Reynolds' replacement as commander of the 1st Corps, had told Meade that he should be concerned about a flanking movement by Lee and that Lee would not be "fool enough" to frontally attack the Union army in the strong position into which the first two

---

[75]. Alexander, *Fighting for the Confederacy*, pp. 234-5. Similarly, Gary Pfanz criticized Lee for leaving Ewell, with one-third of Lee's outnumbered infantry, in an isolated position unsuited to offensive operations. Pfanz, *Second Day*, p. 426.

[76]. Pfanz faulted Lee for his hands-off supervision of Longstreet, whom Lee ". . . seems not to have hurried...along," and Hill ("He did not rectify Hill's faulty deployment of Anderson's division or his inadequate measures to sustain Anderson's attack ..."). Pfanz, *Second Day*, pp. 426-7. For details on Hill's inadequate performance, see *ibid.*, pp. 99, 114, 386-7.

[77]. For details of the third day, see Gallagher, *Third Day*, pp. 1-160; Coddington, *Gettysburg Campaign*, pp. 442-534.

[78]. Coddington, *Gettysburg Campaign*, pp. 465-76; Pfanz, *Culp's Hill & Cemetery Hill*, pp. 284-309; Pfanz, *Second Day*, p. 438.

days' fighting had consolidated it.[79] At around midnight Meade told John Gibbon that his troops in the center of the Union line would be attacked if Lee went on the offensive the next day. Gibbon told Meade that, if that occurred, Lee would be defeated.[80]

Lee, however, saw things differently. Again ignoring the advice and pleas of Longstreet, Lee canceled early morning orders issued by Longstreet for a flank attack and, instead, ordered the suicidal assault which was to be known forever as Pickett's Charge.[81] After studying the ground over which the attack would occur, Longstreet said to Lee, "The 15,000 men who could make a successful assault over that field had never been arrayed for battle."[82]

Longstreet was not alone in his bleak assessment of the chances for success. Brigadier General Ambrose "Rans" Wright said there would be no difficulty reaching Cemetery Ridge but that staying there was another matter because the "...whole Yankee army is there in a bunch."[83] On the morning of the third, Brigadier General Cadmus Wilcox told his fellow brigadier, Richard Garnett, that the Union position was twice as strong as Gaines' Mill at the Seven Days' Battle.[84]

Demonstrating the extreme, almost blind, faith the Confederate troops had in Lee, Alexander commented that, "...like all the rest of the army I believed that it would come out right, because Gen. Lee had planned it."[85] "Planned" may overstate the amount of thought, as distinguished from emotion, that went into Lee's decision.[86]

The famous attack was preceded by a massive artillery exchange -- so violent and loud that it was heard 140 miles away. Just after 1 p.m.,

[79]. Coddington, *Gettysburg Campaign*, p. 450.

[80]. Foote, Shelby, *The Civil War: A Narrative*. (New York: Random House, 1958-74) [hereafter Foote, *Civil War*], II, p. 525.

[81]. On this Lee-Longstreet dispute, see Piston, "Cross Purposes" in Gallagher, *Third Day*, pp. 31-55.

[82]. Coddington, *Gettysburg Campaign*, p. 460. Longstreet later stated that Lee had written to him in the 1863-4 winter that, "If I only had taken your counsel even on the 3d [July 3], and had moved around the Federal left, how different all might have been." Longstreet, James, "Lee's Right Wing at Gettysburg," pp. 339-53, in Johnson, Robert Underwood and Buel, Clarence Clough (eds.), *Battles and Leaders of the Civil War*. (New York: Thomas Yoseloff, Inc., 1956; reprint of Secaucus, New Jersey: Castle, 1887-8) [hereafter Johnson and Buel, *Battles and Leaders*], III, p. 349.

[83]. Coddington, *Gettysburg Campaign*, p. 488.

[84]. Wert, *Longstreet*, p. 287.

[85]. Alexander, *Fighting for the Confederacy*, p. 254.

[86]. Bevin Alexander severely criticized Lee's ordering of Pickett's Charge: "When his direct efforts to knock aside the Union forces failed, Lee compounded his error by destroying the last offensive power of the Army of Northern Virginia in Pickett's charge across nearly a mile of open, bullet-and-shell-torn ground. This frontal assault was doomed before it started." Bevin Alexander, *Great Generals*, p. 26.

then-Colonel E. Porter Alexander unleashed his 170 Rebel cannon against the Union forces on Cemetery Ridge. Two hundred Federal cannon responded. Across a mile of slightly rolling fields, the opposing cannons blasted away for ninety minutes. The Confederate goal was to soften up the Union line, particularly to weaken its defensive artillery capacity, prior to a massive assault on the center of that line. Instead of falling on the Federal batteries, many of the Rebel shells sailed beyond their targets and fell on Union reserves, medical facilities and even General Meade's headquarters (wounding his Chief of Staff, Major General Daniel Butterfield).

Alexander's cannonade continued until his supply of ammunition was dangerously low. A slowdown in the Union artillery response gave the false impression that the Confederate cannonade had inflicted serious damage. Although Alexander received some artillery assistance from Hill's guns to Alexander's north, there were almost no rounds fired from Ewell's five artillery battalions northeast of the main Confederate line. Artillery fire was the one thing that Ewell certainly could have provided, but the Commanding General and his chief of artillery also failed to coordinate this facet of the offensive.[87]

The time of decision and death was at hand for many of the 55,000 Confederates (in 192 regiments) and the 75,000 Yankees (in 270 regiments). The Rebels were about to assault a position that Alexander described as "...almost as badly chosen as it was possible to be." His rationale:

> Briefly described, the point we attacked is upon the long shank of the fishhook of the enemy's position, & our advance was exposed to the fire of the whole length of that shank some two miles. Not only that, that shank is not perfectly straight, but it bends forward at the Round Top end, so that rifled guns there, in secure position, could & did enfilade the assaulting lines. Now add that the advance must be over 1,400 yards of open ground, none of it sheltered from fire, & very little from view, & without a single position for artillery where a battery could get its horses & caissons under cover.
>
> I think any military engineer would, instead, select for attack the bend of the fishhook just west of Gettysburg. There, at least, the assaulting lines cannot be enfiladed, and, on the other hand the places selected for assault may be enfiladed, & upon shorter ranges than any other parts of the Federal lines. Again there the assaulting column will only be ex-

---

[87]. Alexander, *Fighting for the Confederacy*, p. 251.

posed to the fire of the front less than half, even if over one fourth, of the firing front upon the shank.[88]

Around 2:30, Alexander ordered a cease-fire and hurried a note off to General Longstreet. It said, "If you are coming at all, you must come at once or I cannot give you proper support, but the enemy's fire has not slackened at all. At least 18 guns are still firing from the cemetery itself."[89] Longstreet, convinced of the impending disaster, could not bring himself to give a verbal attack order to Major General George E. Pickett. Instead, he merely nodded his indication to proceed after Pickett asked him, "General, shall I advance?"[90]

On the hidden western slopes of Seminary Ridge, nine brigades of 13,000 men began forming two mile-and-a-half-long lines for the assault on Cemetery Ridge. Their three division commanders were Pickett, Dorsey Pender and Brigadier General James J. Pettigrew (in place of the wounded Henry Heth). Pickett gave the order, "Up men, and to your posts! Don't forget today that you are from old Virginia!"[91] With that, they moved out.

The hopelessness of the attack was clear to one of Pickett's more perceptive brigade commanders. North Carolina's Brigadier General Lewis Armistead took off his ring, handed it to Pickett, and asked him to give it to Armistead's fiancée if he fell in the assault. General Armistead bravely put his gray hat on his raised saber and led his men into battle.[92]

After sending his "come at once" message, Alexander noticed a distinct pause in the firing from the cemetery and then clearly observed the withdrawal of artillery from that planned point of attack. Ten minutes after his earlier message and while Longstreet was silently assenting to the attack, Alexander sent a frantic note: "For God's sake come quick! The 18 guns are gone. Come quick or I can't support you."[93] To Alexander's chagrin, however, the Union Chief of Artillery Henry J. Hunt moved five replacement batteries into the crucial center of the line. What Alexander did not yet know was that the Union firing had slowed and virtually ceased in order to save ammunition to repel the coming attack. Hunt had seventy-seven short-range guns in the position the Rebels intended to attack, as well as numerous other guns,

88. *Ibid.*, p. 252.

89. *Ibid.*, p. 258.

90. *Ibid.*, p. 260; Coddington, *Gettysburg Campaign*, p. 500.

91. Freeman, *Lee's Lieutenants*, III, p. 157.

92. Waugh, *Class of 1846*, p. 472.

93. Coddington, *Gettysburg Campaign*, p. 501.

including long-range rifled artillery, along the line capable of raking an attacking army.

The Rebel lines opened ranks to pass their now-quiet batteries and swept on into the shallow valley between the two famous ridges. A gasp arose from Cemetery Ridge as the two long Gray lines, 150 yards apart, came into sight.

It was 3 o'clock, the hottest time of a scorching day. Under the broiling sun, 40,000 Union soldiers were in position to directly contest the hopeless Confederate assault. Many Yankees were sheltered by stone walls or wooden fences. Their awe at the impressive parade coming their way must have been mixed with an understandable fear of battle and a confidence in the strength of their numbers and position.

Their brave Rebel counterparts must have had increasing fear and decreasing confidence with every step they took toward the stronghold on Cemetery Ridge.[94] Their forty-seven regiments (including nineteen from Virginia and fourteen from North Carolina) initially traversed the valley in absolute silence except for the clunking of their wooden canteens. Although a couple of swales provided temporary shelter from most Union view and rifle fire, the Confederates were under constant observation from the dominating 600-foot-high Big Round Top to the southeast. Long-range artillery fire began tearing holes in the Confederate lines. Then they approached and turned slightly left to cross the Emmitsburg Pike. At that point, they had marched into the middle of a Union semi-circle of rifles and cannon. They attempted to maintain their perfect parade order, but all hell broke loose as Federal cannon exploded along the entire ridge line -- from Cemetery Hill on the north to Little Round Top on the south.

The cannons' double loads of canister (pieces of iron) and Minie balls from 40,000 Union rifles decimated the Confederate front ranks. The slaughter was indescribably horrible, but the courageous Rebels closed ranks and marched on. Taking tremendous losses, they started up the final rise toward the copse of trees that was their goal. They had come so far that they were viciously assaulted from the front, both their flanks and even their rear (by riflemen and rifled artillery on the Round Tops). Especially devastating was the rifle fire from Brigadier General George J. Stannard's Vermont Brigade point-blank into the Rebel right

---

[94]. Confederate Captain Joseph Graham, of the Charlotte Artillery, wrote in late July 1863 of Pettigrew's infantry "mov[ing] right through my Battery, and I feared then I could see a want of resolution in our men. And I heard many say, `that is worse than Malvern Hill,' and `I don't hardly think that position can be carried,' etc., etc., enough to make me apprehensive about the result..." Gallagher, "Lee's Army" in Gallagher, *Third Day*, p. 23.

flank. Gaping holes opened in the now-merged Confederate lines, and their numbers dwindled to insignificance. The survivors let loose their Rebel yell and charged the trees near the center of Cemetery Ridge. With cries of "Fredericksburg," the men in blue decimated the remaining attackers with canister and Minie balls. General Armistead led the final surge. He and 150 others crossed the low stone wall, but all of them were killed, wounded, or captured within minutes. Armistead was killed.

During the late stages of the attack, two additional Confederate brigades, those of Brigadier General Cadmus M. Wilcox and Colonel David Lang, moved forward on the right but were quickly repulsed. Amazingly, Lee's third day gamble utilized only eleven of his thirty-eight infantry brigades in the assault; many of the others just observed the grand spectacle.[95] For the second straight day, Lee attacked with a smaller percentage of his army than McClellan did at Antietam.

Just as the Union soldiers recognized a Fredericksburg-like scenario, General Lee, at long last, did so as well. From 1,700 yards away, he watched the smoke-shrouded death throes of his grand assault. He saw his Gray and Butternut troops disappear into the all-engulfing smoke on the ridge and then saw some of them emerge in retreat. Fewer than 7,000 of the original 13,000 were able to make their way through the carnage and return to Seminary Ridge. There was no covering fire from Alexander's cannon because he was saving his precious ammunition to repel the expected counter-attack. As the survivors returned to the Confederate lines, Lee met them and sobbed, "It's all my fault this time."[96] It was.[97]

Lee and Longstreet tried to console Pickett, who was distraught about the slaughter of his men.[98] Lee told him that their gallantry had earned them a place in history, but Pickett responded: "All the glory in the world could never atone for the widows and orphans this day has made."[99] To his death, Pickett blamed Lee for the "massacre" of his division.[100]

The result of Lee's Day 3 strategy was the worst single-charge slaughter of the whole bloody war -- with the possible exception of

[95]. Waugh, *Class of 1846*, p. 489. Pickett's Charge is described well in Coddington, *Gettysburg Campaign*, 502-20; Freeman, *R.E. Lee*, III, pp. 121-32; and Freeman, *Lee's Lieutenants*, III, 157-61.

[96]. Alexander, *Fighting for the Confederacy*, p. 266; Coddington, *Gettysburg Campaign*, p. 526; Wert, *Longstreet*, p. 292.

[97]. Bruce, "Lee and Strategy" in Gallagher, *Lee the Soldier*, pp. 123-4.

[98]. Waugh, *Class of 1846*, p. 487.

[99]. Piston, *Lee's Tarnished Lieutenant*, p. 62.

[100]. Wert, *Longstreet*, p. 292.

Hood's suicidal charge at Franklin, Tennessee, the following year.[101] The Confederates suffered 7,500 casualties to the Union's 1,500. More than 1,000 of those Rebel casualties were killed -- all in a 30-minute bloodbath. Brigadier General Richard Garnett, whose five Virginia regiments led the assault, was killed, and 950 of his 1,450 men were killed or wounded. Virtually wiped out on Cemetery Ridge were three regiments, the 13th and 47th North Carolina and the 18th Virginia.[102]

The only saving grace for Lee's battered army was that General Meade, believing his mission was not to lose rather than to win, failed to immediately follow-up his Day 3 victory with an infantry counter-attack on the stunned and disorganized Confederates. To Lincoln's chagrin, Meade developed a case of the "slows" reminiscent of McClellan after Antietam.

That night Lee rode alone among his troops. At one point, he met Brigadier General John D. Imboden, who said, "General, this has been a hard day on you." Lee responded, "Yes, it has been a sad, sad day to us." He went on to praise Pettigrew's and Pickett's men and then made the puzzling statement, "If they had been supported as they were to have been -- but for some reason not fully explained to me were not -- we would have held the position and the day would have been ours. Too bad. Too bad. Oh, too bad."[103] General Alexander found Lee's comment inexplicable since Lee personally had overseen the entire preparation and execution of the disastrous charge.[104]

Even if Lee was nonplussed, his officers had little difficulty seeing the folly of Pickett's Charge and its parallel to the senseless Union charges at Fredericksburg the previous December. A few days later, as the Confederates waited to cross the Potomac at Williamsport, Maryland, the Reverend Alexander Falk heard Confederate officers wishing that their strong defensive position would be attacked: "Now we have Meade where we want him. If he attacks us here, we will pay him back for Gettysburg. But the Old Fox is too cunning."[105] Similarly General Alexander recalled that time: "...Oh! how we all did wish that the enemy would come out in the open & attack us, as we had done them at

---

[101]. "Properly led on the decisive afternoon at Gettysburg, George Pickett's Virginians and Johnston Pettigrew's Carolinians would not have been sent across the killing fields from Seminary to Cemetery Ridge, against the massed Union army. But their bravery at Chancellorsville had persuaded their general that they were invincible, and so he sent them. And so Gettysburg was lost, and so the war." Furgurson, *Chancellorsville*, p. 350.

[102]. Coddington, *Gettysburg Campaign*, pp. 525-6.

[103]. Freeman, *R.E. Lee*, III, pp. 133-4.

[104]. Alexander, *Fighting for the Confederacy*, pp. 278-80.

[105]. Welch, Richard F., "Gettysburg Finale," *America's Civil War* (July 1993), pp. 50-7.

Gettysburg. But they had had their lesson, in that sort of game, at Fredbg. [Fredericksburg] & did not care for another."[106]

Alexander concluded, "Then perhaps in taking the aggressive at all at Gettysburg in 1863 & certainly in the place & dispositions for the assault on the 3rd day, I think, it will undoubtedly be held that [Lee] unnecessarily took the most desperate chances & the bloodiest road."[107] Similarly, Wade Hampton wrote to Joseph E. Johnston:

> To fight an enemy superior in numbers at such a terrible disadvantage of position in the heart of his own territory, when freedom of movement gave him the advantage of accepting his own time and place for accepting battle, seems to have been a great military blunder...the position of the Yankees there was the strongest I ever saw...we let Meade choose the position and then we attacked.[108]

Having lost over half of his 10,500 men in the July 3 charge, General Pickett submitted a battle report highly critical of that assault--and probably of Lee. Lee declined to accept the report and ordered it rewritten.[109] Pickett refused to do so.

After the war, Lee provided his rationale for having attacked on the second and third days at Gettysburg:

> It had not been intended to deliver a general battle so far from our base unless attacked, but coming unexpectedly upon the whole Federal army, to withdraw through the mountains with our extensive trains would have been difficult and dangerous. At the same time we were unable to await an attack, as the country was unfavorable for collecting supplies in the presence of the enemy who could restrain our foraging parties by holding the mountain passes with local and other troops. A battle had therefore become, in a measure, unavoidable, and the success already gained gave hope of a favorable issue.[110]

Lee, in fact, had not come upon "the whole Federal army." That whole army was not on the battlefield until well into the second day of the Gettysburg struggle. Later, even after suffering three days of terri-

[106]. Alexander, *Fighting for the Confederacy*, p. 271.

[107]. *Ibid.*, p. 92.

[108]. McKenzie, John D., *Uncertain Glory: Lee's Generalship Re-Examined* (New York: Hippocrene Books, 1997) [hereafter McKenzie, *Uncertain Glory*], pp. 170-1.

[109]. Fuller, *Grant and Lee*, p. 118.

[110]. Lee to Samuel Cooper, Battle Report of Gettysburg Campaign, January 20, 1864, Dowdey and Manarin, *Papers*, p. 576.

ble losses, Lee, in fact, was able to retreat safely through the mountains after the three-day battle. In addition, Lee's army managed to live off the country north of the Potomac for nine more days. Thus, Lee's rationale justified neither his series of frontal attacks on the second day nor the suicidal charge on the third day.[111]

Furthermore, Lee's strategic campaign into the North had reaped its inevitable result, the appearance of defeat, and an unforeseen actual military defeat. Archer Jones provided this analysis: "Lee...suffered a costly defeat in a three-day battle at Gettysburg. In losing perhaps as many as 28,000 men to the North's 23,000, the battle became a disaster of depletion for the Confederate army, and his inevitable retreat to Virginia, seemingly the result of the battle rather than his inability to forage, made it a serious political defeat also."[112]

Considering the nearly equal number of combatants at Gettysburg, Lee's losses were staggering in both absolute and relative terms. Of the 75,000 Confederates, 22,600 (30 percent) were killed or injured. The toll of general officers was appalling: six dead, eight wounded, and three captured. Just as significantly, the southern field grade officers suffered very high casualties, and their absence would be felt for the duration of the war. Of the 83,300 Union troops at Gettysburg, 17,700 (21 percent) were casualties.[113] Despite the fact that his losses were higher in absolute and proportional terms, Lee told Davis, "Our loss has been very heavy, that of the enemy's is proportionally so."[114]

The Livermore hit ratios reflected the devastating nature of Lee's loss. While 301 of each 1,000 of his engaged men were hit, they hit 235 of the enemy. Conversely, every 1,000 Yanks suffered 212 hit but inflicted 272 hits on the Rebels.[115]

Fortunately for Lee's devastated army, the Union forces again failed to aggressively and promptly follow up their victory. Lee and his seventeen-mile train of ambulances pulled out of Gettysburg in a torrential rain on the night of July 4 and headed for the Potomac. Five-thousand healthy Rebel soldiers had left their posts that day to get a head start on the trip back to Virginia.[116]

After Meade's cavalry destroyed the pontoon bridge across the Potomac at Falling Waters, thereby trapping the Army of Northern

---

[111]. Lee's attacks at Gettysburg "were an unhappy caricature of the most unfortunate aspects of his tactics." Woodworth, *Davis and Lee*, p. 245.

[112]. Jones, "Military Means," in Boritt, *Why the Confederacy Lost*, p. 68.

[113]. Livermore, *Numbers & Losses*, pp. 102-3.

[114]. Lee to Jefferson Davis, July 31, 1863, Dowdey and Manarin, *Papers*, p. 565.

[115]. Livermore, *Numbers & Losses*, pp. 102-3.

[116]. Lee to Jefferson Davis, July 29, 1863, Dowdey & Manarin, *Papers*, p. 563.

Virginia north of that river, Meade failed to catch the Rebels on the move. Instead, he took nine days to catch up with them and to decide to attack. By then the Rebels were in a strong defensive position backed up against the Potomac. It was entirely too late, and -- much to the chagrin of Lincoln -- the Confederates crossed the river on July 13.[117]

However, the fatal damage had been done. Lee had decimated his own army. Throughout Lee's army and the South there were conflicting views about Gettysburg in the days, weeks and months following that three-day struggle. Many believed that there would have been a Confederate victory on Day 3 if only the Yankees had come out to fight; others wondered who was responsible for sending 13,000 troops into a death-trap.

The Richmond papers, and, thus, many others in the South, initially reported Gettysburg as a grand Confederate victory.[118] The South did not, at first, realize the extent of its losses in Pennsylvania. By July 31, Lee had deluded himself into calling the campaign a "general success."[119] A Virginia private who had fought at Gettysburg expressed a different view to his sister, "We got a bad whiping...they are awhiping us...at every point...I hope they would make peace so that we that is alive yet would get home agane...but I supose Jef Davis and Lee don't care if all is killed."[120] Josiah Gorgas, similarly, was not fooled. On July 28, he bemoaned the rapid change of Confederate fortunes resulting from its defeats at Vicksburg, Port Hudson and Gettysburg. He concluded:

> Lee failed at Gettysburg, and has recrossed the Potomac & resumed the position of two months ago, covering Richmond. Alas! he has lost fifteen thousand men and twenty-five thousand stands of arms. Vicksburg and Port Hudson capitulated, surrendering thirty five thousand men and forty-five thousand arms. It seems incredible that human power could effect such a change in so brief a space. Yesterday we rode on the

---

[117]. Coddington, *Gettysburg Campaign*, pp. 535-74.

[118]. Because of the misleadingly positive newspaper reports, Lee had cautioned his wife, "You will have learned before this reaches you that our success at Gettysburg was not as great as reported." Gallagher, Gary W., "Lee's Army Has Not Lost Any of Its Prestige: The Impact of Gettysburg on the Army of Northern Virginia and the Confederate Home Front," pp. 1-30, in Gallagher, *Third Day*, p. 18. Lee to his wife, July 12, 1863, Dowdey and Manarin, *Papers*, p. 547.

[119]. Lee to Jefferson Davis, July 31, 1863, Dowdey and Manarin, *Papers*, p. 565.

[120]. Wiley, *Road to Appomattox*, pp. 64-5.

pinnacle of success--to-day absolute ruin seems to be our portion. The Confederacy totters to its destruction.[121]

Regardless of what was known when, Lee's strategy and tactics at Gettysburg were the same he had employed for the entire thirteen months he had commanded the Army of Northern Virginia. He attacked too often, and too often he had initiated frontal attacks. Lee's approach had resulted in a terrible toll of death and injury. When he assumed command in June, 1862, his army numbered about 95,000. From the Seven Days' through Cedar Mountain, Second Manassas, Chantilly, South Mountain, Antietam, Fredericksburg, Chancellorsville, and, finally, Gettysburg, Lee's little army had suffered about 80,000 killed and wounded while inflicting about 73,000 deaths and injuries on the enemy.

Not only had the outnumbered army of Lee suffered more casualties in absolute terms, its percentages of losses relative to those of the Federals were staggering. During the Seven Days' Battle, Lee's army had 21 percent killed or wounded (to the enemy's 11 percent), at Second Manassas, it lost 19 percent (to the Federals' 13 percent), at Antietam, Lee lost an appalling 23 percent (to the "attacking" McClellan's 16 percent); at Fredericksburg, Lee's generally entrenched forces lost only 6 percent (to Burnside's 11 percent); in his Chancellorsville "victory" Lee lost 19 percent of his men (to Hooker's 11 percent); and then, at Gettysburg, came the crushing three-day loss of 30 percent of Lee's remaining troops (to Meade's loss of 21 percent).[122] Lee's offensive strategy and tactics were causing his seriously undermanned army to lose irreplaceable troops at an unsustainable rate -- a casualty rate far greater than that of his stronger opponent. Lee was either fighting the wrong war or was fighting for the wrong side.

British Colonel Arthur J. L. Fremantle discussed the flaw of Lee's aggressiveness: "Don't you see your system feeds upon itself? You cannot fill the places of these men. Your troops do wonders, but every time at a cost you cannot afford."[123] Lee's own General Harvey Hill later similarly described the folly of the Army of Northern Virginia's penchant for the tactical offensive:

---

121. Gorgas, *Journals*, p. 75.

122. "Principally, [Gettysburg] cost the Confederacy an immense number of killed and wounded, far greater in proportion to Lee's resources than the battle losses suffered by the Union. As President Davis later wrote, stressing the casualties: 'Theirs could be repaired, ours could not.'" Hattaway and Jones, *How the North Won*, p. 415.

123. Groom, Winston, *Shrouds of Glory. From Atlanta to Nashville: The Last Great Campaign of the Civil War* (New York: The Atlantic Monthly Press, 1995) [hereafter Groom, *Shrouds of Glory*], p. 42.

We were very lavish of blood in those days, and it was thought to be a very great thing to charge a battery of artillery or an earth-work lined with infantry... The attacks on the Beaver Dam intrenchments, on the heights of Malvern Hill, at Gettysburg, etc., were all grand, but of exactly the kind of grandeur which the South could not afford.[124]

All of the attacks mentioned by Hill had been personally ordered by Lee.

In a little over a year, therefore, Lee's army had lost almost as many men as it had when he took command and was losing its strength at a far faster rate than its manpower-rich foe. While the North, with its 4 to 1 manpower advantage, could afford its casualties and replace the men it lost, Lee's aggression had seriously depleted the supply of Confederate men of fighting age in the East and had made his ultimate military defeat inevitable -- unless Lincoln lost the war at the ballot-box in 1864.

In summary, Gettysburg demonstrated all of Lee's weaknesses. He initiated an unnecessary strategic offensive that, because of his army's inevitable return to Virginia, would be perceived as a retreat and, thus, a defeat. He rejected alternative uses for Longstreet's corps that could have avoided or mitigated critical losses of the Mississippi River and middle and southeastern Tennessee, including Chattanooga. His tactics were inexcusably and fatally aggressive on days two and three, he failed to take charge of the battlefield on any of the three days, his battle-plans were ineffective, and his orders (especially to Stuart and Ewell) were vague and too discretionary. Gettysburg was Lee at his worst.

Rhode Islander Elisha Hunt Rhodes' July 9 diary entry typified northern elation over Gettysburg: "I wonder what the South thinks of us Yankees now? I think Gettysburg will cure the Rebels of any desire to invade the North again."[125] Not only would Lee's entire Army of Northern Virginia never again invade the North, it had been so damaged that it had become vulnerable to a war of attrition. All hope of foreign intervention ended as England and France halted deliveries on ships to the Confederates.[126] Perhaps the war already had been lost.

---

124. Wert, *Longstreet*, p. 151.
125. Rhodes, *All for the Union*, p. 117.
126. Glatthaar, Joseph T., "Black Glory: The African-American Role in Union Victory," pp. 133-62 [hereafter Glatthaar, "Black Glory"] in Boritt, *Why the Confederacy Lost*, pp. 149-50.

A cartoon from *Harper's Weekly*. The original caption read:
"Richmond newsboy announcing the Rebel success!" (SK)

Chapter 9

Late 1863:
Mistakes and Disillusion

During the late summer, fall, and winter of 1863, Lee's morale and health deteriorated, and his depleted forces suffered a series of setbacks and disappointments.

Gettysburg was the primary cause of Lee's depression. A month after Gettysburg, Lee submitted his resignation to President Davis. In his resignation letter, Lee took full responsibility for Gettysburg and urged the appointment of someone in whom the army would have greater confidence.[1] Lee certainly had come to realize many of the mistakes he had made at Gettysburg, and perhaps he understood what effects his overall strategy and tactics had wrought on the Army of Northern Virginia. Davis, however, responded to Lee that there was no person in whom the army would have greater confidence and refused to accept Lee's resignation.[2]

Gettysburg, however, did, at least temporarily, reduce Lee's pro-Virginia influence on Davis. Despite Lee's hopes and plans for another offensive against Meade, Davis, at long last yielded to Longstreet's and others' pleas and authorized Longstreet to move west with two divisions to reinforce Bragg. Since August 21, Bragg had been warning Richmond of a massive Tennessee offensive by Rosecrans and Burnside, and Davis began discussing with Lee the possibility of reinforcements from Lee during the last week of August. Lee, who usually argued that Union reinforcements on his front precluded transfers from his army, now argued that transfers away from Meade made him vulnerable to an offensive by Lee's full army.[3] In fact, on August 31, Lee

---

1. Lee to Jefferson Davis, August 8, 1863, Dowdey and Manarin, *Papers*, pp. 589-90.

2. Taylor, Walter H., *General Lee: His Campaigns in Virginia, 1861-1865 with Personal Reminiscences* (Lincoln and London: University of Nebraska Press, 1994; reprint of Norfolk, Virginia: Nusbaum Books, 1906) [hereafter Taylor, *General Lee*], p. 221; Woodworth, *Davis and Lee*, p. 251.

3. Connelly and Jones, *Politics of Command*, pp. 134-5.

even ordered Longstreet to prepare for that offensive.[4] At the same time, Lee declined Davis' request that he take command in the West. Lee declined on the grounds of poor health, ignorance of the West, and expected opposition from generals Lee had shipped to the western front (including William W. Loring, Earl Van Dorn, John B. Magruder, T. Hunter Holmes and Thomas F. Drayton).[5]

The situation in Tennessee worsened with the Confederates' September 3 abandonment of Knoxville that severed the direct rail route from Richmond to Chattanooga. Finally, on September 7, Davis ordered reinforcements from Lee to Bragg.[6] Beginning September 9, McLaws' and Hood's divisions and Alexander's reserve artillery, all without supply wagons and horses, at long last began a time-consuming, circuitous railroad route through the Carolinas and Georgia to join Bragg at Chickamauga. There, 5,000 of those troops, without artillery, had a hand in breaking William Rosecrans' Union lines on the last day of the battle, September 20, and in driving the northerners back into Chattanooga. More of Longstreet's 15,000 troops, as well as his artillery, would have arrived in time to fight and contest the Yankee retreat except for the delay of up to two weeks caused by Lee's reticence to leave Virginia himself or to part with any troops.[7]

Longstreet had pressed Seddon and Lee, in mid-August, for some of Longstreet's troops to be sent west.[8] Lee had first been summoned to Richmond on August 24 to discuss the Tennessee/Georgia situation, but Longstreet's troops were not promptly released for use outside Virginia. During the Davis-Lee consultations on the West, Burnside marched into Knoxville on September 3 and cut the direct rail link (the

---

[4]. *Ibid.*, p. 135; Lee to James Longstreet, August 31, 1863, Dowdey and Manarin, *Papers*, p. 594.

[5]. Thomas, *Lee*, p. 309. In early December, Lee again declined command of the Army of Tennessee and gave similar reasons; on the issue of generals sent west, he wrote, "I also fear that I would not receive cordial co-operation..." Lee to Jefferson Davis, December 7, 1863, Freeman, Douglas Southall and McWhiney, Grady (eds.), *Lee's Dispatches: Unpublished Letters of General Robert E. Lee, C.S.A., to Jefferson Davis and the War Department of the Confederate States of America 1862-65* (Baton Rouge and London: Louisiana State University Press, 1957, 1994; update of Freeman's 1914 original edition) [hereafter Freeman and McWhiney, *Lee's Dispatches*, pp. 130-1.

[6]. Hattaway and Jones compared Lee's ultimate acquiescence with his May 1863 position: "Lee ran less risk, had less emotional investment, and hence less dissonance in September than he had had in the spring. He felt less need to keep all of his forces in Virginia; the need in the West appeared more pressing after the defeats in Mississippi and Tennessee. [Thus] he could easily accede to Davis's desire to apply the conventional strategy and reinforce the west with troops sent by rail from Virginia." Hattaway and Jones, *How the North Won*, p. 374.

[7]. Connelly, *Autumn of Glory*, pp. 152, 191.

[8]. *Ibid.*, p. 150; Freeman, *Lee's Lieutenants*, III, pp. 221-2.

East Tennessee & Virginia and the East Tennessee & Georgia railroads) from Virginia to Chattanooga. After agreeing on September 5 to the movement of Longstreet's troops, Lee and Davis took three more days to agree on the details. As a result, Longstreet's troops did not begin to leave Orange Court House until September 9 and had to take a time-consuming route through the Carolinas (1,000 miles on ten railroads) instead of being able to travel 500 rail-miles directly to the Chattanooga area via Knoxville.[9]

Back in Virginia, after the July retreat of his army, Lee had complained of a serious desertion problem. In an August 17 letter to Davis, Lee wrote, "The number of desertions from the army is so great and still continues to such an extent that unless some cessation of them can be caused I fear success in the field will be seriously endangered."[10] Lee's depressed mental state appears to have aggravated the heart condition that had caused him great pain and disabled him the prior March and April. Between September 20 and October 10, and again from October 31 to November 5, Lee was confined to an ambulance because of the severe chest and back pains brought about by his deteriorating heart.[11]

When Lee reorganized his army again that autumn, he delivered a sharp rebuke to Jeb Stuart. The cavalry was reorganized into two divisions headed by Wade Hampton and Fitz Lee (Robert's nephew), who were promoted to major general. Most telling was the fact that Lee created no formal corps structure above those division commanders. As a result, Stuart remained a major general and was not given the promotion to lieutenant general which the law mandated for corps commanders.

On October 9, Lee launched his brief Bristoe Campaign[12] after he learned that two corps had been moved to the West from Meade's army.[13] Lee's army crossed the Rapidan and Rappahannock Rivers in an effort to get around Meade's right flank. The campaign quickly ended in disaster.[14]

On October 14, at Bristoe Station, Virginia, two brigades under A.P. Hill were lured into a clever Yankee trap and decimated. From high ground, Hill had seen Meade's army marching north along the

9. Connelly, *Autumn of Glory*, pp. 150-3; Hattaway and Jones, *How the North Won*, p. 444.

10. Lee to Jefferson Davis, August 17, 1863, Freeman and McWhiney, *Lee's Dispatches*, pp. 122-3.

11. Thomas, *Lee*, pp. 277-9, 310.

12. Freeman, *R.E. Lee*, III, pp. 169-87.

13. Hattaway and Jones, *How the North Won*, p. 471.

14. Thomas, *Lee*, pp. 210-1.

Orange and Alexandria Railroad toward Manassas Junction. Believing that they would catch the Union troops in a vulnerable condition while on the move, three Confederate brigades incautiously attacked the Union rear. Hidden Union forces along the railroad caught the attackers in a bloody ambush, killed almost 1,400 of them (including two brigadier generals) and captured another 500. This disaster, caused by inadequate reconnaissance and rash offensive tactics, was one Lee could ill afford. The adverse impact on morale was significant.

Although Lee was not personally responsible for Bristoe Station, the same cannot be said for another disaster that occurred the following month. Lee himself, aggressive as ever, helped bring about the loss of 2,000 men at a Rappahannock Station bridge and Kelly's Ford along the Rappahannock. Lee hoped to lure Meade's forces across the river at Kelly's Ford and then to hit them with overwhelming force. To do this, he had Jubal Early establish and hold a bridgehead a few miles away at Rappahannock Station. Lee, however, played right into the hands of Meade, who ordered a demonstration at Kelly's Ford while planning an attack on the Confederates' vulnerable Rappahannock Station bridgehead.[15]

Lee, conferring late on November 7 with Early about the two Rebel brigades that had been advanced across the single pontoon bridge at Rappahannock Station, approved their being kept north of the bridge even in the face of hostile fire. This specific direction led to those 1,700 men being cut off and then killed, wounded, or captured by Meade's attacking force. The combined fighting at the two crossings cost Lee 2,000 troops and four guns. Lee's adjutant, Major Walter Taylor, wrote to his fiancé that this debacle was "...the saddest chapter in the history of this army." The Army of Northern Virginia then retreated to Culpeper and spread out along the Rapidan River.[16]

The Mine Run Campaign followed.[17] To Lee's delight, Meade advanced across the Rapidan on November 26. Lee, of course, went on the offensive. His 2nd and 3rd Corps attacked the next day at Locust Church. The battle resulted in 550 Confederate deaths. Then both armies entrenched along Mine Run just west of Virginia's Wilderness -- the old Chancellorsville battlefield. On the 29th, Union Major General Gouverneur K. Warren discovered that his corps overlapped Lee's exposed right flank but delayed attacking until too close to nightfall.

---

[15]. Hattaway and Jones, *How the North Won*, p. 477.

[16]. Popchock, Barry, "Daring Night Assault," *America's Civil War*, IV, No. 6 (July 1993), pp. 50-7.

[17]. See Freeman, *R.E. Lee*, III, pp. 188-205.

Lee, in a transition from his practice at Gettysburg and earlier, and anticipating his 1864 modus operandi, entrenched his troops.[18] After correcting his erroneous alignment and strengthening his line, Lee unsuccessfully tried to entice Meade into attacking his well-entrenched Confederates. When Meade refused to go for the bait, Lee, characteristically, decided to attack.

In the hope of repeating Chancellorsville, Lee sent two divisions on a frozen, nighttime march around the Union left. When they reached the Union trenches at dawn on the second of December, the frozen Confederates found nothing. Meade had retreated to the north.

The year 1863 had been as disastrous for the Confederates in the West as it had been in the East. During the summer and autumn months, the Confederacy had suffered severe setbacks in the West -- despite one tactical victory gained when Longstreet finally got his chance to fight on the western front. Vicksburg, the Queen City, had been surrendered to Ulysses Grant, along with Pemberton's army of 30,000, on July 4, and the surrender of Port Hudson later that month gave the Union army control of the entire Mississippi River.

The other Confederate western army, under the contentious Braxton Bragg, was not doing much better. A series of brilliant flanking movements across three mountain ranges by Rosecrans' Army of the Cumberland from late June to early September forced Bragg's Army of Tennessee into a succession of retreats from Mid-Tennessee, through Chattanooga and into northwestern Georgia. Lee's refusal to reinforce Bragg played a significant role in Bragg's outnumbered army losing southeastern Tennessee, its direct rail connection with Richmond, and Chattanooga, the gateway city into the industrial heart of the Confederacy.[19]

Rosecrans then became careless, scattered his four corps (one cavalry) in pursuit of the Rebels, and reassembled them barely in time to repel a major offensive by Bragg on September 19 along Chickamauga Creek. Longstreet arrived by rail that night with 5,000 reinforcements from Virginia to give Bragg a slight numerical edge, took command of the Rebel army's left wing the next morning, and broke through and collapsed the right side of the Union line. While Rosecrans fled back to Chattanooga with many troops, Major General George H. Thomas

---

18. Freeman argues that Mine Run was not Lee's first use of field works, but that he had used them at Fredericksburg and Chancellorsville. *Ibid.*, p. 204. Their use there, however, was not widespread and was not repeated at Gettysburg.

19. For details of the struggle for Chattanooga, see Cozzens, Peter, *The Shipwreck of Their Hopes: The Battles for Chattanooga* (Urbana and Chicago: University of Illinois Press, 1994) [hereafter Cozzens, *Shipwreck of Their Hopes*].

earned the name "The Rock of Chickamauga" by organizing and leading the remaining Union forces in a desperate, all-afternoon, army-saving defense. Although Bragg had inflicted 11,000 casualties on the forces of Rosecrans, the constantly-attacking Confederates lost 17,000 men in the two-day battle.

For the next month, the military situation looked promising for the Confederates as they besieged and brought to near-starvation Rosecrans' army in Chattanooga. By October 1, however, Confederate intelligence reported that two eastern Union corps (25,000 troops) under Hooker and two corps from Grant in Mississippi were headed for Chattanooga. In response, Beauregard devised a plan for a massive Confederate concentration and preemptive offensive at Chattanooga. The plan called for 25,000 soldiers from Lee in Virginia and 10,000 from Johnston in Mississippi. At an October 11 council of war, however, Davis rejected the plan because Lee would provide no more troops.

Meanwhile, Bragg rekindled a pre-existing and debilitating dispute between himself and all his corps commanders when he accused one of them, Lieutenant General Leonidas Polk, of failing to timely attack at dawn on September 20 at Chickamauga. Longstreet fueled the anti-Bragg insurrection that followed by participating in anti-Bragg meetings and co-signing a petition to President Davis urging Bragg's removal. Even Davis' trip to Tennessee and personal intervention failed to heal the rift. After hearing most of Bragg's subordinates call for his removal (in Bragg's presence), Davis made the egregious error of retaining his good friend Bragg and allowing him to sack all his corps commanders.

On the Union side, things began looking up. By October 23, Grant, now theater commander of the armies of the Cumberland, Tennessee, and Ohio, replaced Rosecrans with Thomas as commander of the Army of the Cumberland and arrived in Chattanooga to take personal charge of the desperate, near-starvation situation. Within a week, Union forces captured an important ferry downstream on the Tennessee River and established the famous "Cracker Line" to get critical food and supplies into Chattanooga. To more than match Longstreet's 15,000-man movement from Virginia to the West, Hooker continued his 25,000-troop drive from Virginia to Chattanooga.

Within days of his temporary loss of Longstreet's 15,000 troops to the West, however, Lee began his efforts to get them back and, thereby, helped bring about a major military disaster for the Confederacy. Even before all those troops reached Bragg, Lee twice (on September 11 and 14) wrote to Davis about getting them back. On both September 23 and 25, he suggested to Davis that Longstreet and his two divisions move northeasterly from Chattanooga to take on Burnside in Knoxville.[20] This, conveniently, would move Longstreet's forces toward Virginia and back to Lee, who stressed to Davis his urgent need for them. At the same time, Lee wrote to Longstreet, "Finish the work before you, my dear general, and return to me. I want you badly and you cannot get back too soon."[21] On October 26 Lee wrote to Longstreet, "I missed you dreadfully...I hope you will soon return to me."[22]

On October 29 Davis passed Lee's idea for a Knoxville move on to Bragg, who knew that Longstreet had aggravated the discontent among Bragg's generals and suspected that Longstreet wanted his command.[23] Bragg discussed Lee's and Davis' suggestion with Longstreet on November 3; they agreed to separate, and, only two days later, Longstreet departed for Knoxville. Bragg had so weakened his forces besieging the Union troops in Chattanooga that he soon was outnumbered 2 to 1 (80,000 to 36,000) and had no reserve in the event of a Union break-through.

Less than three weeks later, the undermanned Confederates lost Chattanooga. With Grant personally in charge, the reinforced Union armies, on November 24 and 25, fought their way over Lookout Mountain and up Missionary Ridge to liberate Chattanooga and drive Bragg back into Georgia. The turning point occurred when Union soldiers reached the crest of the very defensible Missionary Ridge and Bragg had no reserve forces to drive them back. Bragg's army fled in total disarray and was saved from destruction only by the presence of an impregnable defensive position in the nearby mountains of northwest Georgia. Meanwhile, Longstreet launched a futile November 29 assault on Knoxville, was repelled by Burnside, and retreated into the mountains for the winter.

As Private Sam Watkins of Tennessee watched Bragg's demoralized soldiers retreat from Chattanooga, he observed,

> It was the first defeat our army had ever suffered, but the prevailing sentiment was anathemas and denunciations hurled against Jeff Davis for ordering Longstreet's corps to Knoxville, and sending off [Major] General [Joseph] Wheeler's and [Brigadier General Nathan Bedford] Forrest's

[20]. Connelly, "Lee and the Western Confederacy," p. 129.

[21]. Wert, *Longstreet*, pp. 320-1.

[22]. Cited in Connelly, "Lee and the Western Confederacy" in Gallagher, *Lee the Soldier*, p. 207.

[23]. "Davis's suggestion that Bragg detach Longstreet was quixotic, reflecting both his lack of appreciation of the gravity of the Union buildup at Chattanooga and the degree to which he was swayed by Robert E. Lee." Cozzens, *Shipwreck of Their Hopes*, p. 103.

cavalry, while every private soldier in the whole army knew that the enemy was concentrating at Chattanooga.[24]

Little did Watkins know that Lee's recommendation was behind Davis' actions in Tennessee. Lee's concern for his own theater of the war had hobbled the Confederate Army of Tennessee in the West, resulted in its retreat from Tennessee to Georgia, and cleared the way for William Tecumseh Sherman's decisive 1864 march through Georgia.

In summary, Lee's singular, grudging instance of supporting the western Confederate forces came about because of his weakened standing after Gettysburg, led to a less-than-fulfilling victory at Chickamauga, and then was undermined by Lee's own impatient efforts to retrieve Longstreet's two divisions. Although Bragg and Longstreet, for their own reasons, agreed with Davis' suggestion that Longstreet go off to Knoxville, it was, in fact, Lee's idea that they had implemented.

In December, 1863, when he had no option but to remove Bragg, Davis again offered Lee command of the western army. Unsurprisingly, Lee, concerned exclusively about preserving the Old Dominion, declined the appointment. Once again, Lee's stated reason for doing so was that he would not likely receive support from the subordinate generals in the West, which Lee had used as a dumping ground for failed eastern generals.[25]

While Lee had negatively affected Confederate fortunes in the West, he was even more responsible for the fact that 1863 also had been a Confederate disaster in the East: the extremely costly "victory" at Chancellorsville, the death of Jackson, the lost opportunities and disastrous decimation at Gettysburg, the retreat to Virginia, Bristoe Station, Rappahannock Station, Locust Church, and Mine Run.

The reality was that the South was running out of men. The Confederacy had started with a real manpower shortage, but, under the leadership of Lee it had squandered that precious resource in the East. As a result, the Confederacy would reap the whirlwind in 1864.

---

24. Watkins, Sam R., "*Co. Aytch,*" *Maury Grays, First Tennessee Regiment; or, A Side Show of the Big Show* (Nashville: Cumberland Presbyterian Publishing House, 1882, 1987) [hereafter Watkins, "*Co. Aytch*"], p. 128.
25. Connelly, "Lee and the Western Confederacy," p. 119.

Chapter 10

1864:
Reaping the Whirlwind

It was only a matter of time until the Union realized that Lee no longer had adequate forces to prevail if those forces were kept engaged. Lincoln did come to that realization, and he elevated Ulysses S. Grant, who shared his views. Grant's target was Lee's army, and that army had been fatally weakened by Lee in 1862 and 1863.[1]

At Lincoln's request, Congress, in early 1864, created the rank of lieutenant general and confirmed Lincoln's nomination of Grant to be the first three-star general of the United States since George Washington. Grant's unparalleled record of success at Forts Henry and Donelson, Iuka, Corinth, Jackson, Champion's Hill, Vicksburg and Chattanooga -- tempered by the near-disaster and brilliant recovery at Shiloh -- had convinced the President that, at last, he had found a general capable of tenaciously fighting, and eventually defeating, Robert E. Lee. He had.

Grant became Commander-in-Chief of the Union Armies and retained George Meade to the end of the war as Commander of the Army of the Potomac. Grant devised a specific grand strategy to use all of the Union's military forces to keep the Confederates on the defensive everywhere and, thereby, preclude their sending reinforcements to each other. This strategy, generally, deprived the Rebels of the advantage they possessed by virtue of their inner, shorter lines of communication and reflected Grant's determination to take advantage of the Union's manpower superiority.[2] Even General Alexander grudgingly conceded that Grant "...was no intellectual genius, but he understood arithmetic."[3]

---

[1]. Hattaway and Jones, *How the North Won*, pp. 516-7.
[2]. One exception was Jubal Early's breaking loose in July 1864; Lee, however, kept him in the Virginia theater instead of using him to reinforce Atlanta.
[3]. Alexander, *Fighting for the Confederacy*, p. 346.

Grant's grand plan for 1864[4] contemplated Sherman pushing Joseph Johnston's Army of Tennessee in northwestern Georgia back to Atlanta (the seizure of which was a major or even primary objective of Grant),[5] Nathaniel Banks joining Sherman after capturing Mobile, Franz Sigel clearing out the Shenandoah Valley, Major General Benjamin F. Butler surprising Richmond-Petersburg via the James River, and the Army of the Potomac attaching itself to Lee's Army of Northern Virginia -- to the death. Grant's instructions to Meade were simple: "Lee's army will be your objective point. Wherever Lee's army goes, you will go also."[6]

Instead of subjecting himself to the political pressures of Washington, Grant took to the field and accompanied Meade's Army until the war was over. In Virginia, Grant intended to continuously fight Lee in order to reduce Lee's dwindling manpower further and to keep Lee so engaged that he could not send forces to aid Johnston against Sherman.[7] In a May 2 letter to his wife, Grant expressed confidence: "I know the greatest anxiety is now felt in the North for the success of this move, and that anxiety will increase when it is once known that the Army is in motion. I feel well myself."[8] With the addition of Burnside's 9th Corps, the Army of the Potomac had 120,000 soldiers against Lee's depleted force of 65,000.[9]

Lee spent the winter and spring of 1865 simplistically urging an offensive by Johnston through barren mountains (with few foraging opportunities) into middle Tennessee -- even though Johnston had virtually no mobile supply capability and had half the strength of Sherman.[10] Relying on false rumors that five western Union corps were being moved to Virginia, Lee insisted that a Johnston offensive was necessary to relieve pressure on Virginia.[11] In sharp contrast, Grant contemplated coordinated campaigns by Sherman and himself. Grant wrote to Sherman:

---

4. Hattaway and Jones, *How the North Won*, pp. 516-33. Lincoln told Grant, "The particulars of your plans I neither know nor seek to know. You are vigilant and self-reliant; and, pleased with this, I wish not to obtrude any constraints or restraints upon you." Abraham Lincoln to Ulysses Grant, April 30, 1864, Johnson and Buel, *Battles and Leaders*, IV, p. 112.

5. Hattaway and Jones, *How the North Won*, p. 532.

6. *Ibid.*, p. 524; McFeely, William, *Grant: A Biography* (New York and London: W.W. Norton & Company, 1981), p. 157.

7. Hattaway and Jones, *How the North Won*, p. 528.

8. McFeeley, *Grant*, p. 165.

9. *Ibid.*, p. 538.

10. Connelly and Jones, *Politics of Command*, pp. 143-52.

11. *Ibid.*, p. 192.

What I now want more particularly to say is, that if the two main attacks, yours and the one from here, should promise great success, the enemy may, in a fit of desperation, abandon one part of their line of defense, and throw their whole strength upon the other, believing a single defeat without any victory to sustain them better than a defeat all along their line, and hoping too, at the same time, that the army meeting with no resistance, will rest perfectly satisfied with their laurels, having penetrated to a given point south, thereby enabling them to throw their force first upon one and then on the other.

With the majority of military commanders they might do this. But you have had too much experience in traveling light, and subsisting upon the country, to be caught by any such ruse. I hope my experience has not been thrown away. My directions, then, would be, if the enemy in your front shows signs of joining Lee, follow him up to the full extent of your ability. I will prevent the concentration of Lee upon your front, if it is in the power of this army to do it.[12]

Grant's sweeping national strategy led Sherman, later, to contrast Lee unfavorably to Grant:

[Lee] never rose to the grand problem which involved a continent and future generations. His Virginia was to him the world... He stood at the front porch battling with the flames whilst the kitchen and house were burning, sure in the end to consume the whole... Grant's `strategy' embraced a continent, Lee's a small State; Grant's `logistics' were to supply and transport armies thousands of miles, where Lee was limited to hundreds.[13]

Given Grant's desire to seek out and destroy Lee's Army, Lee played right into his hands. During 1862 and 1863, Lee's hyper-aggression had reduced the Army of Northern Virginia to a mere shadow of what it had been or what it still could have been.[14] Because of the North's virtually unlimited manpower resources (especially since it would employ as many as 180,000 African-Americans in its army and Navy by

---

12. Connelly and Jones, *Politics of Command*, pp. 180-1.
13. Coburn, Mark. *Terrible Innocence: General Sherman at War* (New York: Hippocrene Books, 1993) [hereafter Coburn, *Terrible Innocence*], p. 123.
14. On February 17, 1864, the Confederate Congress did attempt to address the manpower problem by extending conscription to 17-year-old boys and men between 45 and 50 years old. Wiley, *Road to Appomattox*, p. 68.

war's end), Lee probably had lost the military war by the beginning of 1864.[15] That is, if the war continued to its military conclusion, the Confederacy would lose.

However, if Lee could find some way to preserve the forces he had left and perhaps even provide some support to the defense of Atlanta, Lee might still have a chance to maintain a sufficient stalemate to win the war at the northern ballot-boxes in November 1864.[16] Longstreet described this connection between the military events of 1864 and that year's presidential election: "Lincoln's re-election seems to depend upon the result of our efforts during the present year. If he is re-elected, the war must continue, and I see no way of defeating his re-election except by military success."[17]

But it was a long time from April to November, and Lee was not a patient man. Lee aggressively sought out the Army of the Potomac, underestimated Grant's tenacity and cunning, launched attacks as though he had a surplus of manpower, and, periodically, committed costly blunders. As a result, the leadership and manpower of Lee's Army were further decimated -- despite his efforts to strip the Carolinas to reinforce his own army -- and the war went so badly for the South that Lincoln was reelected and the Confederacy thereby, was doomed.

As he had done on many prior occasions, Lee sought to strengthen his own army at the expense of forces elsewhere. That April, while the Army of Tennessee faced a massive offensive by Sherman, Lee made his familiar argument that "...the great effort of the enemy in this campaign will be made in Virginia."[18] On April 7, Lee wrote to Bragg: "I think every preparation should be made to meet the approaching storm, which will apparently burst on Virginia, & unless its force can be diverted by an attack in the West, that troops should be collected to oppose it."[19] Based on that hypothesis and (false) rumors Lee passed on to Richmond about western Federals coming east, Lee, astoundingly, requested part of Johnston's cavalry and recommended that Johnston's army should take the offensive against Sherman. At that time, the Un-

---

[15]. Hattaway and Jones, *How the North Won*, p. 272.

[16]. "Grant aimed to keep Lee so occupied that he could not emulate the Chickamauga campaign by sending men to help oppose Sherman. Although Grant had hopes of capturing Richmond...the essence of his strategy lay in Sherman's taking Atlanta and beginning his raid." Jones, "Military Means," in Boritt, *Why the Confederacy Lost*, p. 71.

[17]. James Longstreet to Brigadier General Thomas Jordan, March 27, 1864, quoted in McPherson, *Battle Cry of Freedom*, p. 721 and Piston, *Lee's Tarnished Lieutenant*, pp. 85-6.

[18]. Connelly, "Lee and the Western Confederacy" in Gallagher, *Lee the Soldier*, p. 198; Weigley, *American Way of War*, p. 125.

[19]. Lee to Braxton Bragg, April 7, 1864, Dowdey and Manarin, *Papers*, p. 692.

ion numerical advantage was 198,000 to 74,000 in the West and 148,000 to 82,000 in the East.[20] Contrary to Lee's advice, Johnston went on the defensive and preserved his forces much more effectively than did Lee. Persistent to a fault, Lee, in May, requested Davis to send him all the organized forces, other than Johnston's, in Florida, Georgia and South Carolina.

May 4, 1864 was the beginning of the end. All of the Union's armies began their coordinated movements, but three failed. The quickest failure among them was that of the incompetent Ben "Beast" Butler. Navy vessels promptly landed his 40,000-man Army of the James on May 5 at Bermuda Hundred, a peninsula formed by the James and Appomattox rivers between Richmond and Petersburg. Butler, however, wasted a week building defenses around his operational base before moving toward Richmond. This gave Beauregard time to assemble reinforcements at Petersburg and march north to intercept Butler at Drewry's Bluff about six miles south of Richmond. There, aided by severe fog, Beauregard shocked Butler by attacking him and driving him back into Bermuda Hundred. This vicious battle cost each side 3,000 casualties. The incompetent Butler, thereafter, was so bottled up in Bermuda Hundred that Grant eventually siphoned off many of Butler's troops for productive use elsewhere.

Instead of moving on Mobile, Banks went on a useless and unsuccessful campaign up the Red River in Louisiana. Another disappointment were the cavalry raids conducted by Grant's new cavalry chief, Major General Philip H. Sheridan. Between May 9 and 24 and then June 7-28, Sheridan galloped his troopers all over eastern Virginia but accomplished little more than fatally wounding Jeb Stuart at Yellow Tavern near Richmond on May 11.

Even less effective was the Shenandoah Valley campaign of Franz Sigel. From Cedar Creek, on May 1, Sigel headed south up the Valley with about 9,000 troops. His campaign was short-lived, however, as Major General John C. Breckinridge organized troops at Staunton, headed north with 5,300 troops (including 247 Virginia Military Institute cadets), and pummeled Sigel at New Market on May 15. On May 26, Grant replaced Sigel with Major General David Hunter.

While all these Union defeats and disappointments were occurring, the centerpiece in the East was Grant's movement south.[21] As the

---

20. Connelly, *Autumn of Glory*, pp. 303-13.

21. For details of Grant's 1864 campaign, see Trudeau, Noah Andre, *Bloody Roads South: The Wilderness to Cold Harbor, May-June 1864* (Boston, Toronto, London: Little, Brown and Co., 1989); Trudeau, Noah Andre, *The Last Citadel: Petersburg, Virginia June 1864-April 1865* (Baton Rouge: Louisiana State University Press, 1991) [hereafter Trudeau, *The Last*

120,000-man Army of the Potomac crossed the Rapidan River at Germanna and Ely's fords on May 4, Lee began rushing his three corps, totaling 65,000 men, to intercept them. Lee had been prepared to meet the enemy in his Mine Run works if Grant had moved southwest, but he thought and hoped Grant would move south-southeast through the Wilderness. In that event, Lee's intent was to meet the invading force in the Wilderness, a defending army's place of dreams and an attacking army's worst nightmare, and, thereby, negate Grant's superiority in numbers and artillery.[22] Instead of meeting and harassing the Union forces with all of his troops and remaining on the defensive in the Wilderness, however, Lee ended up engaging the northerners, with less than a full complement of his forces, in a series of uncoordinated attacks and counter-attacks. The results were devastating for both armies.[23]

Given Lee's desire to attack Grant's forces in the Wilderness, it is surprising how slowly he brought his three corps to bear. After the Federal movement was detected, Lee was able to get Ewell's 2nd Corps and A.P. Hill's 3rd Corps into the fighting on May 5, but Longstreet's poorly-positioned 1st Corps did not arrive until May 6.[24] If Lee's intent was to use Longstreet to protect the important railroad junction back at Gordonsville, he took a tremendous gamble by using all of one of his

---

Citadel]; Lowry, Don, *No Turning Back: The Beginning of the End of the Civil War: March-June 1864* (New York: Hippocrene Books, 1992); Lowry, Don, *Fate of the Country: The Civil War from June-September 1864* (New York: Hippocrene Books, 1992) [hereafter, Lowry, Fate of the Country]; Rhea, Gordon C., *The Battle of the Wilderness May 5-6, 1864* (Baton Rouge and London: Louisiana State University Press, 1994) [hereafter Rhea, *Wilderness*]; Rhea, Gordon C., *The Battles for Spotsylvania Court House and the Road to Yellow Tavern, May 7-12, 1864* (Baton Rouge and London: Louisiana State University Press, 1997); Wheeler, Richard, *On Fields of Fury: From the Wilderness to the Crater: An Eyewitness History* (New York: HarperCollins Publishers, 1991).

22. Freeman, *R.E. Lee*, p. 273.

23. For details of the Wilderness, see Rhea, Gordon C., *Wilderness*; Scott, Robert Garth, *Into the Wilderness with the Army of the Potomac* (Bloomington: Indiana University Press, 1985) [hereafter, Scott, *Into the Wilderness*]. For details of the first day's fighting at the Wilderness, see Mertz, Gregory A., "No Turning Back: The First Day of the Wilderness," *Blue & Gray Magazine*, XII, Issue 4 (April 1995) [hereafter Mertz, "No Turning Back Part I"]; Freeman, *R.E. Lee*, III, pp. 269-83.

24. After the war, Lee criticized Longstreet for being slow in arriving at the Wilderness-- and, in fact, said Longstreet often was slow. Johnston, William Preston, "Memoranda of Conversations with General R.E. Lee," pp. 29-34, May 7, 1868, in Gallagher, *Lee the Soldier*, p. 29. Lee made these statements after Longstreet's published criticism of Lee's actions at Gettysburg. During the war, however, Lee had said that Jackson, famed for his "foot-cavalry," was "by no means so rapid a marcher as Longstreet." Piston, *Lee's Tarnished Lieutenant*, p. 30. Robert Scott noted that Longstreet marched 38 miles via Richards' Shop instead of the 28-mile route via Orange Court House to avoid a road clogged with Hill's supply train. Scott, *Into the Wilderness*, p. 198.

three corps for that purpose when a lesser force could have provided sufficient security, or at least an adequate warning capability.

General Alexander was especially critical of Lee's poor positioning of Longstreet's corps at Mechanicsville, some forty-three miles from the battlefield behind the Confederates' left flank. He found it particularly puzzling in light of Lee's May 2nd statement that he expected Grant to turn the Confederates' right flank. Alexander described what he saw as a grand missed opportunity:

> The first day, naturally, offered [by] us far the greatest chances. Grant's army was not all in hand, & had had no time to make breastworks. It was at a great disadvantage in the Wilderness & could not use its superiority in artillery. We had here the one rare chance of the whole campaign to involve it in a panic such as ruined Hooker on the same ground... What proved a drawn battle when begun by three divisions reinforced by two more after six hours & by three more 18 hours later might have proved a decisive victory if fought by all eight from the beginning.[25]

Because of Lee's failure to have his forces at full strength and in place to meet Grant's army as it entered the Wilderness, May 4 was a successful day for the Blue army. Although still strung out at the end of the day, they had moved all their forces across the Rapidan with no opposition.

The Union cavalry failed to detect and provide early or adequate notice to Grant and Meade that the Confederates were moving to oppose them. However, those generals, as soon as they learned of the approach of Lee's army, decided to strike first with whatever forces were at hand at the threatened points. Their aggressiveness deprived Lee of the opportunity to bring up Longstreet before a general engagement erupted.

During the early afternoon of the 5th, the Union 5th Corps under Major General Warren, attacked Ewell at Saunders' Field on the Orange Turnpike, the northernmost east-west road south of the Rapidan and near the site of Jackson's last attack the previous year. The Rebel defenders, however, held their ground and then successfully counterattacked. The fierce fighting for control of the Turnpike spread south to Higgerson's Field and north along the Culpeper Mine Road, continued all afternoon and evening, and resulted in severe casualties to both sides.

---

25. Alexander, *Fighting for the Confederacy*, p. 349.

Meanwhile, on the virtually-parallel road to the south, the Orange Plank Road, Hancock's 2nd Corps halted the advance of A.P. Hill's 3rd Corps in a fierce battle that began in mid-afternoon and also continued into the darkness. All of this intense, confused, bloody fighting of the 5th was a mere prelude to that of the 6th.

On the night of the 5th, Lee left Hill's battered and disorganized forces in an advanced and exposed position on the Orange Plank Road. He failed to withdraw them, as Hill himself had requested, under cover of darkness despite the fact that Hill's flanks were exposed to attack from a massive accumulation of Federal forces and the non-arrival of Longstreet. Lee, inexplicably, was relying upon Longstreet's early arrival although he knew that Longstreet had said he would march at 1 a.m. from a point from which it had taken a messenger ninety minutes to ride to Lee.[26] That same night, Grant decided to have Burnside's 9th Corps pierce the unguarded center between the Confederate forces on the Turnpike and the Plank Road and then swing left (south) to hit Hill's left flank and rear. The attack was set for 5 a.m.[27]

Thus, Grant took advantage of the opportunity Lee had offered and attacked Hill at dawn. The result was a rout of Hill's forces and a near-total disaster for the Gray. Only the long-awaited arrival of Longstreet's 1st Corps saved the day. Lee was so excited by their arrival that he announced, "I want to lead the Texas Brigade in this charge!" He was dissuaded by Brigadier General John Gregg's Texans, who yelled, "Go back, General Lee, go back! We won't go on unless you go back!" The Confederates then completed and stabilized their line.[28]

Not satisfied with that, Lee authorized Longstreet to launch a flanking attack on the south (left flank) of the Union line via an abandoned railroad bed. The initial success of that attack came to a screeching halt when Longstreet was hit in the throat and shoulder by a Confederate bullet as his attackers moved across the front of the main Confederate line. Lee called off the attack until 4:15 that afternoon, when the Confederates launched a typically costly and unsuccessful thirteen-brigade assault on Union fortifications along Brock Road and perpendicular to the Orange Plank Road. Historian Gregory Mertz de-

[26]. Trudeau, Noah Andre, "'A Mere Question of Time': Robert E. Lee from the Wilderness to Appomattox Court House," pp. 523-58 [hereafter Trudeau, "Question of Time"], in Gallagher, *Lee the Soldier*, pp. 527-8.

[27]. For details of the second day's fighting at the Wilderness, see Mertz, "No Turning Back: The Second Day of the Wilderness," *Blue & Gray Magazine*, XII, Issue 5 (June 1995), pp. 8-20, 48-50 [hereafter Mertz, "No Turning Back Part II"]; Freeman, *R.E. Lee*, III, pp. 283-303.

[28]. Freeman, *R.E. Lee*, III, pp. 287-8.

scribed how two Confederate generals viewed that final assault as a failure:

> Artilleryman E. P. Alexander felt that the final assault should not have been made, comparing it to "sending a boy on a man's errand." The attack cost the Confederacy "good soldiers whom we could not spare." Confederate general Evander M. Law indicated that between the time Longstreet was wounded and the time of the attack, "the tide had turned, and we received only hard knocks instead of victory."[29]

Meanwhile, on the north end of the battlefield, the increasingly incompetent Ewell, relying on the faulty advice of Jubal Early, all afternoon rejected accurate, eye-witness information from John Gordon that the Union right flank was vulnerable to a flank attack. When Lee finally learned about the disagreement and ordered Gordon to attack at dusk, it was too late. Gordon was, initially, successful, but soon was swallowed up and repulsed by the more numerous Union troops.

Two days of bitter, confused, and horrendous fighting in the Wilderness ended in a stalemate and were capped by the dreadful nightmare of wounded soldiers being burned alive in the forest between the lines. These first two fighting days of Grant's campaign had cost him 18,000 men. With a smaller loss of 12,000, Lee superficially appeared to be the winner, but he had cooperated perfectly with Grant's plans to go after Lee's army and had again suffered large losses that he could not make up. While Grant lost 15 percent of his soldiers, Lee lost a critical 20 percent of his strength.[30] Lee's offensive had destroyed any reserve he might assemble[31] and reduced Lee's army so significantly that he never again put his entire army on the tactical offensive.[32]

Unlike his predecessors, Grant did not allow the massive bloodletting or any concern about Lee's possible movements dissuade him

---

[29]. Mertz, "No Turning Back Part II," p. 20.

[30]. The absence of many Confederate records for 1864-5 made additional Livermore hit ratios for Lee's army unavailable for those years.

[31]. "...Had [Lee] refrained from attacking Grant on May 5, which was an act of doubtful wisdom, he would have reached Richmond with his army almost intact." Fuller, J.F.C., *The Generalship of Ulysses S. Grant* (Bloomington: Indiana University Press, 1929, 1958) [hereafter, Fuller, *Generalship of Grant*], p. 362.

[32]. "Robert E. Lee assumed the tactical defensive after the Battle of the Wilderness until the end of the year, and did some of the best fighting of his career." McWhiney & Jamieson, *Attack and Die*, p. 108. However, Grant had achieved his strategic goal of attaching himself to Lee's army and had done so within forty-eight hours of the start of his campaign. Arnold, James R., *The Armies of U.S. Grant* (London: Arms and Armour Press, 1995), p. 186.

from his mission. On the night of May 6, one of his generals warned Grant that a crisis existed and that Lee would throw his whole army on the Union rear and cut off its communications. Grant took the opportunity to send a message to the entire Army of the Potomac by responding,

> Oh, I am heartily tired of hearing about what Lee is going to do. Some of you always seem to think he is suddenly going to turn a double somersault and land in our rear and on both of our flanks at the same time. Go back to your command, and try to think what we are going to do ourselves instead of what Lee is going to do.[33]

Grant, who had told Lincoln "...there would be no turning back," ordered a southeasterly movement around Lee's right flank.[34]

After the two days of vicious fighting on May 5 and 6 and a day of respite on May 7, Lee erroneously assumed that Grant, as all his eastern predecessors would have done, was retreating during the night toward Fredericksburg.[35] Therefore, Lee gave orders to move at 4 a.m. on the 8th toward the east in pursuit of what he believed were the fleeing Federals. Fortunately for Lee, a new corps commander, "Fighting Dick" Anderson, replacing the injured Longstreet, could find no place to bivouac in the smoke-filled Wilderness, decided to begin the eastward trek three hours early at 1 a.m., and kept going once he saw the slow progress being made.

Anderson's men had to follow a newly cut, stump-filled trail as they paralleled the Union army's southeasterly march. Ahead of and parallel to Anderson, on the Brock Road northwest of Spotsylvania Court House, Confederate cavalry delayed the Union infantry for critical hours before giving way to superior numbers and firepower. As a result of the cavalry's delaying tactics, Anderson's early start, and an all-night forced march, his infantrymen were able to intercept and block -- by a matter of seconds or minutes -- the southward advance of the Union forces near Spotsylvania Court House. Lee's army entrenched in the vicinity of the Brock Road northwest of the courthouse,

---

[33]. Gilbert, Thomas D., "Mr. Grant Goes to Washington," *Blue & Gray Magazine*, XII, Issue 4 (April 1995), 33, 37.

[34]. Foote, *Civil War*, III, p. 186.

[35]. On the morning of May 8, Lee advised Secretary Seddon that the "enemy had abandoned his position and is moving toward Fredericksburg." Trudeau, "Question of Time," in Gallagher, *Lee the Soldier*, p. 530. Lee to James A. Seddon, May 8, 1864, Dowdey and Manarin, *Papers*, p. 724.

and Grant's army moved in and sought a way to get around or through Lee's position.

Spotsylvania deteriorated into another bloodbath, primarily because of a defective alignment and tactics condoned and authorized by Lee himself. The initial battlefield array at Spotsylvania was the haphazard result of the Confederates rushing southeast and frantically blocking the Union advance around the Rebel right flank. As the armies settled in, it became obvious that a half-mile-wide central portion of the Army of Northern Virginia's line jutted northward one mile from a generally-straight alignment and that this projection was vulnerable to an attack on both flanks. Because of its shape, this salient became known as the "Mule Shoe." Lee strengthened the position with artillery but did not straighten his line.

Before realizing the vulnerability of the Mule Shoe, Grant, on May 9, attempted to get around Lee's left flank by having his forces cross the Po River. When, however, the Yankees attempted to re-cross the twisting Po farther south the next day, they were repelled at the Block House Bridge and retreated in the face of a Rebel counter-attack. That same day, Grant's men unsuccessfully attacked Laurel Hill to the east of the Po. Finally, at dusk that evening, Union Colonel Emory Upton led a well-conceived, twelve-regiment, surprise attack on the left flank of the Mule Shoe. He carried the Confederate trenches and failed to succeed in a major rout only because his attack was unsupported on his flanks. Although forced to retreat, Upton had confirmed the already-apparent vulnerability of the Mule Shoe -- a confirmation noted by Grant but, apparently, not by Lee.

On May 11, therefore, Grant and Meade made plans for a full-scale attack early on May 12 against the Mule Shoe similar to Upton's of the previous evening. Although the Mule Shoe was slightly elevated, that vulnerable projection could not be properly defended unless covered by substantial artillery. Despite that, Lee played into Grant's hands by personally approving the removal of the Mule Shoe's protective artillery during the night of May 11. Lee had received reports that Grant was on the move, did not know whether Grant was retreating or advancing, and withdrew the artillery from the salient in order either to launch an attack elsewhere or to guard against a flanking movement by Grant.[36] No sooner had the big guns been moved when Rebel pickets in front of the Mule Shoe began hearing sounds indicating the pos-

---

[36]. McWhiney & Jamieson, *Attack and Die*, p. 116. That evening Lee told Heth, "My opinion is the enemy are preparing to retreat tonight to Fredericksburg." Freeman, *Lee's Lieutenants*, III, p. 398.

sibility of a massive Union assault. Desperate attempts to recall the guns were too late; they merely resulted in the guns being brought back just in time to be captured.

Before dawn, 20,000 Union troops under Hancock attacked in a massive column formation and overran virtually the entire Mule Shoe area. The absence of Confederate artillery greatly assisted the attack. The Union attackers captured two generals, 4,000 other prisoners, 20 artillery pieces and 30 Rebel colors. Lee then organized a frantic and violent counter-attack. Although the Confederates were able to recapture the area after many hours of fierce, often hand-to-hand, combat, they lost thousands of irreplaceable men in the struggle to defend, recapture and then hold the Mule Shoe -- especially at its most fiercely-contested point, known ever after as the "Bloody Angle." At long last, on May 13, Lee moved the survivors out of the Mule Shoe and back to the security of a new, straightened line.

After a total of twelve days of Union assaults failed to break the Confederate lines at Spotsylvania, Grant, on May 20, once again moved by the Confederate right flank to get closer to Richmond. Lee followed the next day. The struggle at Spotsylvania had resulted in casualty lists remarkably similar to those of the Wilderness; Grant had lost 18,000, and Lee almost 12,000. Given the 2:1 ratio of their respective armies, Grant could militarily afford casualties at a 3:2 ratio. Lee, on the other hand, could not tolerate the 24,000 casualties his army had suffered in less than three weeks.

Lee requested Davis to provide replacements from the Southeast, and, on May 15, Beauregard and virtually all Rebel infantry and cavalry in South Carolina, coastal Georgia, and eastern Florida were ordered to Virginia. Having been reinforced from the Shanandoah Valley, Lee moved south with 55,000 men toward the North Anna River. They arrived on May 22 and were attacked the next day by Hancock's 2nd Corps, which captured Chesterfield Bridge on Telegraph Road across the North Anna. Upstream near Jericho Mill, other Yankees crossed the river on the 23rd and repulsed a fierce but foolish attack by A.P. Hill. The next day Lee rebuked Hill by saying, "Why did you let these people cross the river? Why did you not drive them back as General Jackson would have done?"[37]

Lee then brilliantly organized his defenses into an inverted "V". The "V" not only was inherently strong but also, by resting its point on

---

[37]. Robertson, James I., Jr., *General A.P. Hill: The Story of a Confederate Warrior* (New York: Random House, 1987), p. 276; Trudeau, "Question of Time" in Gallagher, *Lee the Soldier*, p. 533.

the North Anna, split the Union attackers so that either wing would have to cross the river twice to reinforce the other. On May 24, some of Burnside's troops foolishly attacked the point of the "V" at Ox Ford and sustained heavy losses.

May 25 was the day Lee could have attacked the divided Blue army, but he did not. Lee was ill, bedridden, and unable to personally oversee his army in the field; no attack was made. Lee was extremely disappointed and kept muttering, "We must strike them a blow. We must not let them pass us again. We must strike them a blow."[38] Unable to push back the "V" and recognizing their vulnerability to a Confederate attack while badly divided, the Union forces, on May 27, abandoned the North Anna front and, once again, moved southeast ever closer to Richmond.

Grant next crossed the Pamunkey River just above its confluence with Totopotomoy Creek. Federal cavalry effectively screened the army's May 28 movement by engaging in a fierce battle at Haw's Shop southwest of the Pamunkey crossing. Concerned about the Federal threat to the Virginia Central Railroad (Richmond's link to the Shenandoah), Lee blocked possible westward movement by Grant. On May 30, near Bethesda Church, Colonel Edward Willis' Brigade of Rodes' Division of Early's (formerly Ewell's) Corps unwisely attacked Major General Samuel Wylie Crawford's Union Division and was mauled. Willis was mortally wounded, and two of his colonels were killed. Lee had personally ordered the attack on the enemy force of unknown strength by telling General Early to "send out a brigade and see if those people are in force."[39] They were.

Grant returned the favor in spades. After Sheridan's cavalry seized the Cold Harbor crossroads ten miles from Richmond on June 1, both armies moved to that point. Grant sent Major General Horatio G. Wright's 6th Corps to relieve Sheridan and prepare to attack. Grant was anxious to break through the partially-formed Confederate lines that day. His attack, however, was delayed by the late arrival of Major General William F. Smith's 18th Corps from the Army of the James. Grant had ordered that corps north from Ben Butler's Bermuda Hundred position, but it had marched in the wrong direction under outdated orders. The Union attack finally came at 5 p.m., broke through a gap in the Rebel lines, but then was sealed off by a counter-attack.

---

[38]. Dowdey, Clifford, *Lee* (Gettysburg: Stan Clark Military Books, 1965, 1991), p. 464.

[39]. "Grant and Lee, 1864: From the North Anna to the Crossing of the James," *Blue & Gray Magazine*, XI, Issue 4 (April 1994), pp. 11, 20.

The Rebels spent that night and the entire day on June 2 constructing strong fortifications to repel an expected Union attack. Meanwhile Hancock's 2nd Corps marched during the night to the left of the 6th Corps. Grant's strong desire to attack promptly before the Confederates fortified yielded to the reality that his own forces were not ready to launch the required full-scale attack. Grant planned to renew his attack at 5 a.m. on the 2nd but pushed the time back to 5 p.m. when Hancock's men did not arrive until 6:30 that morning. The fate of the planned Union attack was sealed when Grant postponed the attack again -- until 4:30 the next morning -- because of the exhausted condition of Hancock's men. This meant the Rebels had more than a day-and-a-half to prepare for Grant's attack.

Grant, apparently over-anxious due to the proximity of Richmond, made, perhaps, his worst mistake of the war. At 4:30 on the morning of June 3, 50,000 men of three corps initiated a suicidal assault on Lee's well-entrenched lines. The attack was undertaken without adequate reconnaissance of the impregnable Confederate line and was so doomed to failure that, the previous night, many Union soldiers had written farewell letters to their loved ones and pinned their names on their uniforms so their bodies could be identified. This mistaken assault, which Grant regretted until his death, resulted in 7,000 Union casualties (most of them in less than a half-hour) -- compared to Lee's loss of only 1,500.[40]

After the Cold Harbor debacle, Union forces entrenched, and the two sides settled down to a stalemate under the broiling summer sun, with the monotony broken only by deadly sharpshooting from both armies. During the two-week series of struggles along the Totopotomoy and at Cold Harbor, Lee finally achieved the kind of 3:1 casualty ratio he had needed all along. The Union forces had suffered 12,000 casualties to the Confederates' mere 4,000. But these results came too late and were too inconsequential in the big picture to be decisive. Between the Wilderness and Cold Harbor, Lee had lost about 32,000 of his 70,000 troops (46%) while Grant had lost about 50,000 of his 122,000 troops (41%).[41] Between May 4 and June 3, 22 of the 58 generals in Lee's Army had been casualties (eight killed, twelve wounded and two captured).[42]

Now thoroughly convinced that movement rather than assault was the way to achieve victory, Grant decided to move around Lee's

[40]. *Ibid.*, pp. 11-22, 44-58.
[41]. McWhiney and Jamieson, *Attack and Die*, p. 116.
[42]. Freeman, *Lee's Lieutenants*, III, pp. 512-3.

right once again. On June 12, Grant started a brilliantly screened, three-day movement south to the James River, across the river by pontoon bridge and ferries, and then west to Petersburg, the key to capturing Richmond. Grant moved his troops secretly and by several routes and modes of transportation. Corps by corps, Grant abandoned his Cold Harbor lines without discovery and moved most of his army across the Chickahominy by three different routes east of the old Seven Days' battlefields. Behind a screen established just east of Malvern Hill by Warren's 5th Corps, the other corps headed for the James River. On the 14th, Hancock's 2nd Corps crossed the James by boat from Wilcox's Landing to the south side to establish a bridgehead around Windmill Point.

Grant's daring move was not without risk. Warren's isolated corps faced Lee's entire army north of the James River. General Alexander described the situation that existed on June 13 as Grant moved across the James:

> We [Lee's army] could only successfully oppose Grant's movement in two ways. First, by having an adequate force in the Petersburg intrenchments to meet him on his arrival there. Second, by taking advantage of the isolated position of the 5th Corps, on the afternoon of the 13th, & crushing it. The only trouble about that was that we were entirely ignorant of the fact that it was isolated. On the contrary, by a well devised piece of strategy (the suggestion of [Major] Gen. [Andrew A.] Humphreys), Warren's corps had taken up its line so near to Riddell's Shop as to give us the idea that it was the advance corps of Grant's whole army pushing toward Richmond on the road from Long Bridge.[43]

Meanwhile, Grant had sent W.F. Smith's 18th Corps east from Cold Harbor to White House on the Pamunkey River, where they embarked on vessels for the trip back to Butler's command in the Bermuda Hundred area between Richmond and Petersburg. The vessels carried them down the Pamunkey and York rivers, south on the Chesapeake Bay, through Hampton Roads and then up the James to Bermuda Hundred, where they arrived on the 14th. All the rest of Grant's army crossed the James River on the 15th and 16th on a mile-long pontoon bridge at the same place Hancock had crossed. Federal cavalry and Warren's Corps had prevented prying southern eyes from learning of this massive movement by Grant and had Lee baffled as to

---

43. Alexander, *Fighting for the Confederacy*, p. 420.

where Grant would strike next. Grant had stolen a march on Lee, and a prompt, competent attack on Petersburg by the relocated army would have cost Lee both Petersburg and Richmond, which was dependent on supply by rail through Petersburg.

All the while Grant was moving his entire army toward Petersburg, Lee was totally in the dark.[44] His ignorance of Grant's massive movement is demonstrated by a telegram he sent to Beauregard on the 17th: "Warren's Corps, the 5th, crossed Chickahominy at Long Bridge on 13th, was driven from Riddell's Shop by Hill, leaving many dead & prisoners in our hands. That night it marched to Westover... Have not heard from it since."[45] In sharp contrast, Beauregard had predicted Grant's movement in June 7 and 9 dispatches to Bragg, who had been brought to Richmond as Davis' chief of staff.[46]

As early as during the day on the 14th, Lee had warnings from Beauregard and an opportunity to march troops the necessary 28 miles to join Beauregard in the Petersburg trenches before the arrival of Grant's men. Beauregard was desperately telegraphing warnings of an impending attack and requests for reinforcements from Lee. Sensing that telegraphic requests would be insufficient to convince Lee of the danger, Beauregard sent Colonel Samuel B. Paul to personally solicit support from Lee. Late on the 14th, Lee rejected the request -- apparently firmly and with some hostility.

That night, however, Lee decided to improve his options by moving Hoke's Division of Beauregard's own army south from Drewry's Bluff and by moving some of Lee's own troops early the next morning in the direction of Petersburg. Thus, some of Lee's men marched, on the 15th, toward the pontoon bridge over the James between Chaffin's and Drewry's Bluffs. Nevertheless, Lee halted even that movement of his troops because of the presence of Union cavalry in the vicinity of Malvern Hill north of the James. In reality, that cavalry was just checking to make sure Lee was still there.

At 7 p.m. that evening, June 15th, the leading elements of Grant's army attacked Petersburg with Lee twenty-five miles away. General Alexander believed that this attack could have been another Cold Harbor disaster for Grant, but "General Lee did not have a soldier there to meet him! Grant had gotten away from US completely & was fighting *Beauregard*. The Army of Northern Virginia had lost him, & was suck-

---

44. Hattaway and Jones, *How the North Won*, p. 589.
45. Lee to P.G.T. Beauregard, June 17, 1864.
46. Fuller, *Grant and Lee*, p. 223.

ing its thumbs by the roadside 25 miles away, & wondering where he could be!"[47]

But Lee's reticence to support Beauregard did not stop on the 15th. Here are some telegrams he sent to Beauregard after the Union assaults had begun at Petersburg: June 16 at 10:30 a.m.: "I do not know the position of Grant's army and cannot strip north bank of James River. Have you not force sufficient?"[48] June 16 at 4 p.m.: "The transports you mention have probably returned Butler's troops. Has Grant been seen crossing James River?"[49] June 16-17 at midnight: "Until I can get more definite information of Grant's movements, I do not think it prudent to draw more troops to this side of river."[50] June 17 at 6:00 a.m.: "Can you ascertain anything of Grant's movements?"[51] June 17 at 4:30 p.m.: "Have no information of Grant's crossing James River, but upon your report have ordered troops up to Chaffin's Bluff." (still north of the James River!).[52]

Finally, at 6:40 that same evening, two days since the start of the Union attacks on Petersburg, Beauregard began getting Lee's attention with a dispatch of desperation:

> The increasing number of enemy in my front, & inadequacy of my force to defend the already much too extended lines, will compel me to fall within a shorter one, which I will attempt tonight. This I shall hold as long as practicable, but without reinforcements, I may have to evacuate the city very shortly.[53]

Having had his telegraphic pleas insultingly ignored for days, Beauregard, understandably, decided to resort to extraordinary means of getting Lee's attention when Beauregard was compelled by overwhelming force to retreat to inner lines on the night of the 17th. One after the other, he sent Colonel A.R. Chisolm, who, by 2 a.m. on the 18th, had been told by Lee that he doubted that any significant part of Grant's

---

[47]. Alexander, *Fighting for the Confederacy*, p. 422.

[48]. Lee to P.G.T. Beauregard, June 16, 1864, 10:30 a.m., Dowdey and Manarin, Papers, p. 784; Thomas, *Lee*, p. 337; Alexander, *Fighting for the Confederacy*, p. 429.

[49]. Lee to P.G.T. Beauregard, June 16, 1864, 4 p.m., Dowdey and Manarin, Papers, p. 785; Alexander, *Fighting for the Confederacy*, p. 429.

[50]. Lowry, *Fate of the Country*, p. 53; Freeman, *R.E. Lee*, III, p. 417; Alexander, *Fighting for the Confederacy*, p. 430.

[51]. Thomas, *Lee*, p. 337.

[52]. Lee to P.G.T. Beauregard, June 17, 1864, 4:30 p.m., Dowdey and Manarin, *Papers*, p. 789; Alexander, *Fighting for the Confederacy*, p. 430.

[53]. Foote, *Civil War*, III, p. 438; Lowry, *Fate of the Country*, p. 56; Freeman, *Lee's Lieutenants*, III, p. 534; Freeman, *R.E. Lee*, III, p. 421; Trudeau, *The Last Citadel*, p. 51; Alexander, *Fighting for the Confederacy*, p. 430.

forces had crossed the James; Colonel Alfred Roman, who was turned away by Lee's aides; and, finally, Major Giles B. Cooke, who, after 3 a.m. on the 18th, convinced Lee that the broad representation of three Union corps among captured prisoners demonstrated that Grant, indeed, was across the James in strength.[54]

At long last, Lee realized that he had been duped and was in danger of losing Petersburg, Richmond -- and the war. Lee then sent an urgent 3:30 a.m. message to the Superintendent of the Richmond and Petersburg Railroad asking whether trains could run to Petersburg, directing that cars be sent for troops wherever they could be picked up, and stating finally, "It is important to get troops to Petersburg without delay."[55] He also telegraphed Early, who had been sent to defend Lynchburg, that Grant was in front of Petersburg and that Early should attack quickly and then either carry out the original plan to move down the Valley or move to Petersburg "without delay."[56] Finally, about three days late, Lee got his army underway to Petersburg.

As a result of Lee's three-day delay, only competence and aggressiveness were needed for Grant's army to break through at Petersburg and virtually end the war. Grant's generals, however, demonstrated neither. The Union assaults on Petersburg from June 15 to 18 were sufficiently inept and tepid to allow Lee's belated reinforcements to reach Beauregard and repel the assaults. Grant's plan was for Smith's Corps to move out of Bermuda Hundred, supported by the 2nd Corps, and take Petersburg before reinforcements arrived. Smith dawdled away most of the day before attacking late on the 15th. Since he had 16,000 troops against 2,200 defenders, Smith's assault succeeded in taking part of the Petersburg fortifications and driving the defenders back to a new position. Instead of completing the capture of this crucial town, Smith replaced his "weary" troops with 2nd Corps men and rested.[57]

By the 16th, Beauregard, while continuing to plead with Lee for reinforcements, had consolidated his Bermuda Hundred line between Richmond and Petersburg and sent more troops south to Petersburg. His skimpy force at Petersburg gave ground but was able to hold off rather half-hearted attacks by the 2nd, 18th and newly-arrived 9th corps. Yet another corps, the 5th, had arrived at Petersburg by the 17th, but still uncoordinated attacks, amazingly, lost, rather than gained,

---

[54]. Alexander, *Fighting for the Confederacy*, pp. 430-1.

[55]. Lee to E.H. Gill, June 18, 1864, 3:30 a.m., Dowdey and Manarin, *Papers*, p. 791; Alexander, *Fighting for the Confederacy*, p. 431.

[56]. Lee to Jubal A. Early, June 18, 1864, Dowdey and Manarin, *Papers*, p. 791; Alexander, *Fighting for the Confederacy*, p. 431.

[57]. Hattaway and Jones, *How the North Won*, pp. 589-90.

ground. That night, Beauregard, realizing the extreme danger of his forward position, withdrew to a new, fortified line.

By dawn on the 18th, the Federals had added the 6th Corps, and they launched a 70,000-man, five-corps attack. They overran the Rebels' abandoned trenches and appeared about to sweep aside the defenders of the new line. Miraculously, Lee's reinforcements, from north of the James River, arrived just in time to repulse the attackers. From 7:30 to 11 that morning, Lee's troops poured into the Confederate lines. At noon, Major General David B. Birney launched an unsupported attack and was beaten back. At 4 p.m., one of his regiments did the same, and its 850 men suffered 632 casualties, the greatest percentage lost in a single battle by any Union regiment in the entire war. Later that afternoon, a frustrated Grant called off the assaults. During the preceding three days, he and his corps commanders had missed a golden opportunity presented to them by Lee to capture a virtually undefended Petersburg. That action would have ensured the evacuation of Richmond and significantly shortened the war.

The two armies then settled into siege warfare, a situation Lee had previously said would spell defeat for his army. Lee, earlier had told Early, "We must destroy this army of Grant's before he gets to the James River. If he gets there, it will become a siege, and then it will be a mere question of time."[58] Although Lee had inflicted 65,000 casualties on Grant's army between May 5 and June 18 while his own suffered "only" 37,000 casualties, Lee's army had been so weakened by the losses of 1862 and 1863 that it had no chance to defeat Grant's forces.

Between June 1, 1862, when he assumed command, and December 31, 1863, Lee's army had lost nineteen of its generals, including four in the Antietam Campaign and five more at Gettysburg. These losses were followed by the deaths of eight more generals in May, 1864, including three during Lee's last major tactical offensive at the Wilderness, two at Spotsylvania, and two at Yellow Tavern.[59] As the war progressed, Lee found it increasingly difficult to find suitable replacements for his dead generals.

With the partial siege of Petersburg and Richmond, the first moment had arrived when Lee should have considered ending the slaughter. He must have known that military victory, in the long run,

---

[58]. Nolan, Alan T., *Lee Considered: General Robert E. Lee and Civil War History* (Chapel Hill and London: University of North Carolina Press, 1991) [hereafter Nolan, *Lee Considered*], p. 85.

[59]. Fox, *Regimental Losses*, pp. 571-2; Warner, Ezra J., *Generals in Gray: Lives of the Confederate Commanders* (Baton Rouge and London: Louisiana State University Press, 1959, 1991) [hereafter Warner, *Generals in Gray*].

was impossible. General Alexander later explained that Lee had the ability, but not the will, to halt the proceedings:

> It is, indeed, a fact that both the army and the people at that time would have been very loth to recognize that the cause was hopeless. In the army, I am sure, such an idea was undreamed of. Gen. Lee's influence could doubtless have secured acquiescence in it, for his influence had no bounds; but nothing short of that would. He would not have opposed any policy adopted by President Davis; so the matter was really entirely within the president's power.[60]

Although Alexander believed peace then would have saved thousands of lives and up to a billion dollars of property for the South, he agreed with the decision to fight to the bitter end in order to save the honor of the Army of Northern Virginia.[61]

On June 12, meanwhile, Lee had sent Jubal Early and his 2nd Corps west to defend Lynchburg from Union attack. David Hunter had relieved Sigel, successfully moved up the Shenandoah Valley, won a battle at Piedmont, burned the Virginia Military Institute at Lexington, and then crossed the Blue Ridge Mountains to threaten Lynchburg. Early's reinforcements arrived there from June 17 to 19, just in time to repel Hunter's probes on the 18th. Outnumbered about 14,000 to 11,000, Hunter abandoned his offensive and retreated all the way to the Kanawha Valley in West Virginia.

On June 27, Lee authorized Early to march northward down the Shenandoah Valley, to cross into Maryland, and then to approach Washington from the north.[62] Early's orders from Lee even authorized a hare-brained scheme to send cavalry around, and far southeast of, Washington to free the Confederate prisoners at Point Lookout, the intersection of the Potomac River and Chesapeake Bay in St. Mary's County, Maryland.

The fortifications and forts surrounding Washington ensured that Early would do no damage there. In any event, Early was slowed for a day by a small Union force at Monocacy Creek south of Frederick, Maryland, on July 9. On July 11, Early was repulsed at Fort Stevens on the north side of Washington, and he, thereafter, fled back into northern Virginia. There he engaged in a couple of skirmishes and then

---

[60]. Alexander, *Fighting for the Confederacy*, p. 433.

[61]. *Ibid.*

[62]. For details of Early's campaign, see Judge, Joseph, *Season of Fire: The Confederate Strike on Washington* (Berryville, Virginia: Rockbridge Publishing Co., 1994).

headed north on a senseless revenge mission to burn Chambersburg, Pennsylvania, on July 30.

Lee probably regarded Early's quixotic five-week expedition as a success because it forced Grant to send two corps (the 6th and 19th) from Petersburg by vessel to defend Washington. However, those troops were not going to enable Grant to take Petersburg anytime soon in any event and did not make Grant vulnerable to a counter-attack by Lee. Lee had simply used one corps to draw two of the enemy's to Washington while Grant still had five others to face Lee's remaining two in the Petersburg-Richmond area.

With Atlanta critically threatened by Sherman, there was a much better use for any surplus troops that Lee could spare. Instead of sending Early on an imaginative, but futile, thrust toward Washington and then into Pennsylvania, Lee would have produced more effective results by sending a comparable number of troops south to oppose Sherman in Georgia. By sending those 18,000 surplus troops to Georgia, Lee could have increased Johnston's 57,000-man army defending Atlanta by almost 30 percent. That increase would have had a substantial impact whether Johnston attacked or stayed on the defensive against Sherman. Such a movement was the very thing Grant was concerned about preventing during all of his 1864 campaign.[63]

Unlike Grant, however, Lee was a theater, not a national, general. General Alexander criticized Lee's futile attempt to bluff Grant, whom he said could not be bluffed, and Lee's failure to use the Rebels' internal lines to reinforce Sherman, "...the very strongest play on the military board. Then every man sent might have counted for his full weight in a decisive struggle with Sherman &, if it proved successful, then Early might return bringing a large part of Johnston's army with him to reinforce Lee."[64] The perceptive Grant sent a message to Sherman, in early July, expressing his concern that Early's men were going to reinforce Johnston against Sherman; on July 15, Grant wrote Halleck that his greatest fear was that the Confederates would do just that.[65] But, fortunately for Sherman, Lee had a different idea.

By the time Lee sent Early north from Lynchburg on June 27, it should have been clear to Lee that Sherman's three armies in Georgia, originally totaling 110,000 men, presented a serious threat to the Confederacy, to the chance to beat Lincoln in November's election, and even to Lee's own army. Beginning on May 3, Sherman had pushed

---

63. Gallagher, Gary W., "`Upon Their Success Hang Momentous Interests': Generals," pp. 79-108 [hereafter Gallagher, "Generals"] in Boritt, *Why the Confederacy Lost*, p. 91.

64. Alexander, *Fighting for the Confederacy*, p. 440.

65. Hattaway and Jones, *How the North Won*, p. 604.

toward Atlanta with Major General James B. McPherson's Army of the Tennessee, Major General John M. Schofield's Army of the Ohio, and George Thomas' Army of the Cumberland. Through a series of flanking moves, interspersed with a couple of foolish direct assaults, Sherman had relentlessly moved 70 miles from the Tennessee-Georgia border southeasterly to the environs of Atlanta, the railroad and manufacturing center of the Confederate heartland. The absence of major battles had resulted in Sherman's forces suffering 11,000 casualties and Johnston's 66,000 troops incurring 9,000 casualties -- low casualties for two months of constant contact.

By June 19, Sherman had reached Kennesaw Mountain, a mere twelve miles from Atlanta. Lee had notice, by telegram, that Atlanta was in real trouble -- and with it the South. There was plenty of time -- a few weeks -- to get troops to Atlanta while the city could still be saved. But, instead of sending Early's Corps, or a comparable number of troops, to assist in the defense of Atlanta, Lee sent no one and then proceeded to make the situation in Georgia even worse.

Joseph E. Johnston and Jefferson Davis had had a long history of acrimony which had developed into deep, mutual hatred by July, 1864. Johnston believed that Davis had not given him appropriate seniority among Confederate generals at the outset of the war, that Davis had placed him in a powerless position as Commander of the Department of the West while Pemberton and Bragg were losing Vicksburg and Chattanooga respectively, and that Davis was constantly second-guessing his strategy and tactics. Sherman's persistent and successful campaign not only brought his armies across the Chattahoochee River and within five miles of Atlanta on July 8 and 9, but it also brought the Davis-Johnston feud to a head.

By that time, Davis was disconcerted by the series of retreats to Atlanta by Johnston, was totally frustrated by Johnston's refusal to explain his future plans, and, thus, resolved to replace him immediately in a last desperate effort to save Atlanta. This move was encouraged by Braxton Bragg, who had caused so much discord among western Confederate generals, had been relieved for cause after losing Chattanooga, and now, implausibly, was serving as chief military advisor to Davis, his long-time friend.

Davis and Bragg both disliked Johnston, and John Bell Hood, a new major general and new corps commander under Johnston, had been sending both of them secret, self-serving, and false reports critical of Johnston's campaign. Hood lied to them about his own battlefield failures during the campaign and about the alleged willingness to retreat of Johnston and William J. Hardee (Hood's major competitor to replace Johnston) -- when, in fact, Hood had opposed attacks and urged retreats over Johnston's and Hardee's opposition. Hood's calculated campaign for Johnston's command won the crucial support of Bragg, who also remembered Hardee's earlier opposition to Bragg when Bragg commanded the Army of Tennessee.[66]

Not only did Davis plan to remove Johnston, but he decided to replace him at this crucial juncture with the conniving and hot-headed Hood. Before taking these actions, however, Davis consulted with his trusted military advisor, Robert E. Lee. At that point, Lee had the opportunity to prevent what Bruce Catton has called the most grievous error of the war. Explaining how "the roof fell in" on the Democrats' opportunity to push Lincoln out of the White House, Catton said:

> Worse yet, William Tecumseh Sherman captured Atlanta. Sherman had moved against Joe Johnston's Confederate army the same day Grant crossed the Rapidan. From the distant North his campaign had looked no more like a success than the one in Virginia. If it had not brought so many casualties, it had seemed no more effective at ending Rebel resistance. Wise old Joe Johnston, sparring and side-stepping and shifting back, had a very clear understanding of the home-front politics behind the armies. His whole plan had been to keep Sherman from forcing a showdown until after the election, on the theory that victory postponed so long would look to the people up North like victory lost forever, and his strategy had been much more effective than his own government could realize. To President Davis, Johnston's course had seemed like sheer faintheartedness, and he had at last dismissed Johnston and put slugging John B. Hood in his place. Hood had gone in and slugged, and Sherman's army had more slugging power--so now, with the Democrats betting the election on the thesis that the war effort was a flat failure, decisive success had at last been won [by Sherman].[67]

Replacing Johnston with Hood was inexcusable. Hood, who had lost the use of an arm at Gettysburg and who had lost a leg at Chickamauga, was an overly-aggressive general whom even Lee had described as "all lion, none of the fox."[68] His record of costly frontal assaults included not only the Seven Days' and Gettysburg. His men also

---

66. Connelly, *Autumn of Glory*, pp. 321-5, 371, 391-421; Watkins, *"Co. Aytch"*, pp. 166-7.

67. Catton, Bruce, *The Army of the Potomac: A Stillness at Appomattox* (Garden City, New York: Doubleday & Company, Inc., 1953), pp. 294-5.

68. Hattaway and Jones, *How the North Won*, p. 607.

had been slaughtered at Antietam the previous September; when afterwards asked the whereabouts of his division, Hood had responded, "...dead on the field."[69] Again, as recently as June 22 at Kolb's Farm near Atlanta, Hood's troops had been decimated in battle. Hood, who had commanded a corps for only a few months, was a protege of Lee. Lee knew and admired Hood and his over-zealousness and, when consulted by Davis, made no effort to forcefully dissuade the President from making this disastrous appointment.

Lee knew Davis' decision was unwise but refused to use his great influence to veto it. On July 12, Davis sent Lee a telegram stating that he was relieving Johnston and asking for Lee's evaluation of Hood as Johnston's successor. Lee responded as follows: "Telegram of today received. I regret the fact stated. It is a bad time to release the commander of an army situated as that of Tennessee. We may lose Atlanta and the army too. Hood is a bold fighter. I am doubtful as to other qualities necessary."[70] Obviously concerned about this matter, Lee wrote to Davis later that same day:

> I am distressed at the intelligence conveyed in your telegram of today. It is a grievous thing to change commander of an army situated as is that of the Tennessee. Still if necessary it ought to be done. I know nothing of the necessity. I had hoped that Johnston was strong enough to deliver battle... Hood is a good fighter, very industrious on the battlefield, careless off, & I have had no opportunity of judging of his action, when the whole responsibility rested upon him. I have a high opinion of his gallantry, earnestness & zeal. [Lieutenant] Genl [William J.] Hardee has more experience in managing an army...[71]

A couple of days later, Secretary of War Seddon visited Lee and discussed the matter further. As had Davis, Seddon told Lee, Johnston was being relieved and sought Lee's advice on a successor. Lee expressed his regret about the apparent need for a change but did not provide definitive counsel concerning a replacement.

Although Douglas Southall Freeman, reading between the lines, claims that Lee opposed Johnston's removal and Hood's appointment, the record supports a contrary conclusion. Lee failed to affirmatively oppose Hood, which was necessary in light of Davis' stated intention to select him. Lee also made several positive statements concerning Hood

---

69. Groom, *Shrouds of Glory*, p. 34.
70. Lee to Jefferson Davis, July 12, 1864, Dowdey and Manarin, *Papers*, p. 821.
71. Lee to Jefferson Davis, July 12, 1864, 9:30 p.m., Dowdey and Manarin, *Papers*, pp. 821-2.

(calling him a bold fighter with gallantry and zeal) that would have pushed Davis toward naming Hood. These statements were particularly helpful to Hood because Davis was fed up with Johnston's constant retreats and was looking for someone who would fight. The worst part of Lee's advice was his statements that Hood was good on the battlefield and questionable otherwise; the truth was that Hood's greatest flaw was that he was dangerously reckless on the battlefield. Hood's recklessness on the field was capable of destroying his own army, and it did.

Perhaps Lee saw and admired something of himself in Hood and therefore, did not criticize Hood's battlefield performance. In that regard, it is interesting to consider Johnston's comparison of himself to Lee in Johnston's response to Davis' July 17 order relieving him of command:

> ...Sherman's army is much stronger compared with that of Tennessee than Grant's compared with that of Northern Virginia. Yet the enemy has been compelled to advance much more slowly to the vicinity of Atlanta than to that of Richmond and Petersburg, and has penetrated much deeper into Virginia than into Georgia.[72]

Davis' appointment of Hood drew a mixed reaction; Confederates had their doubts, and the Yankees were elated. Confederate General Arthur M. Manigault later remembered that "...The army received the announcement with very bad grace, and with no little murmuring."[73] Sam Watkins called Hood's appointment "...the most terrible and disastrous blow that the South ever received," and described how fellow Army of Tennessee soldiers cried or deserted after the elevation of the "over-rated" Hood.[74] The only place where Hood's appointment brought joy was in the Union command. John Schofield, Hood's West Point roommate, told Sherman that Hood was bold, rash, and courageous and would quickly hit Sherman "like hell."[75] Sherman alerted his commanders to the risk of attack, advised them that "each army commander will accept battle on anything like fair terms,"[76] and wrote to

72. Castel, Albert, *Decision in the West: The Atlanta Campaign of 1864* (Lawrence: University Press of Kansas, 1992), p. 362.

73. Davis, Stephen, "Atlanta Campaign. Hood Fights Desperately. The Battles of Atlanta: Events from July 10 to September 2, 1864," *Blue & Gray Magazine*, VI, Issue 6 (August 1989), pp. 8, 11.

74. Watkins, "*Co. Aytch*", pp. 167-9, 174-5.

75. Groom, *Shrouds of Glory*, p. 25.

76. Marszalek, John F., *Sherman: A Soldier's Passion for Order* (New York: Macmillan, Inc., 1993), p. 277.

his wife that he was pleased by the change.[77] He had good reason to be happy.

After replacing Johnston as commander of the Army of Tennessee, Hood did, predictably and immediately, go on the offensive. Beginning on July 20, Hood launched frontal assaults on strong Union positions at Peach Tree Creek, then Decatur (Atlanta) (July 22), and, finally, at Ezra Church (July 28). The results were so disastrous that, on August 5 Davis, who must have been having second thoughts, provided his newly-appointed army commander with some belated tactical advice: "The loss consequent upon attacking the enemy in his entrenchments requires you to avoid that if practicable."[78]

During the preceding months of the Atlanta campaign, Johnston had lost 9,000 men to Sherman's 11,000. In a little more than a week, Hood lost an appalling 14,000 more to Sherman's mere 4,000.[79] Parenthetically, Early's 18,000 troops would have made up all, and prevented some, of Hood's losses if Lee had sent them to Georgia, instead of Maryland, in late June or early July.

A month later, on August 31, Hood lost over 4,000 more men (15 percent casualties) at Jonesboro, where he criticized his subordinate Hardee's assault as feeble because of the low percentage of casualties.[80] With their win at Jonesboro, the Union forces controlled all the railroads into Atlanta, which Hood, therefore, was compelled to evacuate on September 1.

Once Hood took command, the struggle for Atlanta became a bloodbath. The 100-day campaign had cost the Union 32,000 killed, injured and missing and the Confederates 35,000 -- two-thirds of these Rebel casualties occurring after Hood succeeded Johnston.[81] Because Sherman had a 2-to-1 manpower advantage, the southerners could not afford to trade casualties of this scope. Their weakened condition compelled Hood to flee westward and make some attempt to destroy Sherman's railroad supply line. Sherman at first followed Hood, but finally convinced Grant that Sherman's superiority was so great that he could split his army and break loose on his famous March to the Sea.

Only three months later, on November 29, Hood allowed Schofield's 20,000-man, augmented Army of the Ohio to escape a trap Hood had carefully set at Spring Hill, Tennessee. The next day, in disgust and fury, Hood deliberately ordered the slaughter of the Army of Tennes-

---

[77]. *Ibid.*
[78]. Connelly, *Autumn of Glory*, p. 433.
[79]. Hattaway and Jones, *How the North Won*, p. 609.
[80]. Groom, *Shrouds of Glory*, p. 53.
[81]. *Ibid.*, p. 54.

see (21 percent casualties) in a suicidal attack at Franklin, Tennessee.[82] Captain Sam Foster, of Texas, said that Franklin, where six Confederate generals were killed, five were wounded, and one was captured, was not war: "It can't be called anything else than cold-blooded murder."[83] More Confederates were killed at Franklin than in any single day of the war. Two weeks later, the remnants of Hood's Army were routed (with 26 percent casualties) in the Battle of Nashville, where Hood foolishly used his 25,000 remaining soldiers to challenge 77,000 of the enemy.[84]

Hood's Livermore hit ratios demonstrate the manner in which he destroyed an army in six months. At Peach Tree Creek, his ratio was 133 (of each 1,000) hit to 85 hitting the enemy. In his attack at the Battle of Atlanta (July 22), Hood's negative ratio was 190 to 53. On July 28 (Atlanta), the ratio worsened further to 222:30. Unbelievably, things deteriorated further at Jonesboro (August 31) to 72:7. In the slaughter at Franklin, the ratio was 206:45. There are no official records of Confederate losses at Nashville because Hood's army fell apart there.[85] In a mere six months, Hood had reduced a proud army of 50,000 to a battered collection of 18,000 survivors, who retreated across the Tennessee into Alabama in the middle of winter.[86] This was the man known to, mentored by, and whose elevation to army command was acquiesced to by Robert E. Lee.

Lee made a positive reference to the one man qualified to replace Johnston: Lieutenant General William J. Hardee, a corps commander in Johnston's army. Although Hardee had refused command of that army after the firing of Bragg, there was no indication that he would refuse again under different circumstances. In fact, his disgust at Hood's appointment and disputes with Hood led to his request for a transfer away from Hood within weeks of Hood's assumption of command. When he made that request, he remarked that his first refusal of the army command was not permanent.[87]

The documentary evidence shows that Lee did not recommend to Davis that he reject Hood and, instead, select Hardee. It shows that perhaps Lee thought this would be the proper action. But, given Davis' stated predisposition to name Hood, and given Bragg's well-known dislike for Johnston and Hardee, Lee's dancing around the issue and failure to make a straight-forward recommendation could only have

82. Livermore, *Numbers & Losses*, p. 132.
83. Groom, *Shrouds of Glory*, p. 218.
84. *Ibid.*, p. 224; Hattaway and Jones, *How the North Won*, pp. 650-3.
85. Livermore, *Numbers & Losses*, pp. 120-133.
86. Groom, *Shrouds of Glory*, p. 273.
87. Warner, *Generals in Gray*, pp. 124-5.

one result: Davis' proceeding to make the disastrous appointment of Hood.[88]

Lee's error in acquiescing to Hood's appointment eventually eliminated the Army of Tennessee as a southern buffer for Lee's own army.[89] It allowed Sherman to move his unchallenged force on a destructive march through Georgia and the Carolinas (causing thousands of desertions from Lee's army) and was about to result in Sherman's and Grant's encirclement of the Army of Northern Virginia when Petersburg and Richmond fell in April, 1865.

The ultimate results of Hood's assumption of command, however, were not immediately apparent. After Hood's initial, three, costly assaults, he assumed a defensive position in Atlanta, kept open two vital rail lines to the south, and held off Sherman for another month. Hood, nevertheless, had so weakened his army that it was only a question of how much time it would take before Atlanta fell. Would Sherman take Atlanta in time to keep Lincoln in the White House?

The North was growing impatient. During July and August 1864, Grant and his army were tied down in a siege of Petersburg and Richmond while Sherman and his armies were locked in a siege at Atlanta. These stalemates were particularly frustrating and depressing when considered in light of the monstrous casualties the Union armies, particularly Grant's, had suffered since the beginning of May. Peace Democrats were successfully causing many northerners to question whether the war was worth fighting. Many appeals were blatantly racist; they asked whether it was worth shedding white blood to free Negro slaves. When the Democrats adopted a Peace Platform and nominated popular ex-Union General George McClellan as their presidential candidate in late August, things looked very bleak for Lincoln and the Union.

Grant's continuing failure to break Lee's now-formidable lines at Petersburg was a major cause of this gloom. On June 22 and 23, the Yankees had tried to sweep southwest to capture the Weldon and Pe-

---

[88]. For still another view, see Hughes, Nathaniel Cheairs, Jr., *General William J. Hardee: Old Reliable* (Baton Rouge and London: Louisiana State University Press, 1965), pp. 215-8. Hughes argues that the Confederacy needed a miracle to turn the tide and only Hood believed he could produce one. That argument overlooks the fact that, with the Presidential election looming, the potentially fatal offensive burden was on Sherman, not the Confederates, and since the Atlanta environs had now been reached, Sherman could no longer simply sidestep the Rebels and move on; he had to take Atlanta for political reasons. By turning to Hood and going on the offensive, Davis doomed Atlanta and the Confederacy.

[89]. Connelly, *Autumn of Glory*, pp. 429-513.

tersburg Railroad but had been severely repulsed, with a loss of 3,000 men, by the three divisions of Hill's 3rd Corps.

The biggest fiasco of the Petersburg siege came a month later, on July 30, when Pennsylvania miner-soldiers set off a horrendous explosion near the center of the Rebel lines, killing hundreds of Confederates, and creating the opportunity for a major break-through. The opportunity was especially great since, during previous days, Grant had duped Lee into moving four of his seven infantry divisions from Petersburg to north of the James. Incompetence and cowardice among Union generals, however, led to a half-hearted assault and the ultimate slaughter of up to 4,000 Union troops, most of them trapped in "The Crater" created by the explosion; the Confederates lost only 1,500 men.[90]

Feeling more confident after this debacle, Lee, in early August, sent Major General Joseph B. Kershaw's division to reinforce Early in the Valley. By doing so, he missed another opportunity to reinforce the Confederate forces (then under Hood) in their continuing struggle against Sherman outside Atlanta.[91]

The advantages of being on the defensive were again demonstrated in late August when, in additional attacks on the Weldon Railroad, the Union lost 4,500 men (to 1,600 Confederates) in securing a hold on the tracks at Globe Tavern on August 18-21. Then lost 2,700 more (to 700 Rebels) in a trap sprung on Hancock at Reams Station several miles to the south on August 25. However, in between these defensive victories for Lee was a foolish August 21 attack in the same Weldon Railroad area. Lee directed an assault on Union breastworks that resulted in 1,500 casualties to the enemy's 300. On both sides of the action, Lee continued to demonstrate the tremendous advantage of being on the defensive.

Lincoln was renominated for President on the Union ticket, but he seriously doubted that he would win another term because of the bleak battlefield situation. In August he told a friend, "You think I don't know I am going to be beaten, but I do and unless some great change

---

90. Hattaway and Jones, *How the North Won*, pp. 614-5; Livermore, *Numbers & Losses*, p. 116.

91. Grant was not alone in considering the possibility of Confederate troops being moved from Virginia to Georgia. Brigadier General Josiah Gorgas, Chief of Confederate Ordnance, wrote, "I think still that my notions were correct at the outset of Sherman's movement when I advocated the detachment of 10,000 men to Georgia, even at the risk of losing Petersburgh & the Southern R.R. It would have ruined Sherman, & with his ruin, gone far to make the north tired of the war." Wiggins, *Journals*, pp. 143-4.

takes place, badly beaten."[92] On August 23, Lincoln despairingly wrote the following note at a Cabinet meeting:

> This morning, as for some days past, it seems exceedingly probable that this administration will not be re-elected. Then it will be my duty to so cooperate with the President-elect as to save the Union between the election and the inauguration, as he will have secured his election on such ground that he cannot possibly save it afterward.[93]

He had all the Cabinet members sign the statement.[94] Three days later, Jedediah Hotchkiss, a skilled Confederate cartographer, came to a similar conclusion in a letter to his wife: "The signs are brightening, and I still confidently look for a conclusion of hostilities with the ending of 'Old Abe's' reign."[95]

Nevertheless, Lincoln persisted in his efforts to save the Union and to end slavery, and he refused to back down from his carefully-crafted position on those two issues. Fortunately for Lincoln, the underlying conditions in both Virginia and Georgia guaranteed ultimate Union military victories -- if the November elections did not stop the war. Lee had so devastated his own army that it was tied down in a siege situation he had long regarded as making defeat inevitable. In addition, he had acquiesced to Hood's taking command in Georgia and, thus, in a similar, fatal weakening of the Army of Tennessee. The issue was whether the Confederate position in either situation was bad enough that the Union forces would emerge victorious in time to affect the Presidential election.[96]

The first good omen for the North was Admiral David Farragut's capture of Mobile Bay. His success there began with his "Damn the torpedoes. Full speed ahead" charge into the Bay on August 5 and ended with the capture of critical Fort Morgan on August 23. As a result, the South had run out of major ports on the Gulf of Mexico.

That same month, Grant expressed his clear recognition of the overriding significance of the manpower disparity between North and South when he urged that the Government continue its policy of not engaging in prisoner exchanges:

---

92. Donald, David Herbert, *Lincoln* (New York: Simon and Schuster, 1995), p. 529.

93. Nevins, *Ordeal*, VIII, pp. 92-3.

94. *Ibid.*, p. 92.

95. Miller, William J., *Mapping for Stonewall: The Civil War Service of Jed Hotchkiss* (Washington: Elliott & Clark Publishing, 1993), p. 143.

96. "...Most Confederates agreed that they needed to mobilize Union discontent and undermine Union will sufficiently so that voters would select a peace candidate to replace Lincoln." Beringer et al, *Why the South Lost*, p. 347.

It is hard on our men held in southern prisons not to exchange them, but it is humanity to those left in the ranks to
fight our battles. Every man we hold, when released on parole or otherwise, becomes an active soldier against us at
once either directly or indirectly. If we commence a system of
exchange which liberates all prisoners taken, we will have to
fight on until the whole South is exterminated. If we hold
those caught they amount to no more than dead men. At this
particular time to release all rebel prisoners...would insure
Sherman's defeat and would compromise our safety here.[97]

The prior day, he had more succinctly written, "We ought not to make
a single exchange nor release a prisoner on any pretext whatever until
the war closes. We have got to fight until the military power of the
South is exhausted, and if we release or exchange prisoners captured it
simply becomes a war of extermination."[98]

Lee's concerns, expressed in an August 24 letter to the Secretary of
War, confirmed Grant's view: "Unless some measures can be devised
to replace our losses, the consequences may be disastrous... Without
some increase of our strength, I cannot see how we are to escape the
natural military consequences of the enemy's numerical strength."[99]

The "great change" that Lincoln needed for re-election occurred
the day after the Democrats' August 31 nomination of McClellan as
their Presidential candidate. Sherman had moved a large force south of
Atlanta, had seized the last open railroad by pushing Hardee off the
Macon and Western at Jonesboro on September 1, and had compelled
Hood to begin abandoning the city that very night. Lee's failure to provide reinforcements and Hood's decimation of the forces he did have
finally had proven too much to overcome. On September 2 Sherman
occupied Atlanta and telegraphed Halleck, "Atlanta is ours, and fairly
won."[100] With the fall of Atlanta, the North went wild, and both Lincoln's re-election and ultimate Union victory were assured.

The icing on Lincoln's cake was provided by Phil Sheridan's defeats of Jubal Early in the Shenandoah Valley during the pre-election
months of September and October.[101] By early September, Sheridan had

---

97. McWhiney and Jamieson, *Attack and Die*, p. 9.
98. *Ibid.*
99. Lee to James A. Seddon, August 23, 1864, Dowdey and Manarin, *Papers*, pp. 343-4.
100. Hattaway and Jones, *How the North Won*, p. 673.
101. For details of the 1864 Shenandoah Valley campaign, see Wert, Jeffrey D., *From Winchester to Cedar Creek: The Shenandoah Campaign of 1864* (Carlisle, Pennsylvania: South
Mountain Press, Inc., 1987).

20,000 troops to take on Early's 12,000. Sheridan's early cautiousness led to the departure of Kershaw's Division from the Valley for Petersburg. Learning of this, Sheridan decided to attack a portion of Early's force at Winchester at the north end of the Valley. Early concentrated his remaining forces just in time for the September 19 battle, held off the strong frontal assaults, but was flanked and forced to retreat. Early lost 4,000 men but inflicted 5,000 casualties on Sheridan, who had been the attacker. Sheridan followed up this victory by again flanking Early's forces at Fisher's Hill three days later and by forcing them to retreat southward far up the Valley.

Sheridan, who had suffered only 500 casualties at Fisher's Hill to his enemy's 1,200, then proceeded to systematically burn and destroy most of the Valley, one of Lee's important breadbaskets. Early came back for one more pre-election effort when, at dawn on October 19, he surprised and routed Sheridan's troops at Cedar Creek. That afternoon, however, the absent Sheridan returned to lead his troops in a counter-attack, which swept the stunned Confederates back up the Valley for the duration of the war. Although Sheridan had lost 5,700 men to Early's 2,900 in this final 1864 struggle in the Valley, he had won three major battles in about a month, cleared the lower Valley of Confederates, and helped set the stage for Lincoln's November success at the ballot-box.

Meanwhile, the Confederacy's military situation near Richmond was continuing to prove costly. Grant, hoping to break through to either Richmond or Petersburg, decided to test the Confederate line by attacking it on both ends. Thus, he launched simultaneous, costly assaults on the morning of September 29. The northern assault on Confederate fortifications in the Chaffin's Bluff area, under the command of Ben Butler, succeeded in capturing New Market Heights, the critical Fort Harrison, and the minor Fort Hoke. Other attacks that day on Forts Gilmer, Gregg, and Johnson, north of Fort Harrison on the Confederate line, met with failure and death.

Nevertheless, Lee was so upset by the loss of Fort Harrison that he desperately, but unsuccessfully, counter-attacked the next day. That frontal assault cost him most of the 2,000 Rebel casualties suffered on the northern sector. The Confederates were compelled to establish a new line slightly closer to Richmond, and the two sides resumed their trench warfare. Total Union casualties of 3,300 in this struggle on the northern end of the line compared unfavorably with the Rebels' 2,000 and again demonstrated the cost of frontally assaulting strong defensive positions. At the other end of the line, Grant was successful in extending his line to Poplar Springs Church and, thus, stretching Lee's lines -- but at a cost to Grant of 2,900 men and to Lee of only 900.

After that September fighting, Lee, in October, proposed to Grant that the two sides resume their prisoner exchanges, which had been halted when the southerners refused to exchange black soldiers with the Union. Grant agreed to Lee's request but only if Blacks were exchanged "...the same as white soldiers." Lee responded that "...negroes belonging to our citizens are not considered subjects of exchange and were not included in my proposition." Grant then turned down the exchange in accordance with Lincoln's policy on the issue, which cost the President votes in the following month's election.[102]

The November election, nevertheless, brought Lincoln a spectacular 212-21 Electoral College victory. He garnered 78 percent of the military vote and 54 percent of civilian ballots. The relative closeness of the popular vote -- 2,200,000 to 1,800,000 -- provided an inkling of what might have been, had the Confederates used their forces more wisely and conservatively and kept Atlanta from falling. Jefferson Davis refused to accept the fact that the game was up and insisted that Lincoln's reelection had changed nothing. But southern citizens' demoralization and southern soldiers' desertions spoke to the contrary.[103] Based on his own earlier statements, Lee should have known that further resistance was futile and would only bring more death and destruction to the South and its armies. Nevertheless, on November 12, he wrote to his wife that she should "...make up [her] mind that Mr. Lincoln is reelected President," and "...we must therefore make up our minds for another four years of war."[104]

From November 1864 until the following April, Lee, with his unparalleled standing among Confederate leaders, had the power to bring the war to a halt by simply resigning. There is no indication that he attempted to tell Davis that further resistance was hopeless, and it is likely that Davis would have rejected any advice to stop the war -- particularly given his later hopes that the struggle could be continued even after Lee surrendered at Appomattox the following April. Nevertheless, Lee's stature and standing were so great that his resignation would have caused massive desertions and brought virtually all the fighting to an end. Lee could have presented Davis with a *fait accompli*, but he chose to carry on the war in the glorious cavalier tradition and,

102. McPherson, *Battle Cry of Freedom*, p. 800.

103. Jones, "Military Means," in Boritt, *Why the Confederacy Lost*, p. 73, citing Confederate Vice President Stephens' statement that southern aspirations of prevailing had been sustained only by hopes that the northern peace advocates would succeed.

104. Thomas, *Lee*, p. 346.

thereby, caused the loss of thousands of lives and the destruction of hundreds of millions of dollars worth of southern property.

Lee should have realized the importance of ominous developments occurring in the Deep South. After the capture of Atlanta, Sherman had pursued Hood into Alabama until Sherman determined to undertake a more creative and effective campaign. Specifically, in late September and on into October and November, Hood went after Sherman's Western and Atlantic Railroad supply line and then moved into northern Alabama for a planned invasion of Tennessee. Initially Sherman pursued Hood across the Alabama border, but Sherman then had second thoughts.

Sherman decided that his most effective course of action would be to break loose of his supply line, live off the countryside, and bring war to the southern people by sweeping through Georgia to the coast, where he could establish a new supply base. To obtain Lincoln's and Grant's consent to this daring gamble, Sherman had sent George Thomas and John Schofield to defend Tennessee, and, possibly, the Ohio River Valley, with 55,000 troops against Hood's desperate, northward movement from northern Alabama. Hood's abysmal failures and the disintegration of his army confirmed the validity of Sherman's strategy and made his campaign an unmitigated success. On November 16, shortly after the Presidential election, Sherman marched out of Atlanta and embarked on a five-month campaign of total destruction through Georgia, then South Carolina, and finally North Carolina. While Lee must have watched in horror, Sherman's unchallenged 60,000-man force moved southeast across Georgia, lived off the resources of the countryside, and left a swath of destruction and depression in its wake. After a 280-mile march, they reached the beautiful coastal city of Savannah and obtained its surrender on December 21 in time for Sherman to make it a Christmas present to Lincoln. Although Hardee's small defending force escaped from Savannah to South Carolina, Thomas, by that time, had annihilated Hood's Army of Tennessee and had 50,000 troops which could be moved to the East. By December 1864, therefore, Lee had to have seen that there was no military force capable of blocking the inevitable movement by Sherman to join Grant in Virginia and obliterate or compel the surrender of Lee's army. If Lincoln's reelection had, somehow, not opened Lee's eyes to the inevitability of a Union victory, the military events of November and December 1864 should have finally made the point.

Southern despair had reached some true believers in the Confederate cause. As early as October 8, 1864, Varina Davis, the President's wife, was writing to Charleston, South Carolina diarist Mary Chesnut,

"Strictly between us, *Things look* very *anxious* here..."[105] On November 20, Mrs. Davis wrote to Mrs. Chesnut, "Only I mean that I am so forlorn that they do not tell me how forlorn they think I am..."[106] In December and January, Mrs. Chesnut reflected her own concerns: "Savannah--a second Vicksburg business. Neither the governor of Georgia nor the governor of South Carolina moving hand or foot. *They have given up.*"[107] And, "here is startling news. Politely but firmly the Virginia legislature requests Jeff Davis and all of his cabinet to resign...And we have sent [Alexander] Stephens, [John Archibald] Campbell--all who never believed in this thing--to negotiate for peace. No hope--no good. *Who dares hope?*"[108] In Richmond, Josiah Gorgas reflected a mixture of despondency and dependency on Lee:

> Jan 15 [1865] In this dark hour of our struggle there is of course strong feeling against the administration for having mismanaged our affairs. This must be expected in adversity.
>
> Jan 25 [1865] I have outlived my momentary depression, & feel my courage revive when I think of the brave army in front of us, sixty thousand strong. As long as Lee's army remains intact there is no cause for despondency. As long as it holds true we need not fear. The attacks of the enemy will now all be directed against that Army. Sherman from the South, Thomas from the West and Grant in front.[109]

With despondency turning to despair throughout the South, Lee, nevertheless, carried on the hopeless struggle to preserve the honor of his Army – and, perhaps, to preserve his own honor.

---

[105]. Woodward, C. Vann, *Mary Chesnut's Civil War* (New Haven and London: Yale University Press, 1981), p. 664.

[106]. *Ibid.*, p. 675.

[107]. *Ibid.*, p. 694 (December 19, 1864 diary entry).

[108]. *Ibid.*, pp. 706-7 (late January 1865 diary entry).

[109]. Gorgas, *Journals*, pp. 148-9.

Chapter 11

1865:
Inevitable Defeat

As 1865 dawned, the Union forces stood ready to annihilate the remainder of the Confederate armies. Grant had Lee's forces at Richmond and Petersburg tied down and stretched to their limits. Lee was requesting that General E. Kirby Smith's Trans-Mississippi Army be transferred to Virginia.[1] Sherman was poised to head into the Carolinas virtually unmolested. The Union was threatening to close the Confederacy's last major port. Tens of thousands of western troops stood ready to move from Tennessee to Virginia.

The end was clearly inevitable. About 40 percent of Confederate soldiers east of the Mississippi had deserted during the fall and early winter.[2] On December 31, 1864, less than half of the Confederacy's soldiers were present with their units.[3] Therefore, 1865 should have witnessed no fighting. But Lee had yet to call a halt to the bloody proceedings. The thousands of deaths that year were a macabre tribute to his chivalry and sense of honor and duty.

As the result of a January 19, 1865, act of the Confederate Congress and Davis' grudging appointment, Lee became Commander-in-Chief of all Confederate forces and, in that capacity, continued the hopeless struggle. Lee's appointment demonstrated the unused power he held because it resulted from pressure by the Confederate Congress and the Virginia Legislature on Davis, who was reluctant to yield any power.[4]

During January and February, Lee consistently underestimated the strength and abilities of Sherman's army and overestimated the numbers and fighting capabilities of the scattered Rebel forces in the Carolinas. In a single dispatch, he spoke of concentrating forces against

[1]. Connelly, "Lee and the Western Confederacy," p. 123.
[2]. Jones, "Military Means," in Boritt, *Why the Confederacy Lost*, p. 74.
[3]. Beringer et al., *Why the South Lost*, p. 333.
[4]. Wiley, *Road to Appomattox*, p. 85.

Sherman and holding Charleston, two mutually inconsistent possibilities.[5]

After a two-month Confederate Government delay following the collapse of Hood's army, Lee, as Commander-in-Chief, on February 22, recalled Davis' old enemy, Joseph Johnston, to active duty as commander of the western army remnants charged with stopping Sherman. Lee's recall order to Johnston reflected unrealistic expectations about what Johnston could accomplish with the limited troops at hand: "Assume command of the Army of Tennessee and all troops in Department of South Carolina, Georgia, and Florida. Assign General Beauregard to duty under you, as you may select. Concentrate all available forces and drive back Sherman."[6] The reality was that Lee's attention to Sherman came far too late to do any good.[7]

In January, 1865, Grant wrote to Sherman, "My own opinion is that Lee is averse to going out of Virginia, and if the cause of the South is lost he wants Richmond to be the last place surrendered. If he has such views it may be well to indulge him until everything else is in our hands."[8] Sherman concurred with Grant and also with a Georgia farmer who was appalled by Sherman's march through Georgia and told him, "Why don't you go over to South Carolina and serve them this way? They started it."[9]

On the Confederate side, Lee's manpower shortage was now so desperate that he wanted a prisoner exchange at a price he previously had been unwilling to pay.[10] In January, 1865, therefore, he and President Davis agreed to exchange Negro soldiers. That month, Lee began putting his persuasive powers to work on President Davis even more desperately[11] and, later, on the Confederate Congress, which passed a

---

5. Connelly, *Autumn of Glory*, p. 529.

6. Hattaway and Jones, *How the North Won*, p. 667.

7. "The delay in appointing Johnston proved disastrous for the West. Johnston was no genius at strategy. But if he had been appointed earlier, he might have wrought some order, and concentration might have been effected. Instead, for almost two critical months in 1865, the Confederacy confronted Sherman in the Carolinas with nothing but chaos." Connelly, *Autumn of Glory*, p. 520.

8. Coburn, *Terrible Innocence*, pp. 191-2.

9. McPherson, *Battle Cry of Freedom*, p. 825.

10. On February 25, Lee wrote, "Hundreds of men are deserting nightly..." Thomas, *Lee*, p. 348. Between February 15 and March 18, Lee's army lost 3,000 deserters, eight percent of its strength. *Ibid.*, p. 349. In March Lee reported 1,094 desertions in a ten-day period; one brigade deserted en masse. Wiley, *Road to Appomattox*, p. 72.

11. Lee to Jefferson Davis, March 2, 1865, Freeman and McWhiney, *Lee's Dispatches*, pp. 373-4.

Blacks' recruitment bill on March 13 — but too late to augment Lee's disintegrating forces.[12]

The noose around the Confederacy was severely tightened that January with the fall of Fort Fisher, which guarded the river entrance to Wilmington, North Carolina, the only significant southern port still open to blockade-runners. After an unsuccessful assault the prior month, the Union assembled a huge fleet of 58 vessels with 627 guns. On January 13 to 15, the Yankees captured critical Fort Fisher on the Cape Fear River with a joint army-navy-marine assault; they then moved inland to finally capture Wilmington on February 22. This capture opened three more supply lines, via railroads radiating west and north from Wilmington, for the northward-moving Sherman.

Between the fall of Fort Fisher and the capture of Wilmington, negotiators made an attempt to end the war. When the respective teams met in Hampton Roads on February 3, however, the Confederate negotiators were operating under fantasyland instructions from Davis. Lincoln and Secretary of State William Seward personally rejected the Confederates' requests for some solution short of abolishing slavery and rejoining the Union. Lee had clearly not made Davis understand that the military situation was hopeless.

Sherman was about to end the few hopes that might have remained among the people of the South. On February 1, he headed north from Savannah. Despite Rebel doubts that Sherman's forces could move through the swamps of South Carolina in the middle of the winter, Sherman's men were truly inspired by the long-awaited opportunity to invade the state that had started the rebellion and moved as though they were on a summer lark on turnpikes. "Boys, this is old South Carolina: let's give her hell," said one Union soldier, reflecting the feelings of most of his comrades. Sherman wrote Halleck that he "almost tremble[d] at her fate."[13] One Union soldier summarized the feelings of Sherman's soldiers as he firmly pronounced, "Here is where treason began, and by God, here is where it will end!"[14]

As he began this campaign, Sherman was concerned about possible opposition from forces cut loose by Lee:

> ...the only serious question that occurred to me was, would General Lee sit down in Richmond (besieged by General Grant), and permit us, almost unopposed, to pass through the

12. Glatthaar, "Black Glory" in Boritt, *Why the Confederacy Lost*, p. 160; Thomas, *Lee*, p. 347; Beringer et al, *Why the South Lost*, p. 373; Hattaway and Jones, *Why the North Won*, p. 272.
13. Marszalek, *Sherman*, pp. 320-1.
14. McPherson, *Battle Cry of Freedom*, p. 826.

States of South and North Carolina, cutting off and consum-
ing the very supplies on which he depended to feed his army
in Virginia, or would he make an effort to escape from General Grant, and endeavor to catch us inland somewhere between Columbia and Raleigh?[15]

Through swamps and across rivers rolled the onslaught.
Sherman's 60,000 men swept across the countryside in two wings --
Major General Henry W. Slocum's on the left and Oliver O. Howard's
on the right. Much of South Carolina's capital of Columbia went up in
flames on February 17. The bypassed coastal city of Charleston was
evacuated the next day, as was its North Carolina counterpart, Wilmington, on the 22nd. On the latter day, Lee wrote in confidence to
Longstreet that he believed he would have to abandon Richmond if the
Union armies continued to unite in threatening his position; he also
revealed his plans to retreat westward.[16]

At that point, Sherman was advancing from the south with 60,000
soldiers, and Schofield was poised along the North Carolina coast prepared to move inland with 30,000 more. Against them, the Confederacy
was able to muster a mere 21,000 troops, the augmented remnants of
Hood's old army then under the command of the restored Joseph E.
Johnston. Once again, Lee should have been able to analyze the 9:2
odds of the "struggle" shaping up about a hundred miles to his south,
to realize that the game was over, and to call a halt to the killing. He
did not -- even when, in March, 1,100 of his men deserted in ten days
and an entire brigade "went over the hill." Lee refused Johnston's
March 1 suggestion that Lee send troops into North Carolina to oppose
Sherman; Lee said he would not do so until Sherman reached the
Roanoke River fifty-five miles south of Petersburg.[17]

As to Lee's capability to affect events, Grant commented of him, at
the time, "All the people except a few political leaders in the South will
accept whatever he does as right and will be guided to a great extent by
his example."[18] This view was shared by Gorgas, who, on March 2,
wrote:

> People are almost in a state of desperation, and but too ready
> to give up the cause... It must be confessed that we are badly
> off for leaders both on the council & on the field. Lee is about

---

15. Sherman, William Tecumseh, *Memoirs of General W.T. Sherman* (New York: Literary
Classics of the United States, Inc., 1990), p. 752.
16. Lee to James Longstreet, February 22, 1865, Dowdey and Manarin, *Papers*, p. 907-8.
17. Bevin Alexander, *Great Generals*, p. 165.
18. Fuller, *Grant and Lee*, p. 123.

all we have & what public confidence is left rallies around him, and he it seems to me fights without much heart in the cause. I do him wrong perhaps, but I don't think he believes we will or can succeed in this struggle. The President has alas! Lost almost every vestige of the public confidence. Had we been successful his errors and faults would have been overlooked, but adversity magnifies them.[19]

During the first week of March, Sherman's army moved into North Carolina, and some of Schofield's troops moved westward, out of New Bern to threaten the Confederate left flank. Schofield's force was temporarily halted by Bragg's 8,500 men at Kinston on March 8 through 10.

Meanwhile, Sherman's massive Union forces were barely hindered by the rest of Johnston's troops. On March 11, Sherman took Fayetteville. He then crossed the Cape Fear and Black Rivers and continued northeast toward a link-up with Schofield at Goldsboro. Sherman's left wing, under Slocum, was delayed at Averasboro between the rivers on March 16 and was attacked on March 19 to 21 at Bentonville, where they inflicted 2,600 casualties on the Confederate attackers while incurring only 1,500 themselves.

At that point, Johnston ordered a retreat to the northwest, which allowed Sherman's army to merge with Schofield's troops coming north from Wilmington and west from New Bern. This merger of well over 90,000 Union troops on March 23 in the vicinity of Goldsboro, with less than 20,000 Confederates to oppose them, presented another missed opportunity for Lee to resign and, thus, to end the war. While Lee was losing Petersburg, Richmond, and the war during the next three weeks, Sherman moved on the North Carolina capital of Raleigh, which he occupied on April 13, four days after Lee's surrender of his army.

Over the winter, Sheridan's and Early's forces, in the Shenandoah Valley, had been greatly reduced by transfers to the Richmond area. Nevertheless, Sheridan decided to permanently terminate the Confederate presence in the valley. He did so by moving south on February 25, pushing aside Early's cavalry at Mount Crawford on March 2, and destroying his infantry at Waynesboro on March 3. Early retreated eastward through the Blue Ridge Mountains toward Charlottesville, and the valley was lost to Lee for the duration. Sheridan's cavalry then was free to return to the Petersburg front.

---

19. Gorgas, *Journals*, pp. 154-5.

On that front, Grant was gradually tightening the noose. From February 5 to 7, Union troops succeeded in pushing back the Confederates at Hatcher's Run southwest of Petersburg and then in extending the Union lines by two additional miles. Throughout February, Colonel Elisha Hunt Rhodes recorded a flood of Confederate deserters. On February 21, he noted that ten deserters had come over to Union lines the prior night and added, "They all tell the same story--that the Southern cause is hopeless." Four days later, he reported the previous night's arrival of 160 Rebel deserters.[20]

Seven weeks after Grant had extended his lines, Lee began the series of actions that terminated the siege and doomed his Rebel army. On March 25, he ordered a desperate, pre-dawn assault on Fort Stedman, just east of Petersburg. The initial attack captured that fort, but Federal counter-attacks from three directions drove the Rebels back with an intolerable loss of 4,000 to the Union's 2,000.

Sensing Lee's desperation, Grant went on the offensive. Humphreys and Warren moved their corps to the left, and Major Generals Wright and Edward O. C. Ord shifted theirs to cover the lines the other two had left behind. This freed Humphreys and Warren to attack the southwest end of Lee's line along White Oak Road south and west of Hatcher's Run. Their March 31 attack coincided with an attempt by Sheridan's cavalry to sweep around Lee's army even farther southwest via Dinwiddie Court House. The Union infantry attack succeeded in breaking through to White Oak Road, where they withstood a Rebel counter-attack, but Sheridan was driven back to Dinwiddie Court House by Rooney Lee's cavalry.

The next day, April 1, the Confederate line finally cracked. Sheridan took his cavalry and Warren's 5th Corps even farther west to hit Pickett at Five Forks. Although Sheridan, unjustly, replaced Warren with Brigadier General Charles Griffin during that day, the Union forces almost encircled Pickett and decimated his corps. This Five Forks victory sprung Sheridan loose on the western Confederate flank, closed down the last railroad (the Southside) into Petersburg, and doomed both Petersburg and Richmond.

On the fateful next day, Grant's forces attacked all along the Rebel lines and broke through at several points. Lee advised Davis to abandon Petersburg and Richmond, and they did so that evening. Lee sacrificed more men to hold the Union forces at bay for the additional hours required for Davis, Lee, and the dwindling Army of Northern Virginia to flee. Although there was no hope that his army would survive more

---

20. Rhodes, *All for the Union*, pp. 214-6.

than a couple of weeks, Lee did not advise surrender or threaten to resign. Thus, the killing continued for one more week.

Playing for time on the second of April, Lee sent three of Anderson's brigades west to assist Pickett's reorganization. Near Petersburg, John Gordon held off the attack of Major General John G. Parke's 9th Corps. Elsewhere along the line that day, the Confederates suffered one disaster after another. West of Parke, Wright's 6th Corps smashed through the Rebels and wrought havoc. To their west, Humphreys' 2nd Corps achieved a similar break-through, chased Henry Heth to the northwest, and moved northeast toward Petersburg. Senseless destruction, at Lee's direction, continued that night with the Confederates' burning of their massive Richmond stores -- and much of the city with them. Union troops occupied the burning city the morning of the third -- followed the next day by President Lincoln.

Meanwhile, the battered and beaten Army of Northern Virginia retreated westward from Richmond and Petersburg. The Rebels generally followed the course of the Appomattox River, but crossing and recrossing that river hindered their 90-mile retreat. The Union forces moved even more quickly out of the Petersburg lines and headed west on the left (south) flank of the fleeing soldiers.

Lee directed all his forces to converge at Amelia Court House on the Richmond & Danville (R&D) Railroad, where he hoped to find a supply of rations which were to have arrived from the west. When the Confederates came together there by April 5, however, no rations were to be found. Even worse, Grant had a major force eight miles southwest of Amelia Court House at Jetersville blocking the R&D Railroad. Farther southwest, Ord's Army of the James arrived at Burke, the crucial intersection of the R&D and the Southside railroads.

Still not willing to give up, the flanked Lee sent his men on a forced march westward toward Farmville in the hope of being supplied from Lynchburg via the Southside Railroad northwest of Burke. On April 6, however, further disaster struck as Lee's rear guard was cut off at Sayler's Creek. Anderson's and Ewell's men lagged behind the main body, were trapped by the 2nd and 6th Union corps, lost most of the precious Confederate wagon train, incurred 1,000 casualties, and had 6,000 men captured. Union losses were only 1,200. Did Lee then give up the hopeless mismatch to halt further bloodshed? No, he continued west.

The next day, his dwindling force at last found rations at Farmville and there repelled Federal attackers before crossing the Appomattox River for the last time. This crossing, however, simply bottled up Lee's army between the Appomattox and James Rivers and forced them toward Appomattox Court House to escape entrapment. While Lee was being delayed at Amelia Court House, Sayler's Creek, and Farmville, however, Union forces had been getting ahead of Lee's retreating army.

Once again it was Sheridan's cavalry that proved decisive. His men raced ahead of the retreating Confederates and, on April 8, blocked them between Appomattox Court House and Appomattox Station on the Southside Railroad, where Sheridan had captured several trainloads of Rebel rations.

Realizing that the end was very near, Grant tried to avoid additional bloodshed by initiating negotiations with Lee on the afternoon of April 7. He wrote:

> General. The results of the last week must convince you of the hopelessness of further resistance on the part of the Army of Northern Virginia, in this struggle. I feel that it is so, & regard it as my duty to shift from myself the responsibility of any further effusion of blood by asking of you the surrender of that portion of the Confederate States Army known as the Army of Northern Virginia.[21]

Lee's response that night, his army's third consecutive night of marching, seemed to reflect a show of determination combined with realistic resignation:

> General, I have received your note of this date. Though not entertaining the opinion you express on the hopelessness of further resistance on the part of the Army of Northern Virginia, I reciprocate your desire to avoid useless effusion of blood, & therefore, before considering your proposition, ask the terms you will offer on condition of its surrender.[22]

A roundabout route delayed delivery of that note until the morning of the 8th, when Grant responded with a single requirement:

> Your note of last evening in reply to mine of the same date, asking the conditions on which I will accept the surrender of the Army of Northern Virginia, is just received. In reply I would say that, peace being my great desire, there is but one condition I would insist upon, -- namely, that the men and officers surrendered shall be disqualified for taking up arms against the Government of the United States until properly

---

21. Thomas, *Lee*, p. 359.

22 . Lee to Ulysses S. Grant, April 7, 1865, Dowdey and Manarin, *Papers*, pp. 931-2.

exchanged. I will meet you, or will designate officers to meet any officers you may name for the same purpose, at any point agreeable to you, for the purpose of arranging definitely the terms upon which the surrender of the Army of Northern Virginia will be received.[23]

Lee's "in-your-face" response that night reflected his reluctance to surrender but, in the end, he appeared to hint at acceptance of the inevitable. Even at that late juncture, however, Lee had hoped to discuss peace instead of surrender:

> General, I received at a late hour your note of today. I did not intend to propose the surrender of the Army of Northern Virginia, but to ask the terms of your proposition. To be frank, I do not think the emergency has arisen to call for the surrender of this army; but, as the restoration of peace should be the sole object of all, I desire to know whether your proposals would lead to that end. I cannot therefore meet you with a view to surrender the Army of Northern Va., but, as far as your proposal may affect the Confederate States forces under my command, & tend to the restoration of peace, I should be pleased to meet you at 10 A.M. tomorrow on the old stage road to Richmond between the picket lines of the two armies.[24]

Longstreet fully understood the depth of Lee's continuing reluctance to surrender. He was approached by General William Pendleton on the 8th, after an informal council of officers had agreed to advise Lee to surrender. Pendleton approached Longstreet because of the latter's special relationship with Lee. Longstreet refused to carry their advice to Lee and indignantly added, "If General Lee doesn't know when to surrender until I tell him, he will never know."[25] Although Longstreet did not intend this meaning, Lee had clearly demonstrated during the preceding several months that he did not know when to surrender.

The end came on April 9. An attempted Confederate breakout that morning revealed Union infantry backing up Sheridan's cavalry. One of Gibbon's officers observed the sorry state of the remnants of Lee's once-grand army: "It was a sad sight -- cavalry, artillery, horses, mules

---

23. Thomas, *Lee*, pp. 360-1.
24 . Lee to Ulysses S. Grant, April 8, 1865, Dowdey and Manarin, *Papers*, p. 932.
25. Freeman, *Lee's Lieutenants*, III, p. 721; Longstreet, James, *From Manassas to Appomattox: Memoirs of the Civil War in America* (New York: Smithmark Publishers, Inc., 1994; reprint of Philadelphia: Lippincott, 1896), p. 620.

and half-starved soldiers in a confused mass. It was a scene to melt the bravest heart."[26] At that point, Lee made his long-overdue decision to seek terms from Grant, who, that morning, had rejected Lee's peace discussion overture. Lee had no choice but to respond to Grant's surrender offer of the previous day:

> General: I received your note of this morning on the picket-line, whither I had come to meet you and ascertain definitely what terms were embraced in your proposal of yesterday with reference to the surrender of this army. I now ask an interview, in accordance with the offer contained in your letter of yesterday, for that purpose.[27]

At long last, and when there was no alternative but ungentlemanly guerilla warfare, Lee had accepted the inevitable. Lee's reluctance, however, was demonstrated by his statement that, "There is nothing left for me to do but to go and see General Grant, and I would rather die a thousand deaths."[28]

The surrender of Lee's army to Grant finally took place that afternoon at Appomattox Court House. The proceedings were held in the home of Wilmer McLean, who, ironically, had moved there from outside Manassas, where his home had been shelled in the First Battle of Bull Run. Grant generously paroled Lee's 30,000 troops and allowed his officers to keep their horses -- conditioned only on their promise to never again take up arms against the United States.

The next day, Lee issued his final order to what was left of his once-grand army. With language that could have been accurately used six months earlier, his General Order No. 9 said:

> After four years of arduous service marked by unsurpassed courage and fortitude, the Army of Northern Virginia has been compelled to yield to overwhelming numbers and resources.

> I need not tell the brave survivors of so many hard-fought battles, who have remained steadfast to the last, that I have consented to this result from no distrust of them; but feeling that valor and devotion could accomplish nothing that could compensate for the loss that must have attended the continuance of the contest, I have determined to avoid the useless

26. Waugh, *Class of 1846*, p. 497.
27. Lee to Ulysses S. Grant, April 9, 1865, Dowdey and Manarin, *Papers*, p. 932.
28. Thomas, *Lee*, p. 362.

sacrifice of those whose past services have endeared them to their countrymen.

With an unceasing admiration of your constancy and devotion to your Country, and a grateful remembrance of your kind and generous consideration for myself, I bid you all an affectionate farewell.[29]

At long last, the bloody struggle was almost over. Over the next month, another 100 minor engagements brought the fighting to a close. A mind-boggling 620,000 Americans -- 260,000 Confederates and 360,000 Yankees -- had died of wounds and disease. Robert E. Lee's offensives of 1862, 1863 and 1864 had accounted for many of those deaths -- on both sides -- and guaranteed the ultimate defeat of the outmanned Confederacy.

Lee's final wartime mistake had been his failure to halt the fighting when it no longer served any sane purpose. This failure accounted for the final tens of thousands of meaningless deaths. After the fall of Atlanta, or certainly after Lincoln's reelection, Lee should have, realized that, "...Valor and devotion could accomplish nothing that could compensate for the loss that must have attended continuance of the contest [and] determined to avoid the useless sacrifice of those whose past services have endeared them to their countrymen."[30]

---

[29]. General Order No. 9, April 10, 1865, Dowdey and Manarin, *Papers*, pp. 934-5.
[30]. *Ibid.*, p. 934.

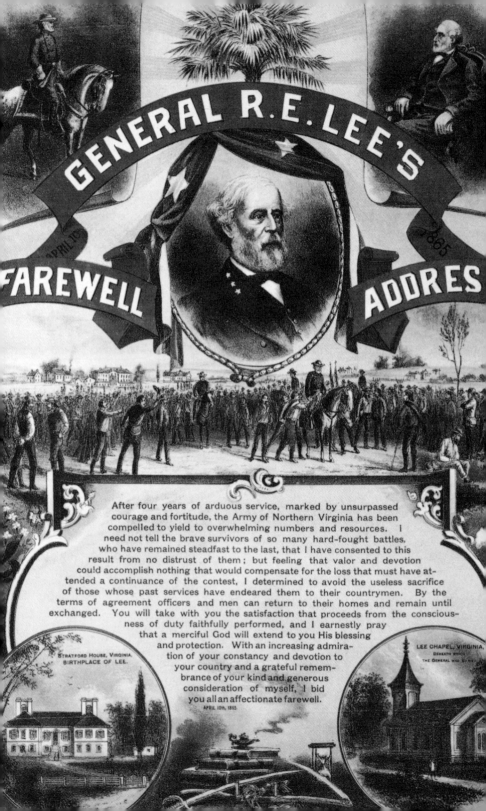

GENERAL R.E.LEE'S
FAREWELL ADDRESS

APRIL 10 1865

STRATFORD HOUSE, VIRGINIA.
BIRTHPLACE OF LEE.

LEE CHAPEL, VIRGINIA.
BENEATH WHICH
THE GENERAL WAS BURIED.

After four years of arduous service, marked by unsurpassed courage and fortitude, the Army of Northern Virginia has been compelled to yield to overwhelming numbers and resources. I need not tell the brave survivors of so many hard-fought battles, who have remained steadfast to the last, that I have consented to this result from no distrust of them; but feeling that valor and devotion could accomplish nothing that would compensate for the loss that must have attended a continuance of the contest, I determined to avoid the useless sacrifice of those whose past services have endeared them to their countrymen. By the terms of agreement officers and men can return to their homes and remain until exchanged. You will take with you the satisfaction that proceeds from the consciousness of duty faithfully performed, and I earnestly pray that a merciful God will extend to you His blessing and protection. With an increasing admiration of your constancy and devotion to your country and a grateful remembrance of your kind and generous consideration of myself, I bid you all an affectionate farewell.

APRIL 10th, 1865.

Chapter 12

Overview

Robert E. Lee is often described as one of the greatest generals who ever lived. He usually is given credit for keeping the vastly superior Union forces at bay and preserving the Confederacy during the four years of the American Civil War.[1]

The Confederacy did lose the Civil War, however, and Lee was the Confederacy's most important military leader. In *The Face of Battle*, John Keegan notes that, "...The only cult general in the English-speaking world -- Robert E. Lee -- was the paladin of its only component community to suffer military catastrophe, the Confederacy."[2] As discussed in Appendix I, the cult of Lee worshippers began with former Civil War generals who had fought ineffectively under Lee and sought to polish their own tarnished reputations and restore southern pride by deliberately distorting the historical record and creating the myth of the flawless Robert E. Lee.

In his capacity as the Confederacy's leading general, however, Lee bears considerable responsibility for the war's outcome. Even more significantly, as we have seen, Lee's own specific strategic and tactical failures cost the Confederates their opportunity to outlast the Union, caused President Abraham Lincoln's electoral defeat in 1864, and thereby won the war.

Lincoln's 1860 election brought about the secession of seven states even before the firing on Fort Sumter, and his resolute stance on the issue of Union caused four more states to secede after Sumter and made war inevitable. The South's primary opportunity for success was

---

[1]. See Appendix I, "Historians' Treatment of Lee." Typical is this statement by Lee's Adjutant-General, Walter H. Taylor: "It is well to bear in mind the great inequality between the two contending armies, in order that one may have a proper appreciation of the difficulties which beset General Lee in the task of thwarting the designs of so formidable an adversary, and realize the extent to which his brilliant genius made amends for paucity of numbers, and proved more than a match for brute force, as illustrated in the hammering policy of General Grant." Taylor, *General Lee*, p. 231.

[2]. Keegan, John, *The Face of Battle* (New York: Dorset Press, 1986; originally New York: The Viking Press, 1976), p. 55.

to outlast Lincoln, and the deep schisms among northerners throughout the War made this a distinct possibility. Northerners violently disagreed on slavery, the draft and the war itself.[3] To exploit these divisions and thereby prevail, the Confederates needed to preserve their
resources, sap the strength of the North, make continuation of the war
intolerable, and thereby compel an acceptable compromise.

At the outset of the war, the North had tremendous population
and resources advantages over the South. The North had 22 million
people, while the South had only nine million. Moreover, of those nine
million southerners, 3.5 million were slaves.[4] Unless therefore the
South found a way to fully involve those slaves in the war effort (and
on the Confederate side), it faced a 4-to-1 general population disadvantage.

More relevantly, the North had 4,070,000 men of fighting age (15
to 40), and the South had only 1,140,000 white men of fighting age.
Considering that immigration and defecting slaves further augmented
the North's forces, the crucial bottom line is that the Union had an effective combat manpower advantage of 4:1 over the Confederacy.

One in ten Civil War soldiers was wounded, one in sixty-five died
in battle and one in thirteen died of disease. Of the nearly three million
men (two million Union and 750,000 Confederate) who served in the
military during the war, 620,000 died (360,000 Union and 260,000 Confederate).[5] While many northerners were in the military for brief peri-
ods of time (many of them serving twice or more), most southern military personnel were compelled to stay for the duration. Amazingly,
almost one-fourth of southern white males of military age died during
the war -- virtually all of them from wounds or war-related diseases.
The primary point of all these statistics is that the South was greatly
outnumbered and could not afford to squander its resources by engaging in a war of attrition. Robert E. Lee's deliberate disregard of this
reality may have been his greatest failure.

The Confederacy, however, was not without advantages of its
own. It consisted of a huge, 750,000-square mile territory which the
Federals would have to invade and conquer.[6] It also had interior lines

---

3. McPherson, *Battle Cry of Freedom*, pp. 591-611.

4. Hattaway and Jones, *How the North Won*, p. 17.

5. *Ibid.*, p. 440.

6. *Ibid.*, pp. 18, 35. "Thus space was all in favour of the South; even should the enemy
overrun her border, her principal cities, few in number, were far removed from the hostile bases, and the important railway junctions were perfectly secure from sudden attack.
And space, especially when means of communication are scanty, and the country affords
few supplies, is the greatest of all obstacles." Henderson, G.F.R., *Stonewall Jackson and the*

and was able to move its troops from place to place over shorter distances via a complex of well-placed railroads. The burden was on the North to win the war;[7] a deadlock would confirm secession and the Confederacy.[8] Historian James McPherson put it succinctly: "The South could `win' the war by not losing; the North could win only by winning."[9]

The Confederates' huge strategic advantage and their missed opportunities were confirmed by an early war analysis of the struggle by a military analyst writing in *The Times* of London. The analyst said, "No war of independence ever terminated unsuccessfully except where the disparity of force was far greater than it is in this case. Just as England during the [American] revolution had to give up conquering the colonies, so the North will have to give up conquering the South."[10] The Confederate Secretary of War agreed with this view at the start of the war: "There is no instance in history of a people as numerous as we are inhabiting a country so extensive as ours being subjected if true to themselves."[11]

Confederate General E. Porter Alexander also confirmed the Confederacy's need to wear down, not conquer, the North:

> When the South entered upon war with a power so immensely her superior in men & money, & all the wealth of modern resources in machinery and transportation appliances by land & sea, she could entertain but one single hope of final success. That was, that the desperation of her resistance would finally exact from her adversary such a price in blood & treasure as to exhaust the enthusiasm of its population for the objects of the war. We could not hope to conquer her. Our one chance was to wear her out.[12]

A southern victory was not out of the question.[13] After all, it had been only eighty years since the supposedly inferior American revolu-

---

American Civil War (New York: Da Capo Press, Inc., 1988; reprint of New York: Grossett & Dunlap, 1943), p. 82.

7. Beringer et al., *Why the South Lost*, p. 49.

8. Union General Henry W. Halleck wrote, "...The North must conquer the South." Henry W. Halleck to Francis Lieber, March 4, 1863, quoted in McWhiney and Jamieson, *Attack and Die*, p. 6.

9. McPherson, *Battle Cry of Freedom*, p. 336.

10. *Ibid.*; Nolan, *Lee Considered*, p. 65.

11. Hattaway and Jones, *How the North Won*, p. 18.

12. Alexander, *Fighting for the Confederacy*, p. 415.

13. "The point is that the South could still have won, save only for the rapid diminution and ultimate death of morale, the will to win, during the last year or two of the war." Beringer et al, *Why the South Lost*, p. 31.

tionaries had vanquished the mighty Redcoats of King George III and it was less than fifty years since the outgunned Russians had repelled and destroyed the powerful invading army of Napoleon. The feasibility of such an outcome is demonstrated by the fact that, despite numerous crucial mistakes by Lee and others, the Confederates still appeared to have political victory in their grasp in the late summer of 1864, when Lincoln himself despaired of winning reelection that coming November.

Had Lee not squandered Rebel resources during the three preceding years, that 1864 opportunity for victory could have been realized. It was Lee's strategy and tactics that dissipated irreplaceable manpower -- even in his "victories." His army lost at Malvern Hill, Antietam, Gettysburg, the Shenandoah Valley, Petersburg and Appomattox. His army took unnecessarily high casualties in those defeats, as well as throughout the entire Seven Days' Battle and at Chancellorsville. Lee's army's 1862-3 casualties made possible Ulysses Grant's successful 1864 campaign of adhesion to Lee's army. Finally, the losses Lee's army suffered at the Wilderness and Spotsylvania were higher than he could afford and helped to create the aura of Confederate defeat that Lincoln exploited to win reelection.[14]

As early as May 1863, Josiah Gorgas noted in his journal the North's susceptibility to a political defeat:

> No doubt that the war will go on until at least the close of [Lincoln's] administration. How many more lives must be sacrificed to the vindictiveness of a few unprincipled men! For there is no doubt that with the division of sentiment existing at the North the administration could shape its policy either for peace or for war.[15]

If Lee had performed differently, the North could have been fatally split, Democratic nominee (and "out-to-pasture" Union Major General) George B. McClellan could have defeated Lincoln, and the South could have negotiated an acceptable settlement with the compromising McClellan, who was running on a Democratic Peace Platform and had demonstrated sympathy for southerners' property interests in slaves.

Lee's strategy was defective in two respects. First, it was too aggressive. With one quarter the manpower resources of his adversary, Lee exposed his forces to unnecessary risks and ultimately lost the

---

14. Fuller concluded that Lee's audacity more than once accelerated the Union's achievement of its strategic goal of conquering the South. Fuller, *Grant and Lee*, p. 267.

15. Gorgas, *Journals*, p. 66.

gamble. The gamble was unwarranted because Lee only needed to play for a tie; instead he made the fatal mistake of going for the win. Lee failed to accept the reality that the North had to conquer the South; instead he tried to conquer the North -- or at least destroy its eastern army.[16]

Twice Lee went into the North on strategic offensives with scant chance of success, lost tens of thousands of irreplaceable officers and men in the disasters of Antietam and Gettysburg, and inevitably was compelled to retreat.[17] These retreats enabled Lincoln to issue his crucial Emancipation Proclamation, created an aura of defeat which doomed any possibility of European intervention, and played a major role in destroying the South's morale and will to fight. Finally, Lee's offensive strategy so seriously weakened the Confederacy's fighting capability that its defeat was perceived as inevitable by the time of the crucial 1864 Presidential election.

Second, Lee's strategy concentrated all the resources he could obtain and retain almost exclusively in the eastern theater of operations while fatal events were occurring in the "West" (primarily Tennessee, Mississippi and Georgia).[18] For example, from 1862 into 1864, grain supplies were stockpiled in Tennessee and Georgia for Lee's army while the western armies lived off the countryside.[19] Both Confederate armies suffered food shortages throughout the war.[20]

Even more significantly, Lee's actions played a role in major Confederate western defeats at Vicksburg, Tullahoma, Chattanooga and Atlanta. He refused to send reinforcements before or during the attack on and siege of Vicksburg, contributed to the gross under-manning of the Confederate forces during the Tullahoma Campaign and at Chatta-

---

16. On his way to Gettysburg, Lee wrote to Jefferson Davis, "It seems to me that we cannot afford to keep our troops awaiting possible movements of the enemy, but that our true policy is, as far as we can, so to employ our own forces as to give occupation to his at points of our selection." Lee to Jefferson Davis, June 25, 1863, Dowdey and Manarin, *Papers*, p. 532. As Nolan pointed out, these were not the words of a general whose grand strategy was defensive--as it should have been. Nolan, *Lee Considered*, p. 73. "For a belligerent with the limited manpower resources of the Confederacy, General Lee's dedication to an offensive strategy was at best questionable." Weigley, *American Way of War*, p. 118.

17. Nolan noted that "...there was a profound difference between Federal casualties and Lee's casualties... Lee's were irreplaceable..." Nolan, *Lee Considered*, p. 85.

18. Connelly and Jones, *Politics of Command*, pp. 31-48. "To all these events in the West, Lee remained remarkably indifferent, despite President Davis's continuing to call upon him as a military adviser. He persistently underrated the strength and importance of Federal offensives in the West." Weigley, *American Way of War*, p. 125.

19. Connelly, "Lee and the Western Confederacy," p. 126.

20. *See* Joinson, Carla, "War at the Table: The South's Struggle for Food," *Columbiad*, 1, No. 2 (Summer 1997), pp. 21-30.

nooga. He also, failed to send expendable troops to defend Atlanta, and played a critical role in the suicidal ascension of Hood to command in the West that led to the fall of Atlanta and destruction of the Army of Tennessee.

Throughout the war, Lee was obsessed with operations in Virginia and urged that additional reinforcements be brought to the Old Dominion from the West, where Confederates defended ten times the area in which Lee operated. Thomas L. Connelly and Archer Jones concluded that, "Lee actually supplied little general strategic guidance for the South. He either had no unified view of grand strategy or else chose to remain silent on the subject."[21] Often Lee prevailed upon President Jefferson Davis to refuse or only partially comply with requests to send critical reinforcements to the West.[22]

In April 1863, for example, Lee opposed sending any of his troops to Tennessee even though the Union had sent Burnside's 9th Corps there. Using arguments that one of his supporters called bizarre, Lee opposed concentration against the enemy and favored concurrent offensives by all Confederate commands against their superior foes. Lee used similar arguments the next month when he declined to involve his soldiers in an effort to save Vicksburg (and a Confederate army of 30,000) and thereby prevent Union control of the Mississippi River. In addition, the lack of eastern reinforcements caused Braxton Bragg's Army of Tennessee to retreat in the Tullahoma Campaign from middle Tennessee through Chattanooga into Georgia, thereby losing Tennessee and the vital rail connection between Tennessee and Richmond.

Only once, in late 1863, did Lee consent to a portion of his army being sent west. On that occasion, Lee delayed of the departure of Longstreet's 15,000 troops, and two-thirds of them arrived at Chickamauga after the battle. Nevertheless, the reinforced Rebels won at Chickamauga and drove the Yankees back into Chattanooga, where they were besieged and threatened by starvation. Almost immediately, however, Lee undercut that grudging assistance by promoting the prompt return to him of his Virginia troops. His promotion of Longstreet's return led to Longstreet's movement away from Chattanooga

---

[21]. Connelly and Jones, *Politics of Command*, p. 33. Earlier, T. Harry Williams had concluded that "Lee was interested hardly at all in 'global' strategy, and what few suggestions he did make to his government about operations in other theaters than his own indicate that he had little aptitude for grand planning." Williams, T. Harry, *Lincoln and His Generals* (New York: Alfred A. Knopf, Inc., 1952) [hereafter Williams, *Lincoln and His Generals*], p. 313.

[22]. Lee's son Robert later described how Lee had advised Davis throughout the war on movements and dispositions of armies other than his own. Fuller, *Grant and Lee*, p. 113.

just before the Union forces broke out of Chattanooga against Bragg's vastly outnumbered army.[23] Lee compounded his erroneous strategic approach to the West by acquiescing in the disastrous elevation of his protege, the obsessively aggressive John Bell Hood, to full general and command of the Rebel Army of Tennessee at the very moment William T. Sherman reached Atlanta in July 1864. Within seven weeks Hood lost Atlanta, and within six months he destroyed that army. During that significant summer, Lee squandered Jubal Early's 18,000-man corps on a demonstration against Washington instead of sending them to Atlanta, where they could have played a vital role defending that city under the command of either Johnston or Hood. These events enabled Sherman to march unmolested through Georgia and the Carolinas and to pose a fatal back-door threat to Lee's own Army of Northern Virginia.

Some may question whether Lee should have sent troops to the West, where allegedly incompetent generals would have simply squandered them. There are several problems with that position. First, many of those western generals were so outnumbered (more than Lee was) that they were simply flanked by their Union opponents (Bragg in mid-1863 and Johnston in mid-1864) in vast areas that afforded greater maneuverability than did Virginia. Second, Lee declined several opportunities to take command in the West, where he could have commanded troops moved from the East but where he had little interest and probably had an inkling things were more difficult than he knew or wanted to know. Third, the success of the few troops under Longstreet Lee finally provided for Chickamauga demonstrates what might have been if Lee had sent more troops in a timely manner. Fourth, Jubal Early's 18,000 troops could have provided invaluable assistance in preventing the fall of Atlanta prior to the crucial 1864 presidential election. Finally, Lee himself squandered the troops in the East (particularly at Gettysburg), lost the war doing what he did, and could hardly have done worse sending some to the undermanned West.

Just as Lee's strategy was flawed, his tactics were fatally defective. His tactical defects were: (1) he was too aggressive on the field, (2) he frequently failed to take charge of the battlefield, (3) his battle plans

23. Lee's myopic view of the war cannot be justified by either (1) his command of a single army or (2) his lack of power to suggest a national strategy. Numerous Confederate army commanders made national strategic recommendations to President Davis and his secretaries of war, and Lee himself had great influence on Davis but chose to use it primarily to aid his own army rather than to recommend national strategy. Connelly and Jones, *Politics of Command*, pp. 33-8.

were too complex or simply ineffective, and (4) his orders were too
vague or discretionary.

First, his tactics, like his strategy, were too aggressive.[24] Although
sometimes creative (particularly when Stonewall Jackson was involved), too often those tactics failed to adequately consider the advantages new weaponry gave to defensive forces. Rifled muskets (ones
with grooves rifled in their bores to spin bullets for accuracy) and bullets which expanded in the bores to follow the grooves (Minie balls)
greatly increased the accuracy and effective range of infantry firepower
(to between 400 and 1,000 yards), thereby providing the defense with
an unprecedented advantage.[25]

Despite the fact that seven of eight Civil War frontal assaults
failed, Lee just kept attacking.[26] Battles in which Lee damaged his army
with overly aggressive tactics include the Seven Days' (particularly
Mechanicsville, Gaines' Mill, and Malvern Hill), Second Manassas,
Chantilly, Antietam, Chancellorsville, Gettysburg, Rappahannock
Station, the Wilderness, and Fort Stedman. Archer Jones has pointed to
Lee's periodically misplaced elation, when he refused to "quit while he
was ahead," and cited Malvern Hill, Chantilly, the end of Chancellorsville, and Pickett's Charge as examples.[27]

The North had more of this advanced weaponry and had it earlier
in the war. Its Model 1861 Springfield rifle, with an effective range of
200-400 yards, could kill at a distance of 1,000 yards or more. Most infantrymen (especially Federals) had rifles by some time in 1862, Union
cavalry had breech-loading (instead of muzzle-loading guns) repeating
rifles by 1863, and even some Union infantry had these "repeaters"
(primarily Spencer rifles) in 1864 and 1865.

Demonstrating this trend, Rhode Islander Elisha Hunt Rhodes
experienced an improvement in weaponry during the war. In June 1861
he was first issued one of many muskets that he described as "old
fashioned smooth bore flint lock guns altered over to percussion
locks."[28] Late the following month, when other Rhode Islanders' enlistments expired after First Bull Run, Rhodes' unit members traded

---

24. "Robert E. Lee suffered his most decisive defeats while on the tactical offensive, at
Malvern Hill and Gettysburg. Even when he was successful on the offensive, Lee used up
thousands of irreplaceable troops in battles such as Second Manassas and Chancellorsville." McWhiney and Jamieson, *Attack and Die*, p. 108.

25. McWhiney and Jamieson, *Attack and Die*, pp. 28-49; Beringer et al., *Why the South Lost*,
pp. 14-6.

26. Fuller, *Grant and Lee*, p. 261.

27. Jones, Archer, "What Should We Think About Lee's Thinking?," *Columbiad*, 1, No. 2
(Summer 1997), pp. 73, 84-5.

28. Rhodes, *All for the Union*, p. 20.

their smooth-bore weapons for Springfield rifles.[29] Three years later, in July 1864 in the Shenandoah Valley, Captain Rhodes wrote: "I have forty of my men armed with Spencer Repeating rifles that will hold seven cartridges at one loading. I have borrowed these guns from the 37th Massachusetts Infantry who are armed with them and have used them for some time."[30]

Appreciation of the great reliance upon rifles by both sides in the conflict can be gleaned from the following estimates provided by Paddy Griffith in his thought-provoking *Battle Tactics of the Civil War*. He estimates that the Confederate Government procured 183,000 smoothbore muskets and 439,000 rifles and that the Union obtained 510,000 smoothbores and an astounding 3,253,000 rifles, including 303,000 breechloaders and 100,000 repeaters.[31]

Musketry and the new lethal force of rifle power accounted for as many as 80 percent of the Civil War's battlefield casualties. The improved arms gave the defense a tremendous advantage against exposed attacking infantry or cavalry. Use of trenches from 1863 on further increased the relative effectiveness of infantry defenders' firepower.

Similar improvements in artillery ranges and accuracy also aided the defense. Rhodes, for instance, wrote on February 14, 1862: "The 4th Battery "C" 1st Rhode Island Light Artillery came over [to Washington, D.C.] from Virginia this morning and exchanged their brass guns for steel rifle cannon."[32] The old smooth-bore cannons had ranges of 1,000 to 1,600 yards while the new rifled artillery had ranges of 4,000 to 6,000 yards.

Despite these significant new advantages held by the defense, during battle after battle, Lee frontally attacked and counter-attacked with his splendid and irreplaceable troops. Military historian Bevin Alexander asserted that Lee's obsession with seeking battle and his limited strategic vision lost the war.[33] The short-term results of Lee's overly aggressive tactics were his troops' injury, death and capture; the long-term results were dissipation of the South's finite resources and loss of the war.[34]

---

[29]. *Ibid.*, pp. 39-40.

[30]. *Ibid.*, p. 172.

[31]. Griffith, *Battle Tactics*, p. 80.

[32]. Rhodes, *All for the Union*, p. 54.

[33]. Bevin Alexander, *Lost Victories*, p. 221.

[34]. "...Casualties, like defeats in battles and campaigns, eventually had nonmilitary consequences. Both casualties and consequences adversely affected the morale of the home front as well as of the soldiers, undermining Confederate will to achieve independence." Beringer et al., *Why the South Lost*, p. 22.

Lee was not alone in failing adequately to compensate for the new effectiveness of defensive firepower, but, as the leading general of a numerically inferior army for almost three years, he could not afford to make that mistake. In fact, Lee lost 20.2 percent of his soldiers in battle while imposing only 15.4 percent losses on his opponents. This negative difference in percentage of casualties (4.8 percent) was exceeded among Confederate generals only by Lee's protege Hood (19.2 percent casualties; minus 13.7 difference) and by Pemberton, who surrendered his army at Vicksburg. For example, neither Joseph Johnston (10.5 percent casualties; minus 1.7 percent difference), Bragg (19.5 percent casualties; minus 4.1 percent difference) nor Beauregard (16.1 percent casualties; minus 3.3 percent difference) sacrificed such percentages of their men in unjustified frontal assaults as did Lee.[35] Lee's statistics were even worse before he generally went on the defensive--finally and much too late--after the Battle of the Wilderness in early May 1864.

Lee's second tactical problem was his frequent failure to take charge of the battlefield--a glaring problem throughout the entire Seven Days' Battle and the three days at Gettysburg. Specifically, he would take a "hands-off" attitude even though, as at the Seven Days' Battle and Gettysburg, he was on the scene and disaster was developing or opportunities beckoned. Lee himself may have provided a partial explanation for some of his army's failures in these situations. After the war, he wrote, "I plan and work with all my might to bring the troops to the right place at the right time; with that I have done my duty. As soon as I order the troops forward into battle, I leave my army in the hands of God." Thirty years after the war, Confederate General Lafayette McLaws provided an analysis of Gettysburg that, intentionally or not, reflected on Lee's failure to take control: "The Battle of Gettysburg has not as yet been analyzed to make the combination of movements comprehensible. The disjointed assaults which could not under any circumstances have produced favorable results, have not yet been explained."[36]

In fact, Lee too often left battle tactics to others who were obviously failing even when Lee was personally present on the battlefield --

---

35. McWhiney and Jamieson, *Attack and Die*, pp. 19-22. In contrast to Lee, Grant suffered 18.1 percent casualties and imposed 31.0 percent casualties on his opponents for a positive difference of 12.9 percent. *Ibid.*, p. 23. The Grant calculations include the 29,396 Confederates of the army that surrendered to him at Vicksburg. Without those captures, Grant's imposed casualties drop to 54,303 from 83,699, his casualties imposed percentage drops to 20.1 percent (compared to Lee's 15.4 percent), and his difference of casualties imposed/suffered drops to a positive 7.2 percent (compared to Lee's minus 4.8 percent).

36. Freeman, *R.E. Lee*, II, p. 347; McLaws, Lafayette, Letter to B.F. Johnson Publishing Co., July 13, 1895, reprinted in *North & South*, I, Issue 1 (November 1997), pp. 38, 40..

effectively leaving those decisions to no one except perhaps his God. Lee's hands-off approach is demonstrated by the dearth of written orders issued by him once a battle had started --something that distinguished him from most other generals in the war. Part of Lee's problem in this area may have been his failure to provide himself with an adequate staff; while his small staff was headed by a colonel or lieutenant colonel, the Army of the Potomac's large staff was headed by a major general and included several brigadier generals.[37] Staffing problems, with resultant poor coordination, had a greater effect on offensive than defensive tactics, and thus would have been a particularly troublesome problem for Lee.[38]

The third problem with Lee's tactics was his propensity to devise battle plans which either required impossible coordination and timing or which dissipated his limited strength through consecutive, instead of concurrent, attacks. For example, the Seven Days' Battle was a series of disasters in which Lee relied upon unrealistic coordination and timing that resulted in Confederate failures and extreme losses. Again, the second day of Gettysburg saw a classic misuse of uncoordinated serial assaults on the Union left when a simultaneous assault might have resulted in a Confederate break-through.

The fourth tactical problem involved Lee's orders themselves. On numerous occasions they were too vague or discretionary, characteristics that were enhanced by the verbal nature of many of Lee's orders.[39] Examples of flawed orders are Lee's confusing and discretionary orders to Stuart as Lee's army moved north prior to Gettysburg and his orders to Ewell to take the high ground "if practicable" at the end of Gettysburg's first day. There are times for discretionary orders, but Lee overused them.

The results of Lee's faulty strategies and tactics were catastrophic. His army had 121,000 men killed or wounded during the war -- 27,000

---

[37]. Williams, *Lincoln and His Generals*, p. 313. Wiley, *Road to Appomattox*, pp. 115-6. When Lee surrendered at Appomattox, his personal staff members signing the parole agreement along with Lee consisted of four lieutenant colonels and two majors. Dowdey and Manarin, *Papers*, p. 935; Taylor, *General Lee*, p. 295. Freeman commented on Lee's small staff: "No general ever had more devoted service than he received from his personal assistants, but surely no officer of like rank ever fought a campaign comparable to that of 1864 with only three men on his staff, and not one of the three a professional soldier." Freeman, *R.E. Lee*, III, p. 230. For details on the various members of Lee's staff throughout the war, see *Ibid.*, I, pp. 638-43. T. Harry Williams stated, "It would not be accurate to say that Lee's general staff were glorified clerks, but the statement would not be too wide of the mark. Certainly his staff was not, in the modern sense, a planning staff, which was why Lee was often a tired general." Williams, *Lincoln and His Generals*, p. 313.

[38]. Griffith, *Battle Tactics*, p. 56.

[39]. Wiley, *Road to Appomattox*, p. 115.

more than any Civil War general on either side, including that alleged "butcher," Ulysses S. Grant, and about 90,000 more than any other Confederate general. Although Lee's army inflicted a war-high 135,000 casualties on its opponents, 60,000 of those occurred in 1864 and 1865 when Lee was on the defensive and Grant engaged in a deliberate war of adhesion against the army Lee had fatally depleted in 1862 and 1863.[40]

In light of his reputation, Lee's relative casualty statistics could be expected to exceed those of his Rebel counterparts. In reality, however, Lee's numbers were worse than those of his fellow Confederate commanders. Lee's soldiers suffered 38 percent of all Confederate battlefield deaths and injuries (121,000 of 320,000) while inflicting only 35 percent of the battlefield deaths and injuries (135,000 of 385,000) suffered by Union troops. Conversely, the men serving under all other Confederate commanders imposed 65 percent of all Union battlefield deaths and injuries (250,000 of 385,000) while suffering only 62 percent of such casualties themselves (199,000 of 320,000).[41]

Similarly, Lee's generals were mortally wounded in battle at a much higher rate than those under other Confederate commanders. After Lee took command of the Army of Northern Virginia, he lost two of the three mortally wounded Confederate lieutenant generals (corps commanders), four of the seven mortally wounded Confederate major generals (division commanders), and 33 of 53 mortally wounded Confederate brigadier generals (brigade commanders).[42] These numbers are out of proportion to the above percentages of casualties inflicted and suffered by Lee's army and thus do not appear to be the result of greater combat by his army than other Confederate troops.

During the first fourteen months that Lee commanded the Army of Northern Virginia, he took the strategic and tactical offensive so often with his undermanned army that he lost 80,000 men while inflicting only 73,000 casualties on his Union opponents. During each major battle in the critical and decisive phase of the war from June 1862 through July 1863, Lee was losing an average 19 percent of his men while his manpower-rich enemies were suffering casualties at a tolerable 13 percent.[43]

---

[40]. "The truth is that in 1864, Lee himself demonstrated the alternative to his earlier offensive strategy and tactics." Nolan, *Lee Considered*, p. 260.

[41]. McWhiney and Jamieson, *Attack and Die*, p. 22; Current, Richard N. (ed.), *Encyclopedia of the Confederacy*, 4 vols. (New York: Simon & Schuster, 1993) [hereafter Current, *Encyclopedia*], I, p. 338.

[42]. Fox, *Regimental Losses*, pp. 571-3; Warner, *Generals in Gray*.

[43]. Livermore, *Numbers & Losses*, pp. 86-103.

Although daring and sometimes seemingly successful, Lee's actions were inconsistent with the North's 4:1 manpower advantage and were fatal to the Confederate cause. By 1864, therefore, Grant had a 120,000-man army to bring against Lee's 65,000 and, by the effective use (unlike Hooker) of the sheer weight of his numbers, imposed a deadly 46 percent casualty rate on Lee's army while losing a bearable 41 percent of his own men, as he drove from the Rappahannock to the James River and created a terminal threat to Richmond.[44]

By June 1864 Lee's diminished forces were tied down by Grant at Richmond and Petersburg. The next month Sherman reached Atlanta. Atlanta fell on September 1, and the Shenandoah Valley was lost in October. Lincoln was reelected in November. The South was doomed, Sherman was marching through Georgia, and Confederate soldiers were dying, nearing starvation and deserting in droves.

The time had come to end the war, but Lee did nothing. Revered and loved by his troops and the entire South, Lee had the power to bring down the curtain on the great American tragedy. Lee's resignation would have brought about a massive return of southern soldiers to their homes and destroyed the will to fight of the Army of Northern Virginia. But he did nothing. For five more months after Lincoln's reelection, up until the last hours at Appomattox, Lee continued the futile struggle. The result was continued death and destruction throughout the South. This senseless continuation of the slaughter was Lee's final failure.

---

[44]. McWhiney and Jamieson, *Attack and Die*, p. 19; Livermore, *Numbers & Losses*, pp. 110-6.

Appendix I

Historians' Treatment of Lee

The following is, by necessity, a very limited and selective summary of the historiography of Lee.[1] In the immediate aftermath of the Civil War, historians dealt with Lee as with most other participants in the war. Although Lee generally was treated positively, his faults also were discussed.

This treatment was consistent with newspapers' treatment of Lee during the war itself -- when Lee was rivaled or surpassed by Stonewall Jackson as the most heroic Confederate general. Both men became idols after their deaths made them martyrs for the Confederacy.

Books published in those first years after the war treated Lee favorably but found fault with his actions at Gettysburg and Malvern Hill -- and sometimes Antietam, Fredericksburg and the Seven Days' Battle. While Jackson, Longstreet, Joseph E. Johnston, Albert Sidney Johnston and others received generally favorable treatment, Richard Ewell and Jubal Early were universally criticized for their timidity on the first day at Gettysburg. These early books included James Dabney McCabe, Jr.'s *Life and Campaigns of Gen. Robert E. Lee* (1866), William Swinton's *The Twelve Decisive Battles of the War* (1867) and *Campaigns of the Army of the Potomac* (1882), John Esten Cooke's *A Life of Gen. Robert E. Lee* (1871), and Edward A. Pollard's *Lee and His Lieutenants* (1867).[2] In an 1866 book, *The Lost Cause*, Pollard concluded that Lee's influence on the Confederacy's general affairs was negative.[3]

After his death on October 12, 1870, however, Lee became a southern and then a national deity. Previously second to Jackson in the literature and hearts of the South, Lee was elevated to the flawless southern embodiment of The Lost Cause. No criticism of him went unchallenged, and the South's other leading generals were seen as a threat to

---

[1]. For a broader analysis and list, see Parrish, T. Michael, "The R.E. Lee 200: An Annotated Bibliography of Essential Books on Lee's Military Career," pp. 561-93, in Gallagher, *Lee the Soldier*.

[2]. Connelly, Thomas L., *Marble Man*, pp. 47-61; Gallagher, *Lee the Soldier*, p. xviii.

[3]. Bruce, "Lee and Strategy" in Gallagher, *Lee the Soldier*, p. 133.

Lee's deification, and thus became fair game for censure and condemnation. One of the major reasons for Lee's elevation to god-like status was that former Confederate officers associated with Lee could promote themselves through idolization of Lee. Wartime incompetents Jubal Early and William Nelson Pendleton were among the leaders of the pro-Lee, anti-Longstreet cabal.[4]

Early had faltered at Gettysburg, lost the Shenandoah Valley and his corps, been relieved of command by Lee, and fled the country for a few years after the war. Through his pro-Lee efforts, he hoped to cover up his own disastrous record and spread the blame elsewhere. He became the power and brains behind the anti-Longstreet movement with his famous January 19, 1872 Lee Birthday speech at Washington and Lee University.[5] In that speech, which was widely distributed as a "Lost Cause" pamphlet, Early created the myth that Lee had ordered Longstreet to attack at dawn on the second day at Gettysburg.[6] Early proved to be a better propagandist than general and dominated the pro-Lee cult for three decades as an author and as president of three Lee-worshipping organizations, the Lee Monument Association, the Association of the Army of Northern Virginia and the Southern Historical Society.[7]

Pendleton, a minister and Lee's mediocre chief of artillery, served as executive director of the Lee Monument Association and developed in his speeches, sermons and writings the parallels between the perfect Jesus Christ and the faultless Robert E. Lee. Pendleton's 1873 Lee Birthday speech further promoted the myth of Lee's July 2, 1863 orders to Longstreet to attack at dawn but contradicted Pendleton's own 1863 after-action report to Lee.[8] Revisionist historian Thomas L. Connelly later explained that Pendleton's attack-at-dawn statement:

> …was pure fabrication, even embarrassing to some members of Lee's staff. Charles Venable admitted the statement was due to Pendleton's obvious emotional illness, `to an absolute loss of memory said to be brought on by frequent attacks resembling paralysis.' Other Lee staff members--A.L. Long,

4. Piston, "Cross Purposes" in Gallagher, *Third Day*, pp. 47-51. "When the Civil War ended, Early and Pendleton were generally viewed as failures. For Early and Pendleton, the worship of Lee seems to have given meaning to otherwise empty lives." *Ibid.*, pp. 48, 50.

5. See reprinted speech in Gallagher, *Lee the Soldier*, pp. 37-73.

6. Piston, *Lee's Tarnished Lieutenant*, p. 118.

7. *Ibid.*, pp. 43-84; Gallagher, "Generals" in Boritt, *Why the Confederacy Lost*, pp. 90-1; Freeman, *Lee's Lieutenants*, III, p. 770.

8. Piston, *Lee's Tarnished Lieutenant*, pp. 37-45, 84-5, 121-2.

Walter Taylor, and Charles Marshall--however much they hated Longstreet, denied that any sunrise order had been given. Venable even lamented, `It is a pity, it ever got into print.'[9]

Another minister, J. William Jones, published his idolizing *Personal Reminiscences of General Robert E. Lee* in 1874,[10] gained control (with Early) of the Southern Historical Society, and used its periodic Papers to worship Lee and damn his critics from 1876 through 1887.[11]

Unabated praise for Lee continued in hundreds of books and articles published in the late nineteenth and early twentieth centuries. In his 1881 book, *The Rise and Fall of the Confederate Government*, Jefferson Davis referred to the *Southern Historical Society Papers* as resolving the issue of responsibility for Gettysburg, thereby implying that the responsibility for failure was Longstreet's. Among the other noteworthy and influential books in this period were Robert E. Lee, Jr.'s *Recollections and Letters of General Robert E. Lee* (1904); the Reverend Jones' 1906 sequel, *Life and Letters of Robert Edward Lee, Soldier and Man*; Thomas Nelson Page's *Robert E. Lee: The Southerner* (1909) and Page's nationalist revision, *Robert E. Lee: Man and Soldier* (1911).[12] Praise for Lee knew no bounds in this period, as demonstrated by the following quote of Senator Benjamin Hill of Georgia's memorial service oration appearing in his nephew Fitzhugh Lee's *General Lee: A Biography of Robert E. Lee* (1894):

> [Lee] was a foe without hate, a friend without treachery, a soldier without cruelty, and a victim without murmuring. He was a public officer without vices, a private citizen without wrong, a neighbor without reproach, a Christian without hypocrisy, and a man without guilt. He was Caesar without his ambition, Frederick without his tyranny, Napoleon without his selfishness, and Washington without his reward. He was as obedient to authority as a servant and royal in authority as a king. He was as gentle as a woman in life, pure and modest as a virgin in thought, watchful as a Roman vestal, submissive to law as Socrates, and grand in battle as Achilles.[13]

---

9. *Ibid.*, pp. 84-5.

10. Jones, J. William, *Personal Reminiscences of General Robert E. Lee* (Richmond, United States Historical Society Press, 1874, 1989).

11. Connelly, *Marble Man*, pp. 39-42, 73-90, 110; Piston, *Lee's Tarnished Lieutenant*, p. 130.

12. Connelly, *Marble Man*, pp. 107-10.

13. Lee, Fitzhugh, *General Lee: A Biography of Robert E. Lee* (New York: Da Capo Press, 1994; reprint of Wilmington, North Carolina: Broadfoot Publishing Company, 1989; original published in 1894 by D. Appleton and Company), p. 418.

Lee's permanent deification is found in the classic seven volumes written by Douglas Southall Freeman, the four-volume, Pulitzer Prize-winning *R. E. Lee: A Biography* (1934-35)[14] and the three-volume *Lee's Lieutenants: A Study in Command* (1942-44).[15] During his twenty-five years of work on these authoritative historical masterpieces, Dr. Freeman, editor of the *Richmond News Leader*, saluted Lee's statue each day as he went to work in Richmond.[16] As early as 1914, in an introduction to *Lee's Dispatches*, Freeman had revealed his view of Lee: "He entered upon the year 1863 with a series of victories unbroken from the time he had taken command [Malvern Hill and Antietam were what?][17] ...He ended the year with the greatest opportunity of his career lost through the blunders and worse of his subordinates...Lee seemed then the very incarnation of knighthood."[18]

In his seven volumes of flowing prose and detailed documentation, Freeman found Lee to be perfect in very nearly every way. According to Freeman, Lee had in his veins the blood of Virginia's finest families, the best families of the finest society America ever has produced. Lee was brilliant, prescient, humane, intelligent and virtually flawless. Unsurprisingly, his flaws only seemed to make him greater. For example, he was so tolerant of the faults in others (his lieutenants, for example) that sometimes their mistakes would result in defeats for which Lee would be held responsible. Like some of his nineteenth-century predecessors, Freeman cited Lee's failure to criticize Longstreet's conduct at Gettysburg as proof of Lee's great Christian morality, instead of as evidence that Lee had in fact found no fault with Longstreet's performance.

Freeman continued in this vein for a couple thousand pages and, like many of his predecessors, lauded Lee by explicitly tearing down Longstreet and deftly denigrating the accomplishments of Jackson, whom he regarded as a threat to Lee's supreme status. In a nutshell, *R.E. Lee* demonstrated how great Lee was, and *Lee's Lieutenants* described how all his subordinates had let him down.[19]

---

14. Freeman, *R.E. Lee*.
15. Freeman, *Lee's Lieutenants*.
16. Savage, *Court Martial*, p. 13.
17. "Since the political definition of losing is retreat, Lee had lost the battle [of Antietam]. Since he would have had to withdraw after any battle, his decision to fight assured a negative political result in the South and a positive one in the North." Jones, "Military Means" in Boritt, *Why the Confederacy Lost*, p. 60.
18. Freeman, *Lee's Dispatches*, pp. xxxiv, xl.
19. Piston, *Lee's Tarnished Lieutenant*, pp. 174-6.

Freeman's works affected those of later writers such as his pro-tege, Clifford Dowdey, who wrote a series of worshipful pro-Lee books in the 1950s and 1960s.[20] A chapter heading in one of his books referred to Lee and said it all: "The God Emerges."[21] Freeman's influence also is present but muted in Emory M. Thomas' excellent 1995 *Robert E. Lee: A Biography*, which contains some adverse criticism of Lee but adopts some of Freeman's strong pro-Lee positions, such as solely blaming Longstreet for the delays on Day 2 at Gettysburg.[22]

Contemporary historian Gary W. Gallagher, argues that Lee was correct in seeing Virginia as the critical battleground, was successful on several occasions and might have enjoyed success at Antietam and Gettysburg, and his propensity for the offensive and the attack-mode was consistent with the hopes and needs of the Southern people.[23]

It was, however, inevitable that the dichotomy between the image of the flawless Lee and the reality of the devastating defeat of his Con-federate army would become the subject of more adverse critical his-torical analysis. One of the first break-throughs was the 1907 publica-tion of Confederate Brigadier General E. Porter Alexander's classic and balanced *Military Memoirs of a Confederate: A Critical Narrative*. Aware of, but ignoring, the plethora of Lee-worshippers, Alexander set forth his frank criticisms of all the leading Civil War generals. All of them, including Lee, received both plaudits and negative criticism for what Alexander deemed their respective strengths and weaknesses. Even more valuable is the unexpurgated 1989 printing of the original version of Alexander's work, *Fighting for the Confederacy: The Personal Recollec-tions of General Edward Porter Alexander*, which was retrieved and edited by Gary W. Gallagher.[24] Among the many valuable insights of Alexan-der's works are his criticisms of Lee's decision to fight a battle he could not win at Antietam, many of Lee's tactical decisions at Gettysburg, and Lee's failure to coordinate his activities with those of Confederate forces unsuccessfully defending Vicksburg and Tennessee in 1863 and Atlanta in 1864.

Another critical evaluation of Lee came from British Major Gen-eral J.F.C. Fuller. In his 1933 book, *Grant and Lee: A Study in Personality and Generalship*, Fuller described Lee as "in several respects...one of the

[20]. Gallagher, *Lee the Soldier*, pp. xix-xx.
[21]. Piston, *Lee's Tarnished Lieutenant*, p. 183.
[22]. Thomas, *Lee*, supra.
[23]. Gallagher, "Generals" in Boritt, *Why the Confederacy Lost*, pp. 98-108; Gallagher, "An-other Look at the Generalship of R.E. Lee," pp. 275-89, in Gallagher, *Lee the Soldier*.
[24]. Alexander, *Fighting for the Confederacy*.

most incapable Generals-in-Chief in history"[25] and found Grant superior to Lee because of the former's broad strategic outlook -- in contrast to Lee's narrow eastern theater perspective.[26] He also criticized Lee for his over-aggressiveness during the Peninsular, Gettysburg and 1864 Virginia campaigns. In his earlier *The Generalship of Ulysses S. Grant* (1929), Fuller combined these ideas in a succinct statement: "Unlike Grant, [Lee] did not create a strategy in spite of his Government; instead, by his restless audacity, he ruined such strategy as his Government created."[27]

Another British military historian, Basil Liddell Hart, wrote two devastating mid-1930s articles critical of Lee in the *Saturday Review of Literature*. In "Lee: A Psychological Problem," he found Lee to be mediocre, overly concerned about Virginia (instead of the entire Confederacy), and guilty of bleeding the South to death with his suicidally aggressive tactics.[28] In "Why Lee Lost Gettysburg," Hart criticized Lee as a strategist for failing to recognize the Confederacy's limited manpower resources.[29]

A pioneer analyst was T. Harry Williams, who began questioning the myths surrounding Lee in a short and shocking *1955 Journal of Southern History* article criticizing Freeman's analysis of Lee. The following excerpts demonstrate Williams' heresy:

> [Freeman] was more like the little girl in Richmond who came home from Sunday School and said "Mama, I can never remember. Was General Lee in the Old Testament or the New Testament?"
>
> * * * * *
>
> Freeman came close to arguing that whatever Lee did was right because he was Lee.
>
> * * * * *
>
> Freeman was a Virginia gentleman writing about a Virginia gentleman.
>
> * * * * *
>
> The emotion that impelled Lee into the war also influenced the way he fought. He fought for Virginia. Freeman did not recognize Lee's limitations because to him too the war is in

25. Fuller, *Grant and Lee*, p. 8.

26. Gallagher, "Generals" in Boritt, *Why the Confederacy Lost*, pp. 90, 95.

27. Fuller, *Generalship of Grant*, p. 375.

28. Hart, B.H. Liddell, "Lee: A Psychological Problem," *Saturday Review*, XI (December 15, 1934), pp. 365ff.

29. Hart, B.H. Liddell, "Why Lee Lost Gettysburg," *Saturday Review*, XI (March 23, 1935), pp. 561ff.

Virginia. It did not occur to him to examine the effect of Lee's preoccupation with Virginia on total Confederate strategy. Nor did he see the tragic result of Lee's limitation. In the end, all the brilliance and fortitude of the greatest Confederate general availed little to save his country. It fell to pieces behind his back, and most of his efforts in Virginia went for nothing.[30]

Thomas L. Connelly followed up Williams' work with a 1969 *Civil War History* article criticizing and detailing Lee's ignorance of the western theater, his obsession with defending Virginia, and his persistent uninformed demands for reinforcements from the West and Deep South.[31] Next, in a 1973 article in the same publication, Connelly described the image of Lee historians had created. In particular, he argued that "Lee was a symbol of victory in a defeated region" and cited 1880s *Southern Historical Society Papers* articles seriously contending that Lee had never lost (Antietam and Gettysburg being strategic withdrawals).[32]

Connelly then teamed with Archer Jones to produce *The Politics of Command: Factions and Ideas in Confederate Strategy* (1973). They focused on a "western concentration bloc" and its running battle with Lee for Davis' attention and scarce troops. They concluded that Lee's close relationship with Davis enabled him to get attention for the Virginia front and special treatment for the Army of Northern Virginia.[33]

Finally, in his remarkable *The Marble Man: Robert E. Lee and His Image in American Society* (1977), Connelly traced the idealized historiography on Lee's life and especially his Civil War activities. He described the myth of The Lost Cause created by former Confederate officers who made Lee, Virginia, the Confederacy and themselves look good by praising Lee and attacking Longstreet. Connelly described how Early and Jones had falsified documents and cut deals with other authors in their quest to praise Lee and Early and to damn Longstreet.[34] For example, they had published Jeb Stuart's report on Gettysburg, deleted a paragraph in which Stuart had criticized Early for failing to watch for Stuart's cavalry, been caught in their fraud by Stuart's former adjutant, and then struck a bargain with him calling for no aspersions on either

---

30. Williams, T. Harry, "Freeman: Historian of the Civil War: An Appraisal," *Journal of Southern History*, XXI (Feb. 1955), pp. 91, 96, 98-100.

31. Connelly, "Lee and the Western Confederacy," pp. 116-32.

32. Connelly, Thomas L., "The Image and the General: Robert E. Lee in American Historiography," *Civil War History*, 19 (March 1973), pp. 50-64.

33. Gallagher, "Generals" in Boritt, *Why the Confederacy Lost*, pp. 95-6.

34. Gallagher, *Lee the Soldier*, p. xxiii.

Stuart or Early and placement of full blame for Gettysburg on Long-street.[35] Connelly also explained how Lee's son Robert and the Reverend Jones promoted Lee as a national, not just a southern, hero by deleting documents or portions of documents written by Lee that reflected pro-slavery or anti-northern views.[36]

Others who followed Connelly's lead in exposing the deliberate but flawed deification of Lee were William Garrett Piston in his *Lee's Tarnished Lieutenant: James Longstreet and His Place in Southern History* (1987)[37] and Alan T. Nolan in *Lee Considered: General Robert E. Lee and Civil War History* (1991).[38] Douglas Savage followed those with a semi-fictional examination of Lee's mistakes in his creative historical novel, *The Court Martial of Robert E. Lee* (1993).[39] The most recent criticism of Lee's overly aggressive approach was John D. McKenzie's *Uncertain Glory: Lee's Generalship Re-Examined* (1997).[40]

Grady McWhiney's and Perry D. Jamieson's *Attack and Die: Civil War Military Tactics and the Southern Heritage* (1982) provided valuable insight into unnecessary and self-defeating aggressiveness during the Civil War, particularly by Confederate generals.[41] They set forth detailed statistics demonstrating the devastating losses suffered by attacking armies and showing that Lee's troops suffered and imposed far more casualties than those of any other general on either side.[42]

Unfortunately for historical accuracy, the deliberate enshrinement of Robert E. Lee and concurrent denigration of James Longstreet, Ulysses Grant and Stonewall Jackson have become deeply ingrained in the American psyche. As J.F.C. Fuller said in his study of Grant, "The truth is, the more we inquire into the generalship of Lee, the more we discover that Lee, or rather the popular conception of him, is a myth..."[43]

---

35. Connelly, *Marble Man*, pp. 87-9.

36. *Ibid.*, pp. 118-9.

37. Piston, *Lee's Tarnished Lieutenant*.

38. Nolan, *Lee Considered*; Gallagher, "Generals" in Boritt, *Why the Confederacy Lost*, p. 97; Gallagher, *Lee the Soldier*, p. xxiii.

39. Savage, *Court Martial*.

40. McKenzie, *Uncertain Glory*.

41. McWhiney and Jamieson, *Attack and Die*, supra.

42. Gallagher, "Generals" in Boritt, *Why the Confederacy Lost*, p. 96.

43. Fuller, *Generalship of Grant*, p. 375.

Appendix II

Casualties of the Civil War

Determination of the number of casualties is one of the most difficult issues in writing about the Civil War. Not only did the Union and the Confederacy calculate their casualties differently, but individual armies on both sides took different approaches to doing so. Sometimes they deliberately changed the way in which they counted casualties.[1] The deterioration of the Army of Tennessee in late 1864 and of the Army of Northern Virginia in 1864 and 1865 resulted in an almost total absence of reliable Confederate records of their casualties for the last two calendar years of the war.

Defining casualties is another aspect of the problem. A full casualty count often includes killed, wounded and missing, but many records and writers include only killed and wounded. Distinctions between killed and wounded became difficult because of battle-related deaths that occurred during the days, weeks and months after a battle.

The "missing" category was particularly amorphous because it might or might not include soldiers who had wandered away or deserted under cover of battle -- as well as those captured by the enemy. Because the "missing" category was so ambiguous, captured soldiers could be exchanged or paroled, and the North could more readily replace missing or captured soldiers, the present volume -- except where specifically indicated--has used only the numbers of killed and wounded in discussing battle casualties.[2]

About twenty pages of Union Army Captain Frederick Phisterer's *Statistical Record of the Armies of the United States* (1883) were devoted to

---

[1]. For example, on May 14, 1863, after Chancellorsville's heavy casualties, Lee issued an order stating that the prevailing practice of counting slight injuries as casualties "...is calculated to mislead our friends, and encourage our enemies, by giving false impressions as to the extent of our losses...," and therefore directed that "...the reports of the wounded shall only include those whose injuries, in the opinion of the medical officers, render them unfit for duty." General Orders, No. 63, quoted in Fox, *Regimental Losses*, p. 559. This order apparently had an immediate impact on Lee's commanders' casualty reports. *Ibid.*

[2]. Bevin Alexander, *Lost Victories*, p. 287.

Civil War casualty numbers.[3] However, the first comprehensive publication on Civil War casualties was Union Lieutenant Colonel William F. Fox's *Regimental Losses in the American Civil War, 1861-1865*, which was published in 1898.[4] It is a voluminous treatise analyzing the numbers and causes of casualties, primarily totals and percentages suffered by every single Union regiment. Although its analysis of Union losses is far more extensive than of Confederate losses, it has many compelling features, such as tables showing the maximum percentages of losses in individual battles by regiments on both sides. (The respective "winners" were the Confederate 1st Texas at Antietam (82.3%) and the Union 1st Minnesota at Gettysburg (82.0%).)

The foremost authority on Civil War casualties is Thomas L. Livermore, whose *Numbers and Losses in the Civil War in America, 1861-1865* (1901) has been the starting point, and often the finishing point, for almost all later writers and statisticians.[5] Livermore's entire little tome explains how he derived his numbers.[6]

In his 1933 classic, *Grant and Lee: A Study in Personality and Generalship*,[7] Major General J.F.C. Fuller included a valuable appendix listing the strength, killed, wounded and missing of both sides in 58 Civil War battles.[8] About two-thirds of his numbers were taken from Livermore, but he expanded some of the lesser-known Confederate numbers. He also analyzed those figures and came to some startling conclusions.

---

[3]. Phisterer, Frederick, *Statistical Record: A Treasury of Information about the U.S. Civil War* (Carlisle, Pennsylvania: John Kallman Publishers, 1996; reprint of *Statistical Record of the Armies of the United States* (1883), a supplementary volume to the Campaigns of Scribner's Civil War series).

[4]. Fox, *Regimental Losses*.

[5]. Livermore, *Numbers & Losses*.

[6]. Joseph B. Mitchell criticized Livermore's calculations for Gettysburg (28,063 Confederate dead, wounded and missing) and questioned his calculations for other battles in "Confederate Losses at Gettysburg: Debunking Livermore," *Blue & Gray Magazine*, VI, No. 4 (April 1989), pp. 38-40. Mitchell argued that it "is patently obvious" that Livermore double-counted about 6,000 Confederate wounded at Gettysburg and concluded that each side had about 24,000 casualties (including missing) at Gettysburg. Mitchell's major basis for concluding that Livermore double-counted apparently was that Livermore overestimated the size of Lee's forces. Even if that were the case, the percentage of casualties taken by Lee remains high; the important point is that Lee could not afford to even equally exchange 24,000 casualties at this stage of the war. In a related discussion, Shelby Foote concluded that Lee had understated his Gettysburg casualties (including missing) at 20,451, when they were probably 25,000 or more. Foote pointed to the absence of reports from some Rebel units, Lee's new policy of not counting lightly wounded, and Lee's counting 5,150 as missing when the Union records included the names of 12,227 captured Confederates. Foote, *Civil War*, II, p. 578.

[7]. Fuller, *Grant and Lee*.

[8]. *Ibid.*, pp. 286-7.

First, in their respective 1862-63 battles, Lee had 16.20 percent of his men killed or wounded while Grant's losses were only 10.03 percent. Second, Grant's 1864-65 losses against Lee were 10.42 percent, and Lee's 1864-65 losses were unknown. Third, where both sides' losses were known, the Federals lost 11.07 percent and the Confederates 12.25 percent -- both higher than Grant's wartime total of 10.225 percent and lower than Lee's 1862-63 total of 16.20 percent even though the Confederate totals include Lee's own numbers.[9]

The culmination of these statistical analyses is found in Grady McWhiney's and Perry D. Jamieson's *Attack and Die: Civil War Military Tactics and the Southern Heritage* (1982).[10] In their opening chapter, "It Was Not War -- It Was Murder," they assembled an illuminating series of statistical tables analyzing the casualties incurred by Union and Confederate commanders.[11] Because of their mastery of the numbers and for purposes of consistency, their casualty figures (killed and wounded) have been used throughout this book.

The following significant statistical nuggets come from the tables in *Attack and Die*. 121,000 of Lee's men were killed and wounded -- an astounding 89,000 more than the Confederate runner-up, Braxton Bragg, and 91,000 more than third place John Bell Hood. Even Ulysses Grant lost only 94,000. While Lee had 20.2 percent (121,042) of his men killed or wounded in battle, he imposed only 15.4 percent (134,602) casualties on his opponents. This minus 4.8 percent difference for killed and wounded was exceeded among all major commanders only by Lee's protege, John Bell Hood. Selected other generals' casualty percentage differences were minus 13.7 for Hood, minus 4.1 for Bragg, minus 1.7 for Joseph Johnston, and plus 12.9 percent for Grant. Some of those calculations, particularly Grant's, include numbers of surrendered troops.[12]

Relevant grand totals of casualties appear in Richard N. Current's *Encyclopedia of the Confederacy* (1993), Vol. 1, "CIVIL WAR: Losses and Numbers."[13] Relying on Livermore and others, this article lists the following respective Union and Confederate casualties: battlefield deaths, 110,100 (U) and 94,000 (C); non-mortally wounded, 275,000 (U) and

---

9. *Ibid.*, p. 274.
10. McWhiney and Jamieson, *Attack and Die*. Beringer et al., *Why the South Lost*, pp. 458-81, contained a statistical analysis that criticized the *Attack and Die* -- conclusion that Confederates self-destructed but conceded that the high Rebel casualties helped depress southern morale.
11. McWhiney and Jamieson, *Attack and Die*, pp. 3-24.
12. *Ibid.*, pp. 19-23, 158.
13. Current, *Encylopedia*.

226,000 (C); and total battlefield casualties, 385,100 (U) and 320,000 (C).[14]

An analysis of the combined *Attack and Kill* and *Encyclopedia* numbers allows us to determine Lee's contributions to casualties inflicted and suffered by Confederate forces. As indicated in the Overview chapter above, Lee's numbers were worse than those of his fellow Confederate commanders. Lee's soldiers suffered 38 percent of all Confederate battlefield deaths and injuries (121,000 of 320,000) while inflicting only 35 percent of the battlefield deaths and injuries (135,000 of 385,000) suffered by Union troops. Conversely, the men serving under all other Confederate commanders imposed 65 percent of all Union battlefield deaths and injuries (250,000 of 385,000) while suffering only 62 percent of such casualties themselves (199,000 of 320,000).

The following are various authors' estimates of killed and wounded (plus missing*) for three major engagements involving Lee's army:

Antietam

Source	Confederate	Union
Current, *Encyclopedia*[15]	11,724	11,657
Foote, *Civil War*[16]	11,000	12,000
Freeman, *R.E. Lee*[17]	10,700*	12,410*
Fuller, *Grant & Lee*[18]	11,724	11,657
Hattaway and Jones, *How the North*[19]	13,724*	12,469*
Livermore, *Numbers and Losses*[20]	11,724	11,657
	13,724*	12,410*
McWhiney and Jamieson, *Attack*[21]	11,724 (22.6%)	11,657(15.5%)
Woodworth, *Davis and Lee*[22]	11,000	12,000

[14]. *Ibid.*, I, p. 338.
[15]. *Ibid.*
[16]. Foote, *Civil War*, I, p. 702.
[17]. Freeman, *R.E. Lee*, II, p. 402.
[18]. Fuller, *Grant and Lee*, p. 286.
[19]. Hattaway and Jones, *How the North Won*, p. 243.
[20]. Livermore, *Numbers & Losses*, pp. 92-3.
[21]. McWhiney and Jamieson, *Attack and Die*, p. 19
[22]. Woodworth, *Davis and Lee*, p. 192.

Chancellorsville

Source	Confederate	Union
Current, *Encyclopedia*[23]	10,746	11,116
Freeman, *Lee's Lieutenants*[24]	13,156*	16,804*
Fuller, *Grant and Lee*[25]	10,746	11,169
Furgurson, *Chancellorsville*[26] (citing Bigelow, *Chancellorsville*	10,293(17%)	11,549(9%)
Hattaway & Jones, *How the North*[27]	10,746	11,368
Livermore, *Numbers & Losses*[28]	10,746	11,116
	12,764*	16,792*
McWhiney and Jamieson, *Attack*[29]	10,746 (18.7%)	11,116 (11.4%)
Sears, *Chancellorsville*[30]	10,957	11,366
	13,460*	17,304*

Gettysburg

Source	Confederate	Union
Current, *Encyclopedia*[31]	22,638	17,684
Foote, *Civil War*[32]	25,000-plus*	17,684
Freeman, *R. E. Lee*[33]	23,371*	28,129*
Fuller, *Grant & Lee*[34]	22,638	17,684
Hattaway & Jones, *How the North*[35]	28,063*	23,049*
Livermore, *Numbers & Losses*[36]	22,638	17,684
	28,063*	23,049*
McWhiney and Jamieson, *Attack*[37]	22,638 (30.2%)	17,684 (21.2%)

These figures demonstrate consistency among several writers and dependence on Livermore. Regardless of which set of numbers is used for analysis, Lee's army incurred a much higher percentage of casualties than its opponent in each of these significant battles. These statistics are typical of Lee's experience at least through the Wilderness in May 1864 and demonstrate that he undermined the fighting capacity of his army.

[23]. Current, *Encyclopedia*, I, p. 338.

[24]. Freeman, *Lee's Lieutenants*, pp. 644, 648.

[25]. Fuller, *Grant and Lee*, p. 286.

[26]. Furgurson, *Chancellorsville*, pp. 364-5.

[27]. Hattaway and Jones, *How the North Won*, p. 384.

[28]. Livermore, *Numbers & Losses*, pp. 98-9.

[29]. McWhiney and Jamieson, *Attack and Die*, p. 19.

[30]. Sears, *Chancellorsville*, p. 442.

[31]. Current, *Encyclopedia*, I, p. 338.

[32]. Foote, *Civil War*, II, pp. 576, 578.

[33]. Freeman, *R.E. Lee*, III, p. 154.

[34]. Fuller, *Grant and Lee*, pp. 200, 286.

[35]. Hattaway and Jones, *How the North Won*, p. 409.

[36]. Livermore, *Numbers & Losses*, pp. 102-3.

[37]. McWhiney and Jamieson, *Attack and Die*, p. 19.

Bibliography

MEMOIRS, LETTERS, PAPERS
AND OTHER PRIMARY DOCUMENTS

Alexander, Edward Porter. *The Military Memoirs of a Confederate: A Critical Narrative*. New York: Charles Scribner's Sons, 1907.

Benson, Susan Williams (ed.). *Confederate Scout-Sniper: The Civil War Memoir of Barry Benson*. Athens and London: University of Georgia Press, 1992.

Blackford, William Willis. *War Years with Jeb Stuart*. Baton Rouge and London: Louisiana State University Press, 1945. 1993 Reprint.

Cox, Jacob Dolson. *Military Reminiscences of the Civil War*. 2 vols. New York: Charles Scribner's Sons, 1900.

Davis, Jefferson. *The Rise and Fall of the Confederate Government*. 2 vols. New York: Da Capo Press, Inc., 1990. Reprint of 1881 edition.

Douglas, Henry Kyd. *I Rode with Stonewall: Being chiefly the war experiences of the youngest member of Jackson's staff from the John Brown Raid to the hanging of Mrs. Surratt*. St. Simons Island, Georgia: Mockingbird Books, Inc., 1961. Reprint of Raleigh: The University of North Carolina Press, 1940.

Dowdey, Clifford and Manarin, Louis H. (eds.). *The Wartime Papers of R.E. Lee*. New York: Bramhall House, 1961.

Freeman, Douglas Southall and McWhiney, Grady. (eds.) *Lee's Dispatches: Unpublished Letters of General Robert E. Lee, C.S.A., to Jefferson Davis and the War Department of the Confederate States of America 1862-65*. Baton Rouge and London: Louisiana State University Press, 1957, 1994. Update of Freeman's original 1914 edition.

Gaff, Alan D. *On Many a Bloody Field: Four Years in the Iron Brigade*. Bloomington and Indianapolis: Indiana University Press, 1996.

Gallagher, Gary W. (ed.). *Fighting for the Confederacy: The Personal Recollections of General Edward Porter Alexander*. Chapel Hill: University of North Carolina Press, 1989.

Gibbon, John. *Personal Recollections of the Civil War*. New York and London: G. P. Putnam's Sons, 1928.

Gordon, John B. *Reminiscences of the Civil War*. Baton Rouge and London, Louisiana State University Press, 1993. Reprint of New York: Charles Scribner's Sons, 1903.

Grant, Ulysses S. *Memoirs and Selected Letters: Personal Memoirs of U.S. Grant, Selected Letters 1839-1865*. Reprint. New York: Literary Classics of the United States, Inc., 1990.

Johnson, Robert Underwood and Buel, Clarence Clough (eds.). *Battles and Leaders of the Civil War*. 4 vols. New York: Thomas Yoseloff, Inc., 1956. Reprint of Secaucus, New Jersey: Castle, 1887-8.

Jones, J. William. *Personal Reminiscences of General Robert E. Lee*. Richmond: United States Historical Society Press, 1874, 1989. Reprint.

Longstreet, James. *From Manassas to Appomattox: Memoirs of the Civil War in America*. New York: Smithmark Publishers, Inc., 1994.

McLaws, LaFayette. Letter to B.F. Johnson Publishing Co., July 13, 1895. Reprinted in *North & South*, I, Issuel 1 (November 1997), pp. 38-40.

Nicolay, John G. *The Outbreak of Rebellion*. New York: Charles Scribner's Sons, 1881. Reprint of Harrisburg: The Archive Society, 1992.

Porter, Horace. *Campaigning with Grant*. New York: Smithmark Publishers, Inc., 1994. Reprint.

Rhodes, Robert Hunt (ed.). *All for the Union: The Civil War Diary and Letters of Elisha Hunt Rhodes*. New York: Orion Books, 1991.

Sherman, William Tecumseh. *Memoirs of General W. T. Sherman*. Reprint. New York: Literary Classics of the United States, Inc., 1990.

Taylor, Walter H. *General Lee: His Campaigns in Virginia, 1861-1865 with Personal Reminiscences*. Lincoln and London: University of Nebraska Press, 1994. Reprint of Norfolk, Virginia: Nusbaum Books, 1906.

Tower, R. Lockwood (ed.). *Lee's Adjutant: The Wartime Letters of Colonel Walter Herron Taylor, 1862-1865*. Columbia, University of South Carolina Press, 1995.

The War of Rebellion: A Compilation of the Official Records of the Union and Confederate Armies. 128 vols. Washington, Government Printing Office, 1880-1901.

Watkins, Sam. R. *"Co. Aytch," Maury Grays, First Tennessee Regiment; or, A Side Show of the Big Show*. Nashville: Cumberland Presbyterian Publishing House, 1882. 1987 Reprint.

Wiggins, Sarah Woolfolk (ed.). *The Journals of Josiah Gorgas 1857-1878*. Tuscaloosa and London: The University of Alabama Press, 1995.

Woodward, C. Vann (ed.). *Mary Chesnut's Civil War*. New Haven and London: Yale University Press, 1981.

STATISTICAL ANALYSES

Fox, William F. *Regimental Losses in the American Civil War, 1861-1865: A Treatise on the Extent and Nature of the Mortuary Losses in the Union Regiments, with Full and Exhaustive Statistics Compiled from the Official Records on File in the State Military Bureaus and at Washington.* Albany: Brandow Printing Company, 1898. Reprinted: Dayton, Morningside House, Inc., 1985.

Livermore, Thomas L. *Numbers & Losses in the Civil War in America, 1861-1865.* Bloomington: Indiana University Press, 1957. Millwood, N.Y.: Kraus Reprint Co., 1977.

Phisterer, Frederick. *Statistical Record: A Treasury of Information about the U.S. Civil War.* Carlisle, Pennsylvania: John Kallmann, Publishers, 1996. Reprint of Statistical Record of the Armies of the United States (1883), a supplementary volume to the Campaigns of Scribner's Civil War series.

PERIODICAL ARTICLES

Bradley, Mark L. "Last Stand in the Carolinas: The Battle of Bentonville, March 19-21, 1865," *Blue & Gray Magazine*, XIII, Issue 2 (December 1995), pp. 8-22, 56-69.

Bruce, George A. "Strategy of the Civil War," *Papers of the Military Historical Society of Massachusetts*, 13, 1913, pp. 392-483.

Cheeks, Robert C. "Failure on the Heights," *America's Civil War*, 5 (November 1992), pp. 42-49.

Connelly, Thomas Lawrence. "The Image and the General: Robert E. Lee in American Historiography," *Civil War History*, 19 (March 1973), pp. 50-64.

_____. "Robert E. Lee and the Western Confederacy: A Criticism of Lee's Strategic Ability," *Civil War History*, 15 (June 1969), pp. 116-32.

Davis, Stephen, "Atlanta Campaign. Hood Fights Desperately. The Battles for Atlanta: Events from July 10 to September 2, 1864," *Blue & Gray Magazine*, VI, Issue 6 (August 1989), pp. 8-39, 45-62.

Fleming, Martin K. "The Northwestern Virginia Campaign of 1861: McClellan's Rising Star -- Lee's Dismal Debut," *Blue & Gray Magazine*, X, Issue 6 (August 1993), pp. 10-17, 48-54, 59-65.

Gallagher, Gary W., "Brandy Station: The Civil War's Bloodiest Arena of Mounted Combat," *Blue & Gray Magazine*, VIII, Issue 1 (October 1990), pp. 8-22, 44-53.

Gilbert, Thomas D., "Mr. Grant Goes to Washington," *Blue & Gray Magazine*, XII, Issue 4 (April 1995), pp. 33-37.

"Grant and Lee, 1864: From the North Anna to the Crossing of the James," *Blue & Gray Magazine*, XI, Issue 4 (April 1994), pp. 11-22, 44-58.

Handlin, Oscar, "Why Lee Attacked," *The Atlantic Monthly*, CXCV (March 1955), pp. 65-66.

Hart, B.H. Liddell, "Lee: A Psychological Problem," *Saturday Review*, XI (December 15, 1934), pp. 365ff.

_____. "Why Lee Lost Gettysburg," *Saturday Review*, XI (March 23, 1935), pp. 561ff.

Holsworth, Jerry W. "Uncommon Valor: Hood's Texas Brigade in the Maryland Campaign," *Blue & Gray Magazine*, XIII (August 1996), pp. 6-20, 50-55.

Joinson, Carla. "War at the Table: The South's Struggle for Food," *Columbiad*, 1, No. 2 (Summer 1997), pp. 21-30.

Jones, Archer. "What Should We Think About Lee's Thinking?," *Columbiad*, 1, No. 2 (Summer 1997), pp. 73-85.

Krick, Robert K. "Lee's Greatest Victory," *American Heritage*, 41, No. 2 (March 1990), pp. 66-79.

Krolick, Marshall D. "Gettysburg: The First Day, July 1, 1863," *Blue & Gray Magazine*, V, Issue 2 (November 1987), pp. 8-20.

Kross, Gary. "Gettysburg Vignettes: Three Mini-Tours of Sites on the Gettysburg Battlefield related to the Fighting on July 1, 1863, that are Unmarked or Seldom Visited," *Blue & Gray Magazine*, XII, Issue 3 (February 1995), pp. 9-24, 48-58.

Matter, William D. "The Battles of Spotsylvania Court House, Virginia, May 18-21, 1864," *Blue & Gray Magazine*, I, Issue 6 (June-July 1984), pp. 35-48.

Mertz, Gregory A. "No Turning Back: The Battle of the Wilderness," *Blue & Gray Magazine*, XII, Issue 4 (April 1995), pp. 8-23, 47-53; Issue 5 (June 1995), pp. 8-20, 48-50.

Miller, J. Michael. "Strike Them a Blow: Lee and Grant at the North Anna River," *Blue & Gray Magazine*, X, Issue 4 (April 1993), pp. 12-22, 44-55.

Mitchell, Joseph B. "Confederate Losses at Gettysburg: Debunking Livermore," *Blue & Gray Magazine*, VI, No. 4 (April 1989), pp. 38-40.

Popchock, Barry. "Daring Night Assault," *America's Civil War*, IV, No. 6 (March 1992), pp. 30-37.

Welch, Richard F. "Gettysburg Finale," *America's Civil War* (July 1993), pp. 50-7.

Williams, T. Harry. "Freeman: Historian of the Civil War: An Appraisal," *Journal of Southern History*, XXI (February 1955), pp. 91-100.

ATLASES

Cobb, Hubbard. *American Battlefields: A Complete Guide to the Historic Conflicts in Words, Maps, and Photos.* New York: Macmillan, 1995.

Davis, George B.; Perry, Leslie J., and Kirkley, Joseph W. *Atlas To Accompany the Official Records of the Union and Confederate Armies.* Washington: Government Printing Office, 1891-95.

Esposito, Vincent J. (ed.) *The West Point Atlas of American Wars.* 2 vols. New York, Washington, London: Frederick A. Praeger, Inc., 1959.

Greene, A. Wilson and Gallagher, Gary W. *National Geographic Guide to the Civil War Battlefield Parks.* Washington, D.C.: The National Geographic Society, 1992.

McPherson, James M. (ed.) *The Atlas of the Civil War.* New York: Macmillan, 1994.

Symonds, Craig L. *Gettysburg: A Battlefield Atlas.* Baltimore: The Nautical & Aviation Publishing Company of America, 1992.

CHRONOLOGIES

Bishop, Chris and Drury, Ian. *1400 Days: The Civil War Day by Day.* New York: Gallery Books, 1990.

Bowman, John S. (ed.). *The Civil War Almanac.* New York: World Almanac Publications, 1983.

Mosocco, Ronald A. *The Chronological Tracking of the American Civil War Per the Official Records of the War of the Rebellion.* Williamsburg: James River Publications, 1994.

OTHER BOOKS

Abbazia, Patrick. *The Chickamauga Campaign, December 1862-November 1863.* New York: Wieser & Wieser, Inc., 1988.

Alexander, Bevin. *How Great Generals Win.* New York and London: W. W. Norton & Co., 1993.

_____. *Lost Victories: The Military Genius of Stonewall Jackson.* New York: Henry Holt and Company, 1992.

Ambrose, Stephen E. *Halleck: Lincoln's Chief of Staff.* Baton Rouge and London: Louisiana State University Press, 1962, 1990.

Arnold, James R. *The Armies of U.S. Grant.* London: Arms and Armour Press, 1995.

Barry, John M. *Rising Tide: The Great Mississippi Flood of 1927 and How It Changed America*. New York: Simon & Schuster, 1997.

Beecham, R.K. *Gettysburg: The Pivotal Battle of the Civil War*. Stamford, Connecticut: Longmeadow Press, 1994. Reprint of Chicago: A.C. McClurg, 1911.

Beringer, Richard E.; Hattaway, Herman; Jones, Archer; and Still, William N., Jr. *Why the South Lost the Civil War*. Athens: University of Georgia Press, 1986.

Boritt, Gabor S. (ed.). *Lincoln's Generals*. New York and Oxford, Oxford University Press, 1994.

_____. *Lincoln, the War President*. New York and Oxford: Oxford University Press, 1992.

_____ (ed.). *Why the Confederacy Lost*. New York and Oxford: Oxford University Press, 1992.

Bowers, John. *Stonewall Jackson: Portrait of a Soldier*. New York: William Morrow and Company, Inc., 1989.

Bradford, Ned (ed.). *Battles and Leaders of the Civil War*. New York: Meridian, 1989.

Buell, Thomas B. *The Warrior Generals: Combat Leadership in the Civil War*. New York: Crown Publishers, Inc., 1997.

Bushong, Millard Kessler. *Old Jube: A Biography of General Jubal A. Early*. Shippensburg, Pennsylvania: White Mane Publishing Company, Inc., 1955, 1990.

Cannan, John (ed.). *War in the East: Chancellorsville to Gettysburg, 1863*. New York: Gallery Books, 1990.

Carmichael, Peter S. *Lee's Young Artillerist: William R.J. Pegram*. Charlottesville: University Press of Virginia, 1995.

Casdorph, Paul D. *Lee and Jackson: Confederate Chieftains*. New York: Paragon House, 1992.

Castel, Albert E. *Decision in the West: The Atlanta Campaign of 1864*. Lawrence: University Press of Kansas, 1992.

Catton, Bruce. *The Army of the Potomac: Glory Road*. Garden City, New York: Doubleday & Company, Inc., 1952.

_____. *The Army of the Potomac: Mr. Lincoln's Army*. Garden City, New York: Doubleday & Company, Inc., 1951, 1962.

_____. *The Army of the Potomac: A Stillness at Appomattox*. Garden City, New York: Doubleday & Company, Inc., 1953.

_____. *Grant Takes Command*. New York: Book-of-the-Month Club, 1994. Reprint of New York: Little, Brown and Company, 1968.

Civil War Times Illustrated. *Great Battles of the Civil War.* New York: W. H. Smith, Inc., 1984.

Clark, Champ (ed.). *Gettysburg: The Confederate High Tide.* (The Civil War Series) Alexandria, Virginia: Time-Life Books, Inc., 1985.

Coburn, Mark. *Terrible Innocence: General Sherman at War.* New York: Hippocrene Books, 1993.

Coddington, Edwin B. *The Gettysburg Campaign: A Study in Command.* New York: Charles Scribner's Sons, 1968, 1979.

Commager, Henry Steele (ed.). *The Blue and the Gray. Two Volumes in One. The Story of the Civil War as Told by Participants.* New York: The Fairfax Press, 1982. Reprint of Indianapolis: Bobbs-Merrill, c. 1950.

Connelly, Thomas Lawrence. *Army of the Heartland: The Army of Tennessee, 1861-1862.* Baton Rouge and London: Louisiana State University Press, 1967.

_____. *Autumn of Glory: The Army of Tennessee, 1862-1865.* Baton Rouge and London: Louisiana State University Press, 1971, 1991.

_____. *The Marble Man: Robert E. Lee and His Image in American Society.* New York: Alfred A. Knopf, 1977.

_____ and Barbara L. Bellows. *God and General Longstreet: The Lost Cause and the Southern Mind.* Baton Rouge: Louisiana State University Press, 1982.

_____ and Archer Jones. *The Politics of Command: Factions and Ideas in Confederate Strategy.* Baton Rouge: Louisiana State University Press, 1973.

Cooling, Benjamin Franklin. *Forts Henry and Donelson: The Key to the Confederate Heartland.* Knoxville: The University of Tennessee Press, 1987.

Cozzens, Peter. *The Shipwreck of Their Hopes: The Battles for Chattanooga.* Urbana and Chicago: University of Illinois Press, 1994.

Current, Richard N. (ed.), *Encyclopedia of the Confederacy* (4 vols.) New York: Simon & Schuster, 1993.

Davis, Burke. *The Long Surrender.* New York: Vintage Books, 1985.

_____. *They Called Him Stonewall: A Life of Lt. General T. J. Jackson, C.S.A.* New York: Rinehart, 1954. Reprint: New York: Wings Books, 1988.

Davis, Kenneth C. *Don't Know Much About the Civil War: Everything You Need to Know About America's Greatest Conflict but Never Learned.* New York: William Morrow and Company, Inc., 1996.

Davis, William C. *Brother Against Brother: The War Begins.* (The Civil War Series) Alexandria, Virginia: Time-Life Books, Inc., 1983.

_____. *The Cause Lost: Myths and Realities of the Confederacy.* Lawrence: University Press of Kansas, 1996.

_____. *Jefferson Davis: The Man and His Hour*. Baton Rouge, Louisiana State University Press, 1991.

_____. *The Orphan Brigade: The Kentucky Confederates Who Couldn't Go Home*. Mechanicsburg, Pennsylvania: Stackpole Books, 1993.

Donald, David Herbert (ed.). *Why the North Won the Civil War*. New York: Macmillan Publishing Co., 1962.

_____. *Lincoln*. New York: Simon & Schuster, 1995.

Dowdey, Clifford. *Lee*. Gettysburg: Stan Clark Military Books, 1991. Reprint of 1965 edition.

Eckert, Ralph Lowell. *John Brown Gordon: Soldier - Southerner - American*. Baton Rouge and London: Louisiana State University Press, 1989.

Eicher, David J. *The Civil War in Books: An Analytical Bibliography*. Urbana and Chicago: University of Illinois Press, 1997.

Faust, Patricia L. (ed.). *Historical Times Illustrated Encyclopedia of the Civil War*. New York: HarperPerennial, 1991.

Fellman, Michael. *Citizen Sherman: A Life of William Tecumseh Sherman*. New York: Random House, 1995.

Fishel, Edwin C. *The Secret War for the Union: The Untold Story of Military Intelligence in the Civil War*. Boston and New York: Houghton Mifflin, 1996.

Foote, Shelby (ed.). *Chickamauga and Other Civil War Stories*. New York: Dell Publishing, 1993.

Foote, Shelby. *The Civil War: A Narrative*. 3 vols. New York: Random House, 1958-1974.

Freeman, Douglas Southall. *Lee's Lieutenants: A Study in Command*. 3 vols. New York: Charles Scribner's Sons, 1942-4 (1972 reprint).

_____. *R.E. Lee*. 4 vols. New York and London: Charles Scribner's Sons, 1934-5.

Fuller, J.F.C. *The Generalship of Ulysses S. Grant. 1929*. Reprint. Bloomington: Indiana University Press, 1958.

_____. *Grant and Lee: A Study in Personality and Generalship*. Bloomington: Indiana University Press, 1957. Reprint of 1933 edition.

Furgurson, Ernest B. *Ashes of Glory: Richmond at War*. New York: Alfred A. Knopf, 1996.

_____. *Chancellorsville 1863: The Souls of the Brave*. New York: Alfred A. Knopf, 1992.

Gallagher, Gary W. (ed.). *Lee the Soldier*. Lincoln and London, University of Nebraska Press, 1996.

_____ (ed.). *The Third Day at Gettysburg & Beyond*. Chapel Hill and London: The University of North Carolina Press, 1994.

Glatthaar, Joseph T. *Partners in Command: The Relationships Between Leaders in the Civil War*. New York: Macmillan, Inc., 1994.

Griffith, Paddy. *Battle Tactics of the Civil War*. New Haven and London: Yale University Press, 1996.

Groom, Winston. *Shrouds of Glory. From Atlanta to Nashville: The Last Great Campaign of the Civil War*. New York: The Atlantic Monthly Press, 1995.

Guernsey, Alfred H. and Alden, Henry M. (eds.). *Harper's Pictorial History of the Civil War*. New York: The Fairfax Press, 1977. (Originally Harper's Pictorial History of the Great Rebellion in the United States. New York: Harper & Brothers, 1866.)

Hattaway, Herman and Jones, Archer. *How the North Won: A Military History of the Civil War*. Urbana and Chicago: University of Illinois Press, 1983, 1991.

Heleniak, Roman J. and Hewitt, Lawrence L. (ed.). *The Confederate High Command & Related Topics: The 1988 Deep Delta Civil War Symposium*. Shippensburg, Pennsylvania: White Mane Publishing Co., Inc., 1990.

Henderson, G.F.R. *Stonewall Jackson and the American Civil War*. New York: Da Capo Press, Inc., 1988. Reprint of New York: Grossett & Dunlap, 1943.

Hendrickson, Robert. *Sumter: The First Day of the Civil War*. Chelsea, Michigan: Scarborough House, 1990.

Hennessy, John J. *Return to Bull Run: The Campaign and Battle of Second Manassas*. New York: Simon & Schuster, 1993.

Hughes, Nathaniel Cheairs, Jr. *General William J. Hardee: Old Reliable*. Baton Rouge and London: Louisiana State University Press, 1965.

Hurst, Jack. *Nathan Bedford Forest: A Biography*. New York: Alfred A. Knopf, 1993.

Jones, Archer. *Civil War Command & Strategy: The Process of Victory and Defeat*. New York, The Free Press, 1992.

_____. *Confederate Strategy from Shiloh to Vicksburg*. Baton Rouge and London: Louisiana State University Press, 1991.

Jones, Terry L. *Lee's Tigers: The Louisiana Infantry in the Army of Northern Virginia*. Baton Rouge and London: Louisiana State University Press, 1987.

Jordan, David M. *Winfield Scott Hancock: A Soldier's Life*. Bloomington and Indianapolis, Indiana University Press, 1996.

Judge, Joseph. *Season of Fire: The Confederate Strike on Washington*. Berryville, Virginia: Rockbridge Publishing Co., 1994.

Katcher, Philip. *The Army of Robert E. Lee*. London: Arms and Armour Press, 1994.

Keegan, John. *The Face of Battle*. New York: Dorset Press, 1986. (originally New York: The Viking Press, 1976).

_____. *The Mask of Command*. New York: Viking, 1987.

Kegel, James A. *North with Lee and Jackson: The Lost Story of Gettysburg*. Mechanicsburg, Pa.: Stackpole Books, 1996.

Kennett, Lee. *Marching Through Georgia: The Story of Soldiers and Civilians During Sherman's Campaign*. New York: HarperCollins, 1995.

Ketchum, Richard M. *The American Heritage Picture History of the Civil War*. 2 vols. New York: American Heritage Publishing Co., Inc., 1960.

Lee, Fitzhugh. *General Lee: A Biography of Robert E. Lee*. New York: Da Capo Press, 1994; reprint of Wilmington, North Carolina: Broadfoot Publishing Company, 1989; original published in 1894 by D. Appleton and Company.

Krick, Robert K. *Stonewall Jackson at Cedar Mountain*. Chapel Hill and London: The University of North Carolina Press, 1990.

Lewis, Thomas A. *The Guns of Cedar Creek*. New York: Harper & Row, 1988.

Longacre, Edward. *General John Buford: A Military Biography*. Conshohocken, Pennsylvania: Combined Books, Inc., 1995.

Lossing, Benson. *A History of the Civil War, 1861-65, and the Causes That Led up to the Great Conflict*. New York: The War Memorial Association, 1912.

Lowry, Don. *Fate of the Country: The Civil War from June - September 1864*. New York: Hippocrene Books, 1992.

_____. *No Turning Back: The Beginning of the End of the Civil War: March-June, 1864*. New York: Hippocrene Books, 1992.

Luvaas, Jay and Nelson, Harold W. (ed.). *The U.S. Army War College Guide to the Battle of Antietam: The Maryland Campaign of 1862*. Carlisle, Pennsylvania: South Mountain Press, Inc., 1987.

_____. *The U.S. Army War College Guide to the Battle of Gettysburg*. Carlisle, Pennsylvania: South Mountain Press, Inc., 1986.

McDonough, James Lee. *Chattanooga: A Death Grip on the Confederacy*. Knoxville: The University of Tennessee Press, 1984.

McFeely, William. *Grant: A Biography*. New York and London: W.W. Norton & Company, 1981.

McKenzie, John D. *Uncertain Glory: Lee's Generalship Re-Examined*. New York: Hippocrene Books, 1997.

McMurry, Richard M. *Two Great Rebel Armies: An Essay in Confederate Military History*. Chapel Hill and London: The University of North Carolina Press, 1989.

McPherson, James. *Battle Cry of Freedom: The Civil War Era*. New York: Ballantine Books, 1988.

McWhiney, Grady and Jamieson, Perry D. *Attack and Die: Civil War Military Tactics and the Southern Heritage*. Tuscaloosa: The University of Alabama Press, 1982.

Marszalek, John F. *Sherman: A Soldier's Passion for Order*. New York: Macmillan, Inc., 1993.

Martin, David G. *Jackson's Valley Campaign, November 1861-June 1862*. New York: Wieser & Wieser, Inc., 1988.

_____. *The Shiloh Campaign, March-April 1862*. New York: Wieser & Wieser, Inc., 1987.

_____. *The Vicksburg Campaign, April, 1862-July, 1863*. New York: Wieser & Wieser, Inc., 1990.

Meredith, Roy. *The Face of Robert E. Lee in Life and Legend*. New York: The Fairfax Press, 1981.

Miers, Earl Schenck. *The Web of Victory: Grant at Vicksburg*. New York: Knopf, 1955. Reprint: Baton Rouge and London: Louisiana State University Press, 1984.

Miller, William J. *Mapping for Stonewall: The Civil War Service of Jed Hotchkiss*. Washington: Elliott & Clark Publishing, 1993.

Morris, Roy, Jr. *Sheridan: The Life and Wars of General Phil Sheridan*. New York: Crown Publishers, Inc., 1992.

Murphin, James V. *The Gleam of Bayonets: The Battle of Antietam and the Maryland Campaign of 1862*. Baton Rouge and London: Louisiana State University Press, 1965.

Nagel, Paul C. *The Lees of Virginia: Seven Generations of an American Family*. New York and Oxford: Oxford University Press, 1990.

Neely, Mark E., Jr.; Holzer, Harold; and Boritt, Gabor S. *The Confederate Image: Prints of the Lost Cause*. Chapel Hill and London: The University of North Carolina Press, 1987.

Nevins, Alan. *Ordeal of the Union*. 8 vols. New York and London: Charles Scribner's Sons, 1947-50.

Newell, Clayton R. *Lee vs. McClellan: The First Campaign*. Washington, D.C.: Regnery Publishing, Inc., 1996.

Nofi, Albert A. *The Gettysburg Campaign, June and July, 1863*. New York: Wieser & Wieser, Inc., 1986.

Nolan, Alan T. *Lee Considered: General Robert E. Lee and Civil War History*. Chapel Hill and London: University of North Carolina Press, 1991.

Perret, Geoffrey. *A Country Made by War: From the Revolution to Vietnam -- the Story of America's Rise to Power*. New York: Random House, 1989.

Pfanz, Harry W. *Gettysburg--Culp's Hill and Cemetery Hill*. Chapel Hill & London: The University of North Carolina Press, 1993.

_____. *Gettysburg: The Second Day*. Chapel Hill and London, The University of North Carolina Press, 1987.

Piston, William Garrett. *Lee's Tarnished Lieutenant: James Longstreet and His Place in Southern History*. Athens and London: The University of Georgia Press, 1987.

Pollard, Edward A. *The Lost Cause. A New Southern History of the War of the Confederates*. New York: Gramercy Books, 1994. Reprint of New York: E.B. Treat & Company, 1866.

Priest, John M. *Antietam: The Soldiers' Battle*. Shippensburg, Pennsylvania: White Mane Publishing Co., Inc., 1989.

Rhea, Gordon C. *The Battle of the Wilderness May 5-6, 1864*. Baton Rouge and London: Louisiana State University Press, 1994.

_____. *The Battles for Spotsylvania Court House and the Road to Yellow Tavern, May 7-12, 1864*. Baton Rouge and London: Louisiana State University Press, 1997.

Robertson, James I., Jr. *General A.P. Hill: The Story of a Confederate Warrior*. New York: Random House, 1987.

_____. *The Stonewall Brigade*. Baton Rouge and London: Louisiana State University Press, 1963 [1991 Reprint].

_____. *Stonewall Jackson: the Man, the Soldier, the Legend*. New York: Macmillan Publishing USA, 1997.

Royster, Charles. *The Destructive War: William Tecumseh Sherman, Stonewall Jackson, and the Americans*. New York: Vintage Books, 1993.

Safire, William. *Freedom: A Novel of Abraham Lincoln and the Civil War*. Garden City: Doubleday & Company, Inc., 1987.

Savage, Douglas. *The Court Martial of Robert E. Lee: A Historical Novel*. Conshohocken, Pennsylvania, Combined Books, Inc., 1993.

Scott, Robert Garth. *Into the Wilderness with the Army of the Potomac*. Bloomington: Indiana University Press. 1985.

Seagrave, Ronald R. *Civil War Books: Confederate and Union*. Fredericksburg, Virginia: Sergeant Kirkland's Press, 1995.

Sears, Stephen W. *Chancellorsville*. Boston and New York: Houghton Mifflin Company, 1996.

_____(ed.). *The Civil War: The Best of American Heritage.* New York: American Heritage Press, 1991.

_____. *George B. McClellan: The Young Napoleon.* New York: Ticknor & Fields, 1988.

_____. *Landscape Turned Red: The Battle of Antietam.* New York: Book-of-the-Month Club, Inc., 1994.

_____. *To the Gates of Richmond: The Peninsula Campaign.* New York: Ticknor & Fields, 1992.

Shaara, Michael. *The Killer Angels.* New York: Ballantine Books, 1974.

Smith, Gene. *Lee and Grant: A Dual Biography.* New York: Promontory Press, 1984.

Stackpole, Edward J. *They Met at Gettysburg.* New York: Bonanza Books, 1956.

Stern, Philip Van Doren. *Robert E. Lee: The Man and the Soldier.* New York: Bonanza Books, 1963.

Stewart, George R. *Pickett's Charge: A Microhistory of the Final Attack at Gettysburg, July 3, 1863.* Boston: Houghton Mifflin Co., 1959.

Tanner, Robert G. *Stonewall in the Valley: Thomas J. "Stonewall" Jackson's Shenandoah Valley Campaign Spring 1862.* Mechanicsburg, Pennsylvania: Stackpole Books, 1996.

Thomas, Emory M. *Robert E. Lee: A Biography.* New York and London: W.W. Norton & Company, 1995.

Tidwell, William A.; Hall, James O.; and Gaddy, David Winfred. *Come Retribution: The Confederate Secret Service and the Assassination of Lincoln.* Jackson and London: University Press of Mississippi, 1988.

Trudeau, Noah Andre. *Bloody Roads South: The Wilderness to Cold Harbor, May-June 1864.* Boston, Toronto, London: Little, Brown and Co., 1989.

_____. *The Last Citadel: Petersburg, Virginia June 1864--April 1865.* Baton Rouge: Louisiana State University Press, 1991.

_____. *Out of the Storm: The End of the Civil War, April-June 1865.* Boston, New York, Toronto, London: Little, Brown and Company, 1994.

Vandiver, Frank E. *Mighty Stonewall.* College Station: Texas A&M University Press, 1989. Reprint of 1957 edition.

Wallace, Willard M. *Soul of the Lion: A Biography of General Joshua L. Chamberlain.* Edinburgh, New York and Toronto: Thomas Nelson & Sons, 1960. Reprint: Gettysburg: Stan Clark Military Books, 1991.

Ward, Geoffrey C.; Burns, Ric, and Burns, Ken. *The Civil War: An Illustrated History.* New York: Alfred A. Knopf, Inc., 1990.

Warner, Ezra J. *Generals in Blue: Lives of the Union Commanders.* Baton Rouge and London: Louisiana State University Press, 1964.

_____. *Generals in Gray: Lives of the Confederate Commanders.* Baton Rouge and London: Louisiana State University Press, 1959.

Waugh, John C. *The Class of 1846: From West Point to Appomattox: Stonewall Jackson, George McClellan and Their Brothers.* New York: Warner Books, Inc., 1994.

Weigley, Russell F. *The American Way of War: A History of United States Military Strategy and Policy.* New York: Macmillan Publishing Co., Inc., 1973.

Weir, William. *Fatal Victories.* Hamden, Connecticut: Archon Books, 1993.

Werstein, Irving. *Abraham Lincoln Versus Jefferson Davis.* New York: Thomas Y. Crowell Company, 1959.

Wert, Jeffrey D. *General James Longstreet: The Confederacy's Most Controversial Soldier--A Biography.* New York: Simon & Schuster, 1993.

_____. *From Winchester to Cedar Creek: The Shenandoah Campaign of 1864.* Carlisle, Pennsylvania: South Mountain Press, Inc., 1987.

_____. *Mosby's Rangers.* New York: Simon and Schuster, 1990.

Wheeler, Richard. *Lee's Terrible Swift Sword: From Antietam to Chancellorsville, An Eyewitness History.* New York: HarperCollins Publishers, Inc., 1992.

_____. *On Fields of Fury: From the Wilderness to the Crater: An Eyewitness History.* New York: HarperCollins Publishers, 1991.

Wicker, Tom. *Unto This Hour.* New York: The Viking Press, 1984.

Wiley, Bell Irvin. *The Life of Billy Yank: The Common Soldier of the Union.* Baton Rouge and London: Louisiana State University Press, 1952, 1991.

_____. *The Life of Johnny Reb: The Common Soldier of the Confederacy.* Baton Rouge and London: Louisiana State University Press, 1943, 1991.

_____. *The Road to Appomattox.* Baton Rouge and London: Louisiana State University Press, 1994 (originally Memphis: Memphis State College Press, 1956).

Wilkinson, Warren. *Mother, May You Never See the Sights I Have Seen: The Fifty-seventh Massachusetts Veteran Volunteers in the Army of the Potomac, 1864-1865.* New York: Harper & Row, 1990.

Williams, T. Harry. *Lincoln and His Generals.* New York: Alfred A. Knopf, Inc., 1952.

Wills, Brian Steel. *A Battle from the Start: The Life of Nathan Bedford Forrest.* New York: Harper Perennial, 1992.

Winders, Richard Bruce. *Mr. Polk's Army: The American Military Experience in the Mexican War.* College Station: Texas A & M University Press, 1997.

Woodworth, Steven E. *Davis and Lee at War*. Lawrence: University of Kansas Press, 1995.

_____. *Jefferson Davis and His Generals: The Failure of Confederate Command in the West*. Lawrence: University Press of Kansas, 1990.

Index

D

V

Valley Campaign · 43, 47
Van Dorn, Earl · 138
Venable, Charles · 208, 209
Vera Cruz, Mexico · 19, 20
Vicksburg, MS · 43, 89, 90, 98, 101, 103, 109, 133, 141, 145, 166, 179, 197, 198, 202, 211
Virginia Central Railroad · 45, 157
Virginia Military Institute · 149, 164
Virginia Militia · 24
Virginia, 6th Cav. · 60
Virginia, 18th Inf. · 130
Virginia's Constitutional Convention · 23, 24

W

Walker, John G. · 67, 69, 71
Warren, Gouverneur K. · 140, 151, 159, 186
Washington and Lee University Lexington, VA · 208
Washington, DC · 19, 21, 23, 27, 30, 32, 36, 37, 39, 40, 44, 57, 59-61, 63, 81, 102, 108, 117, 146, 164, 165, 199, 201
Washington, George · 17, 18, 145, 209
Washington, John A. · 29
Watkins, Sam · 143, 144, 169
Waynesboro, VA · 185
Weldon and Petersburg Railroad · 173
West Point · 18, 20, 169
West Virginia · 27, 29, 58, 164
Western and Atlantic Railroad · 178
Westminster, MD · 107
Westmoreland County, VA · 18
Westover, VA · 160

Wheatfield Gettysburg, PA · 120-122
Wheeler, Joseph · 143
Wheeling, (West) VA · 25
White House Washington, DC · 24
White House Landing, VA · 44, 45, 47, 49, 159
White Oak Road, VA · 186
White Oak Swamp, VA · 49, 50
White's Ferry, MD-VA · 65
Whiting, William H. C. · 50
Wilcox, Cadmus M. · 125, 129
Wilcox's Landing, VA · 159
Wilderness, VA · 91, 95, 96, 140, 150-158, 163, 196, 200, 202, 219
Williams, T. Harry · 212
Williamsburg, VA · 39, 47
Williamsport, MD · 40, 79, 130
Willis, Edward · 157
Willoughby Run Gettysburg, PA · 110
Wilmington, NC · 183-185
Winchester, VA · 40, 108, 176
Windmill Point, VA · 159
Wise, Henry A. · 29, 30
Wofford, William T. · 121
Wool. John E. · 37
Wright, Ambrose · 125
Wright, Horatio G. · 157

Y

Yellow Tavern, VA · 149, 163
York River, VA · 36, 37, 44, 45, 159
York, PA · 108
Yorktown, VA · 26, 37, 39

Z

Zoan Church, VA · 91